Sacred Space, Sacred Thread

Sacred Space, Sacred Thread

Perspectives across Time and Traditions

EDITED BY
John W. Welch
and Jacob Rennaker

FOREWORD BY
Larry Eastland and Varun Soni

⁌PICKWICK *Publications* · Eugene, Oregon

SACRED SPACE, SACRED THREAD
Perspectives across Time and Traditions

Copyright © 2019 Wipf & Stock Publishers. All rights reserved. Except for brief quotations in critical publications or reviews, no part of this book may be reproduced in any manner without prior written permission from the publisher. Write: Permissions, Wipf and Stock Publishers, 199 W. 8th Ave., Suite 3, Eugene, OR 97401.

Pickwick Publications
An Imprint of Wipf and Stock Publishers
199 W. 8th Ave., Suite 3
Eugene, OR 97401

www.wipfandstock.com

PAPERBACK ISBN: 978-1-5326-3523-6
HARDCOVER ISBN: 978-1-5326-3525-0
EBOOK ISBN: 978-1-5326-3524-3

Cataloguing-in-Publication data:

Names: Welch, John W., editor. | Rennaker, Jacob, editor.

Title: Sacred space, sacred thread : perspectives across time and traditions / edited by John W. Welch and Jacob Rennaker.

Description: Eugene, OR: Pickwick Publications, 2019 | Includes bibliographical references.

Identifiers: ISBN 978-1-5326-3523-6 (paperback) | ISBN 978-1-5326-3525-0 (hardcover) | ISBN 978-1-5326-3524-3 (ebook)

Subjects: LCSH: Temples | Temple of Jerusalem (Jerusalem) | Temples—Middle East | Hindu temples | Clothing and dress—Religious aspects

Classification: BL550 W252 2019 (print) | BL550 (ebook)

Manufactured in the U.S.A.   JULY 18, 2019

This scholarly conference and publication are sponsored by the John A. Widtsoe Foundation and the University of Southern California.

Permissions

Scripture Citations marked RSV are taken from the Revised Standard Version of the Bible, copyright © 1946, 1952, and 1971 National Council of the Churches of Christ in the United States of America. Used by permission. All rights reserved.

Scripture Citations marked NRSV are taken from the New Revised Standard Version Bible, copyright © 1989 National Council of the Churches of Christ in the United States of America. Used by permission. All rights reserved.

Scripture Citations marked NJPS are taken from TANAKH: A New Translation of THE HOLY SCRIPTURES According to the Traditional Hebrew Text, copyright © 1985 The Jewish Publication Society. Used by permission. All rights reserved.

Figure 4: Rendering of the Triple Gates, copyright © Ritmeyer Archaeological Design. Used by permission. All rights reserved.

Figure 5: Rendering of the Temple courts, copyright © Ritmeyer Archaeological Design. Used by permission. All rights reserved.

Figure 6: Consecration of the Tabernacle, copyright © Yale University Art Gallery, Dura-Europos Collection, Scanned images. Used by permission. All rights reserved.

Figure 7: Temple of Solomon, Jerusalem, copyright © Yale University Art Gallery, Dura-Europos Collection, Scanned images. Used by permission. All rights reserved.

Figure 10: Reproduction from Michael Avi-Yonah, "A List of Priestly Courses from Caesarea." *Israel Exploration Journal* 12 (1962): plate 13. Courtesy of the Israel Exploration Society.

Figure 11: Reproduction from Michael Avi-Yonah, "A List of Priestly Courses from Caesarea." *Israel Exploration Journal* 12 (1962): figure 1. Courtesy of the Israel Exploration Society.

Figure 12: The Hebrew inscription of the priestly courses found at Bayt Ḥāḍir, Yemen. Photo © Christian Robin, used with kind permission.

Figure 13: Line drawing by Maria Gorea, based on the Hebrew inscription of the priestly courses found at Bayt Ḥāḍir, Yemen, used with kind permission.

McHugh, James. "Seeing Scents: Methodological Reflections on the Intersensory Perception of Aromatics in South Asian Religions." *History of Religions* 51 (2011) 156–177. © 2011 by The University of Chicago. All rights reserved. Used by permission as chapter 5 in this volume.

Table of Contents

List of Contributors ix

Foreword xi
    Larry Eastland and Varun Soni

Introduction xv
    John W. Welch and Jacob Rennaker

SACRED SPACE

1. Theology Enshrined in the Israelite Sanctuary 3
    Roy E. Gane

2. Sacred Space in Judaism after the Temple 15
    Gary A. Rendsburg

3. Navigating the Aqueous and Fluvial Imagery of the Liquid Temple 50
    Ross E. Winkle

4. From Tree to Temple Town: The Sacred Urbanism of Hindu India 66
    Vinayak Bharne

5. Seeing Scents: Space and Sensory Experience in a Hindu Temple 77
    James McHugh

6. Religious Ritual and the Creation of Sacred Space 103
    Alonzo L. Gaskill

SACRED THREAD

7. Symbolism of Ancient Clothing: Conviction in Covering Oneself 127
    Rory Scanlon

8. Arrayed in Dazzling White: The Goddess Ta'it and Clothing in Ancient Egyptian Rituals of the Old Kingdom 134
    John S. Thompson

9. A Few of the Ways by which the High Priest's Sacred Clothing Sets Him Apart 146
   Selena Billington

10. Dressed to Impress: Adam as a Priestly Figure in Eden 158
    Jacob Rennaker

11. The Making and Meaning of the Colored Fabrics of the Temple 171
    Margaret Barker

12. The Veil of the Temple in Second Temple Judaism and Early Christianity 189
    Daniel M. Gurtner

CONVERSATIONS

13. Muslim, Jewish, and Catholic Perspectives on Sacred Spaces and Sacred Clothing: An Interfaith Panel Discussion 203
    Reuven Firestone, Amir Hussain, and Pim Valkenberg

14. Constructive Tensions in Sacred Spaces and Sacred Clothing in Lived Religious Experience: An Interfaith Panel Discussion 213
    Margaret Barker, E. Wayne Gaddis, Edina Lekovic, Patrick Mason, and Varun Soni

List of Contributors

Margaret Barker, Independent scholar

Vinayak Bharne, Lecturer, University of Southern California School of Architecture, and Associated Faculty at the USC Shinso Ito Center for Japanese Religions and Culture

Selena Billington, Independent scholar

Larry Eastland, President, John A. Widtsoe Foundation

Reuven Firestone, Regenstein Professor in Medieval Judaism and Islam at Hebrew Union College

E. Wayne Gaddis, President, California Missionary Baptist State Convention, and Senior Pastor, Greater True Light Missionary Baptist Church

Roy Gane, Professor of Hebrew Bible and Ancient Near Eastern Languages, Seventh-day Adventist Theological Seminary, Andrews University

Alonzo L. Gaskill, Associate Professor of Church History and Doctrine, Brigham Young University

Daniel M. Gurtner, Ernest and Mildred Hogan Professor of New Testament Interpretation, Southern Baptist Theological Seminary

Amir Hussain, Professor of Theological Studies at Loyola Marymount University

Edina Lekovic, Consultant, Muslim Public Affairs Council, and Chair of the Board of Directors, NewGround: A Muslim-Jewish Partnership for Change

Patrick Mason, Howard W. Hunter Chair of Mormon Studies, Claremont Graduate University

James McHugh, Associate Professor of Religion, University of Southern California

Gary A. Rendsburg, Blanche and Irving Laurie Professor of Jewish History, Department of Jewish Studies, Rutgers University

Jacob Rennaker, Scholar in Residence, John A. Widtsoe Foundation

Rory Scanlon, Associate Dean, College of Fine Arts and Communications, Brigham Young University

Varun Soni, Dean, Office of Religious Life, University of Southern California

John S. Thompson, Director for LDS Seminaries and Institutes of Religion, Cambridge, MA and Chaplain at Harvard University

Pim Valkenberg, Professor of Religion and Culture in the School of Theology and Religious Studies at the Catholic University of America

John W. Welch, Robert K. Thomas Professor of Law, Brigham Young University

Ross E. Winkle, Professor of New Testament and Chair, Department of Theology, Pacific Union College

Foreword

Larry Eastland and Varun Soni

"Sacred space" is a term used to describe mosques, temples, churches, and synagogues, as well as private places of worship, meditation, and self-reflection. They are places where individuals, families, and congregations gather for the purpose of devoting time and thought to that god whom they serve. Although coming from a wide variety of faith traditions and cultures, these communities have much in common with the way their sacred space functions for their members in helping to organize and build a community of faith and to create within a meaningful faith identity. They also become places where people of faith not only gather to worship, but also to find ways to help those most in need in their communities.

In addition to sacred space, "sacred clothing" is a term used to describe the ceremonial garments and religious coverings that individuals wear which are unique to their faith community to create a more personal religious identity that also becomes a reminder to the members that affirms their commitment to themselves, to each other, and to their god.

In today's media climate, we're constantly reinforced with narratives about how religion is intractably and inherently a source of conflict; about how violence in the world is really a problem with religion. The reality is very different, though. The history of religion is a history of reconciliation; it's a history of shared sacred space, of shared sacred clothing, of shared hopes, dreams, and aspirations. These fundamental and ancient ideas of space and clothing are ideas that connect all of our religious traditions; they are a theological thread that binds together all the great religious texts of the world. So, at this particular moment in time, when America and the world are really struggling with reconciling our differences and in making our diversity work for us, it is so important for us to come together and affirm our shared values, our common humanity, and our shared goals—the very things that make us human.

Using the lens of sacred space and sacred clothing, this particular conference provided a place to think deeply about how our religious responses to the world around us are so similar and how the core values that connect each of our faith traditions can be part of a solution to the world's great crises, as opposed to being part of the problem. What studies show us is that it's important to learn about other faith traditions in order to combat religious prejudice. With learning comes understanding.

But even more important than learning about other faith traditions is knowing someone of another faith tradition personally. This conference was not just an opportunity to learn about the modes of worship practiced by other faith traditions throughout the world, but it became a place where those in attendance could meet people from other faith traditions, to grow with them, to study with them, to collaborate with them, and to befriend them.

Because of this tragic fragmentation in the world which has accelerated in the past decade, focusing on the commonalities of sacred space and sacred clothing in different faith traditions is more immediately relevant today than at any time in the past several decades. This conference desired to create a gathering where scholars and religious practitioners could talk about these significant commonalities together in a respectful, scholarly, and deeply personal way. In doing so, we also hoped to enrich the understanding and experience of all those involved and in attendance by sharing with one another the linkages between ancient and modern faith traditions, while respecting those traditions which are unique to each one individually.

The conference also was an opportunity to bring together the two faces of scholarship and daily living by inviting leading participants in both religious life and religious studies. By so doing, this conference became something extraordinary and unique. We believe it was able to combine these two areas—religious life and religious studies—in a way that brought out the best in both and enriched all those who attended. All too often there has been a perceived divide between scholarship and practice. The campus and the community are seen as fulfilling two different missions, which all too often seem to be living in two different worlds. And, when they do meet, they often collide between the ideal of theory and the practicality of daily living.

However, if theory cannot translate to serve the community, and the practice of religion does not have the underpinning of a meaningful theology, then all suffer. Thus, our focus on sacred space and sacred clothing was a way to bring together theory and practice across the global community of faith, to stream it live so that this community could be involved in the discussion, and to find ways to expand the reach of faith and theology to the four corners of the globe.

It is our hope that this volume will give you a sense of this truly remarkable gathering of great minds and equally great practitioners, and provide a model for future events.

Introduction

John W. Welch and Jacob Rennaker

Religious Studies scholars, theologians, and faith leaders, as distinctly expert interest groups, each speak their own particular languages, as it were. Naturally, each group is most comfortable speaking to those who are fluent in their own preferred modes and manners of discourse, and as a result, conversations between these groups are far less frequent than they should be. To ameliorate this less-than-ideal situation, on November 3–4, 2016, practitioners in each of these groups came together at the University of Southern California to have just such a conversation. The result was a landmark conference titled, "Sacred Space, Sacred Thread." Together, these participants explored the power, purpose, and meaning of sacred spaces and sacred clothing across time and around the globe.

The list of co-sponsors for this event further demonstrates the breadth of these conversation partners: the John A. Widtsoe Foundation, the University of Southern California's Office of Religious Life, the Academy for Temple Studies, the USC Caruso Catholic Center, the California Missionary Baptist State Convention, the Los Angeles Greek Orthodox Community, as well as the USC Latter-day Saint Student Association and Institute of Religion. In addition to the direct participation of these diverse academic and faith-based organizations, the conference was viewed live online at over 1,500 locations in nine foreign countries (Canada, UK, Germany, Indonesia, Israel, Italy, Greece, Tanzania, and Colombia) as well as across the United States. This resulting publication seeks to make available the remarkable presentations and conversations from such a well-attended and widely enjoyed conference.

Bringing together a variety of speakers from different backgrounds and who use different approaches makes a single systematic organization of the conference's proceedings difficult. Thus, in assembling these conference presentations, we have divided the following papers into three broad sections—Sacred Space; Sacred Thread; and Conversations—and loosely organized the chapters within each section topically.

In the "Sacred Space" section, the first three chapters deal with Judeo-Christian ideas of physical and conceptual sacred spaces. In "Theology Enshrined in the Israelite Sanctuary," Roy Gane insightfully demonstrates that, contrary to the idea that a space is sacred because of the rituals preformed there, Israel's portable sanctuary in the wilderness served as a symbol for what the space was—a dwelling place for God. This sanctuary was a symbol for the sovereignty, immanence, and transcendence of God. Drawing upon comparative evidence from Egypt, Gane shows that the Israelite's mobile sanctuary mirrored the layout of Egyptian military camps, which were arranged around the dwelling place of the Pharaoh. This Israelite sacred space travelled with the people so that God could always be with them. The tabernacle was treated as the temporary home of God, and like the Egyptian camps, it was revered as the dwelling of the Israel's heavenly king.

Gary Rendsburg's chapter, "Sacred Space in Judaism after the Temple," sensitively shows how the memory of a sacred space can be preserved by a religious group well after that sacred space has been violated and its sacred structures have been destroyed. His thesis is that the Jewish temple played a central and unique role in this community's religious traditions for nearly a thousand years, even after its physical destruction by the Romans. Judaism incorporated images and symbols of the temple into the artwork and architecture of synagogues both in the Land of Israel and throughout the Diaspora to evoke this lost sacred space. Furthermore, Rendsburg argues that many ritual acts associated with the temple were transferred to the developing liturgy in the synagogue in a post-temple world. Through numerous avenues, Jewish religious traditions maintained a sustained effort to keep the memory of the temple alive. Thus, no single sacred space has replaced the temple in the Jewish religious imagination.

In the next chapter, "Navigating the Aqueous and Fluvial Imagery of the Liquid Temple," Ross Winkle meaningfully shows that sacred spaces such as temples are sacred not only because of the rituals performed there, but also for the symbols which can instruct worshipers in the deeper things of their deities. Winkle focuses on ways in which water was present in the Jewish temple, as well as those writings which describe it. Through its symbolic representation and its physical presence, he suggests that water was used as an allegory for the teachings and wisdom of God. Winkle then demonstrates how this imagery of temple water was preserved and amplified by Christian writers, who found this particular image theologically compelling.

Then the following chapter takes readers geographically farther east, as Vinayak Bharne discusses how sacred local shrines developed into temples and then towns in India. "From Tree to Temple Town: The Sacred Urbanism of Hindu India" shows how India's rich religious tradition has given rise to vast "faithscapes"—holy cities where religious ritual and community come together. Many of these faithscapes began as holy trees or small shrines where the local communities worshiped and prayed. Through piecemeal growth fueled by the devotion of both commoners and chieftains, these small sacred places grew into formal temples. This practice of small sacred spaces carved out of the mundane continues in today's urban areas in India, often encroaching on the public domain. These sacred spaces should be identified and celebrated, because today's shrines will become tomorrow's centers and monuments. Bharne astutely points out how the hopes and spiritual aspirations of millions of people today are made manifest in and through these seemingly insignificant early shrines established by the common people.

James McHugh's chapter, "Seeing Scents: Space and Sensory Experience in a Hindu Temple," innovatively looks at the concept of sacred space from a different angle—that of the senses. McHugh highlights the fact that East Asian religions used perfumes made of specific ingredients as part of their worship services. While perfumes produced a particular smell which set apart a space as sacred, the visual experience of the worshiper which was associated with the perfume was just as important. The aromatic nature of the perfume is only one aspect of a worshipper's experience; there are also the material aspects—the touch, taste, and visual aspects of the perfume. Without an understanding of the full ritual experience—the visual as well as the aromatic—it is unlikely that anyone studying Hinduism (or any other religious tradition that employs scents in their worship) will ever fully understand these sacred rituals.

The final chapter of this section, "Religious Ritual and the Creation of Sacred Space," is both a bit more theoretical, while at the same time somewhat more practical in nature. Alonzo Gaskill explains that the rituals enacted within sacred spaces provide worshippers with a way to find deep meaning in their personal and religious experiences. Ritual offers peace and place in an otherwise meaningless world. Gaskill argues that sacred spaces are made sacred because of the rituals performed there, not by virtue of the physical location of that space. The rituals performed there mark that place as different from the mundane world and create a sort of spiritual significance to worshipers. However, these rituals only have this transformative power when they are endowed with meaning. Losing the underlying meaning of rituals can lead to confusion among worshipers and a loss of reverence for these sacred spaces.

The book's second section, "Sacred Thread," moves from the concept of sacred spaces in religious thought to that of sacred fabric. It opens with a general approach to sacred clothing in the ancient world: Rory Scanlon's "Symbolism of Ancient Clothing: Conviction in Covering Oneself." Scanlon surveys the many important ways clothing functioned within ancient societies. In religious settings, clothing served as a visual statement of personal belief about one's self, about one's community, and about one's God. Archaeologically speaking, cloth is poorly preserved, and as a result, relatively little is known about the materials ancient societies used in making their clothing and how it was constructed. However, by incorporating the study of textiles, Religious Studies scholars can come to a better understanding of the symbolic role clothing played in a civilization's religious life.

This helpfully orienting discussion of sacred clothing is followed by John Thompson's detailed study, "Arrayed in Dazzling White: The Goddess Ta'it and Clothing in Ancient Egyptian Rituals of the Old Kingdom." Thompson meticulously focuses on the clothing rites described in the Pyramid Texts, whose purposes are to prepare the participant for a heavenly ascent. These rituals invoke the Egyptian goddess Ta'it, a goddess associated with linen and weaving, and demonstrate the sacred nature of clothing in ancient Egyptian religious life. In both rituals for food offerings to the gods and for funerary ceremonies, the associated clothing rituals serve to purify the wearer. Ritual clothing did not only serve purify, however; it also served as a reminder of the internal changes required by the initiate, such as generosity and thoughtfulness.

The next two chapters deal with the concept of priestly clothing in Israelite and later Jewish thought. In "A Few of the Ways by which the High Priest's Sacred Clothing Sets Him Apart," Selena Billington demonstrates that the clothing worn by Israelite high priests was closely related to the type of clothing worn by ancient Near Eastern kings and pharaohs. Several of the high priest's clothing items were dyed, a process typically only employed by the ruling classes of other societies. The color of these dyes was also significant in the wider world of ancient Near Eastern royalty. Billington also examines how the material itself from which the high priest's clothing was made would have ensured that an Israelite high priest would be immediately identified as socially significant by anyone in the wider ancient Near East.

Jacob Rennaker's chapter, "Dressed to Impress: Adam as a Priestly Figure in Eden," looks at the symbolic connections which early Jewish interpreters made between Adam, the first man, and the Israelite high priest. Those early Jewish authors linked the temple and the creation stories recorded in Genesis, even going so far as to describe the Israelite high priest and his clothing in terms of Adam. Rennaker examines several texts written during the Second Temple period in order to tease out what interpreters saw as Adam's priestly role in Eden, and suggests ways in which these authors may have discerned such ideas from the biblical text itself.

Margaret Barker then undertakes to shift our attention from the symbolism of priestly clothing to the symbolic fabrics used in the construction of the Israelite temple in her chapter, "The Making and Meaning of the Colored Fabrics of the Temple." Barker looks at biblical and extra-biblical traditions dealing with the symbolic nature of weaving in general, as well as the weaving of temple-related fabrics in particular. She argues that the woven temple veil was a symbol of creation in the cosmos, separating the heavens from the earth, while at the same time providing a link between the two. She also suggests that the imagery associated with the temple veil was conceptually tied to the high priest's woven robes, which together demonstrate that the temple and its high priest were seen as a reflection of humanity's condition within God's cosmos.

Rounding out this section, Daniel Gurtner's chapter, "The Veil of the Temple in Second Temple Judaism and Early Christianity," focuses entirely on the temple veil and the ways in which early Jews and Christians interpreted this sacred cloth. Gurtner shows that Jewish texts from the Second Temple period that discuss the temple veil often emphasized its separation of sacred spaces within the temple. Christian texts from the same period focus, instead, on the tradition that the temple veil was torn at the death of Jesus, which was said to symbolize an increased access to a heavenly sacred space for believers.

The third and final section of this volume, "Conversations," aims to capture two of the most significant panel discussions from the conference.

In the first, "Muslim, Jewish, and Catholic Perspectives on Sacred Spaces and Sacred Clothing," Jewish scholar Reuven Firestone, Muslim scholar Amir Hussain, and Catholic scholar Pim Valkenberg discuss the importance and significance of sacred spaces and sacred clothing in each of their respective traditions. Each spoke of the development of sacred space in their tradition over time and the importance of ritual in defining the border between sacred and profane spaces. This evolution of the sacred extended to what is considered sacred clothing in these traditions as well. While each of these religious communities has its own distinct sacred spaces and clothing, the importance of the sacred lay in allowing the community to leave behind the mundane world and to enter a spiritual realm—for prayer, worship, or ritual.

The conference's concluding panel, "Constructive Tensions in Sacred Spaces and Sacred Clothing in Lived Religious Experience," also brought together speakers from diverse religious traditions: Methodist theologian Margaret Barker, Baptist Pastor E. Wayne Gaddis, Muslim social activist Edina Lekovic, Mormon scholar Patrick Mason, and Hindu scholar and administrator Varun Soni. This group finds that, while sacred spaces manifest themselves with different degrees of formality in these diverse traditions, each group values the importance of a clean and pure place to connect with the divine. Similarly, the idea of sacred clothing also provides a reminder of the purity and divinity of their respective traditions, while also serving to bind the community together. Both sacred space and sacred clothing, however, are an outward sign of religiosity, and that can sometimes create tension—both among different religions and between the religious and the non-religious. And, when religious ritual becomes divorced from the ethics of the religion, additional tensions can arise. However, in spite of these tensions, each tradition allows for the sacred spaces and clothing of other religious groups to be respected.

As should be evident from the variety of approaches and diversity of participants, the conference fostered many vibrant discussions about sacred space and sacred thread. This ongoing conversation spans and unites many times and traditions. By conveniently providing the proceedings of this rewarding and memorable conference, we hope that scholars, theologians, and faith leaders everywhere can continue this conversation not only within their respective communities, but also among their interdisciplinary networks, and, hopefully, warmly embrace other communities, as well.

Sacred Space

1

Theology Enshrined in the Israelite Sanctuary

Roy E. Gane

As with other ancient Near Eastern (ANE) shrines, the layout, architecture, and furnishings of the Israelite wilderness sanctuary reflected theological concepts that correlated with activities performed there. A synchronic investigation of pentateuchal texts reveals that the physical sanctuary implicitly ascribed sovereignty, immanence, and transcendence to YHWH, Israel's deity.

1. Sovereignty

The Israelites camped around the sanctuary during their journey from Egypt to Canaan (Num 2). Three tribes pitched their tents on each of four sides, in the form of a hollow square, at the center of which was the rectangular sanctuary courtyard around the two-room moveable tabernacle of YHWH. The fact that Numbers 1 records a census of Israelite males of fighting age indicates that their encampment was military in nature, on the way to conquer Canaan.

The ruler of the nation and commander-in-chief of its army was YHWH himself, who issued orders from his sanctuary headquarters (Exod 25:22; Lev 1:1–2; Num 7:89—8:2). Balaam recognized that

YHWH's role included that of a monarch when he looked down on the Israelite camp and exclaimed:

> The LORD their God is with them,
> And their King's acclaim in their midst.
> (Num 23:21)[1]

The Israelite war camp was strikingly similar to that of the Egyptian pharaoh Ramesses II (1279–1213 BC) when he fought against the Hittites at Qadesh (about 1275 BC) in Syria. His rectangular camp is portrayed in a diagram etched on a stone wall inside a temple at Abu Simbel, in southern Egypt. Army divisions surrounded the palatial mobile tent-shrine of the pharaoh, which was comprised of two rooms.[2] This military war camp was like Israel's in that it was commanded by a god-king from centrally located portable headquarters.

In addition to the central position of the sanctuary in the Israelite camp, several other features evidenced YHWH's sovereignty, some of which additionally related to his immanence and transcendence, which we will discuss below.

First, like the palace of a human king, YHWH's tabernacle had a place of enthronement where there were guardian figures, in this case in the form of cherubim on the ark of the covenant (Exod 25:10–22; 1 Sam 4:4).[3] Inside the ark were the tablets on which were inscribed covenant stipulations—the Ten Commandments—that he had given to the Israelite nation as its suzerain (Exod 34:28; Deut 10:1–5; 1 Kgs 8:9).[4]

Second, also like a human monarch, he had authorized house servants to maintain his residence (e.g., Exod 29–30) and guards to control activities and access there (e.g., Num 1:53; 3:6–10).

---

1. NJPS here and in subsequent biblical quotations, unless indicated otherwise.

2. Homan, "The Divine Warrior," 22–33, 55; Homan, *To Your Tents*, 111–16; Wells, "Exodus," 1:250–51; Kitchen, *On the Reliability*, 278, 470.

3. On cherubim, which serve as guardians and bearers of YHWH's throne in the Bible and are counterparts of ANE sphinxes, see Mettinger, "Cherubim," 189–92. For some ANE depictions of cherubim, see Keel, *Symbolism of the Biblical World*, 142–43. For guardian figures at the throne of a human king, see, e.g., Solomon's throne: "Six steps led up to the throne ... Two lions stood beside the arms, and twelve lions stood on the six steps, six on either side" (1 Kgs 10:19–20). Neo-Assyrian royal palaces featured bull colossi in areas leading to thrones (Russell, *Sennacherib's Palace*, 10–14).

4. On the Decalogue and other laws as stipulations in the covenant, a kind of suzerainty treaty between YHWH and Israel, see Walton, *Ancient Israelite Literature*, 103.

Third, his servants blew signal trumpets to control the movements of the camp, deploy the army to meet emergencies, and announce special occasions (Num 10:1–10). Two such signal trumpets have been discovered in the tomb of the pharaoh Tutankhamun.[5]

Fourth, costly materials used for construction of the tabernacle and the garments of its priests, including silver, gold, and expensive blue and purple dyes,[6] as well as the fine craftsmanship of objects and ornate fabrics (Exod 25–28, 30–31, 35–39), testified to the royal status of its resident.

2. Immanence

The Israelite sanctuary structure was the earthly residence of YHWH (Exod 25:8), his *miškan*, "dwelling-place," usually rendered "tabernacle" (v. 9; 26:1). Because he is divine, it was a *miqdaš*, "holy place," i.e., "sanctuary" (25:8; Lev 12:4). Because he was Israel's king, it was a portable palace, so it could also be called an *'ohel mo'ed*, "tent of meeting" (Exod 27:21), where his people could come for an audience with the divine monarch (29:42–43).[7]

As a compact palace, the tabernacle consisted of two apartments,[8] separated by a veil (Exod 26:33). There was a square "throne room" and a rectangular "living room," twice the size of the throne room. The former, called the "holy of holies," contained the place where YHWH was enthroned: the ark of the covenant, a gold-covered box (25:10–22). However, unlike other ANE shrines, there was no material representation of the deity in the inner sanctum, either in anthropomorphic form or as a symbol because, according to the Pentateuch, his living, dynamic presence actually resided there among his people. An idol would have denied his real immanence.[9]

---

5. Kitchen, *On the Reliability*, 280.

6. These dyes signified royalty because only royalty could afford them, due to the fact that they were laboriously extracted from snails found off the coast of northern Israel and Lebanon (Milgrom, *Numbers*, 127; cf. Propp, *Exodus 19–40*, 373).

7. Including at sacred *mo'adim*, "appointed times," including festivals (Lev 23).

8. Like many ANE shrines from early times, including the tent-shrine of Ramesses II (see above).

9. Another problem with idolatry was the fact that nobody had seen YHWH's form, so any material representation of him would be inaccurate (Deut 4:12, 15–19).

An ANE suzerainty treaty text could refer to the deposit of the treaty document in a shrine belonging to the vassal.[10] Similarly, the ark in the sanctuary within the nation of Israel, YHWH's vassal, contained the tablets of covenant stipulations, the Ten Commandments (Exod 25:16; Deut 10:1–5). However, uniquely in the ANE, the suzerain was a deity and he resided in the sanctuary that was located with the vassal, enthroned above the ark containing the covenant stipulations (Exod 25:22; Num 7:89; 1 Sam 4:4). In this way, he demonstrated his intimate connection with Israel and with the covenant principles of the Decalogue, which did not merely constitute his royal policies, but reflected his moral character.[11]

Located in the living room, i.e., the "holy place" or outer sanctum, were three items of furniture that were appropriate for a royal residence: a table for food and drink (Exod 25:23–30), a lampstand with lamps for light (vv. 31–40), and an incense burner to sweeten the atmosphere at mealtime (30:1–10).[12] The branched lampstand was shaped like a stylized tree with "cups shaped like almond-blossoms" (25:33–34). The almond tree (*šaqed*) was associated with watching or wakefulness (verb from the same root *š-q-d*; Jer 1:11–12), due to the fact that it blossomed earlier in the year than other trees.[13] This evokes the idea that the resident deity was watching over his people (cf. Zech 4:2, 10).[14] Reinforcing the immanent

---

10. A fourteenth-century-BC treaty between the Hittite emperor Suppiluliuma I (suzerain) and Shattiwaza of Mitanni (vassal) in the Middle Babylonian Akkadian language includes the following specifications: "A duplicate of this tablet is deposited before the Sun-(goddess) of Ari[nn]a, since the Sun-(goddess) of Arinna directs kingship and queenship. Also, in the land of Mitanni, (a copy) is deposited before the Storm-god, Lord of the *kur[i]nnu* of Kaẕat" (§15a; Kitchen and Lawrence, *Treaty, Law and Covenant*, 1:377).

11. Cf. Ps 97:2—"righteousness and justice are the base of His throne."

12. See Nielsen, *Incense in Ancient Israel*, 90.

13. Koehler and Baumgartner, *Hebrew and Aramaic Lexicon*, 2:1638–39. For the connection between the lampstand and a tree, cf. the observation by Carol Meyers that the lampstand exemplifies a conventional ANE form that "is derived from a stylized tree of life design and symbolizes such themes as the fertility of nature and the sustenance of life" ("Lampstand," 4:142).

14. Cf. Num 17:23 (Eng. v. 8), where Aaron's staff "had sprouted: it had brought forth sprouts, produced blossoms, and borne almonds," reaffirming YHWH's choice of Aaron as his priest (cf. v. 20 [Eng. v. 5]). YHWH told Moses to put this staff in front of the "testimony," i.e., the ark, "as a sign for the rebels, that you may make an end of their grumblings against me, lest they die" (v. 25 [Eng. v. 10]). Here the almonds, etc., appear to signify YHWH's watchfulness to hold the Israelites accountable for accepting the Aaronic priesthood (Gane, "Productive and Protected Ministry," 30–32; Gane, *Leviticus, Numbers*, 645).

presence of YHWH was the complex of regular (*tamid*) rituals by which his servants, the priests, placed bread on the table (Lev 24:1–9), poured out a libation (Num 28:7), burned incense, and tended and lit the lamps (Exod 30:7–8) in his living room.[15]

The presence of YHWH could remain among his people when they traveled because his sanctuary was portable, like similar tabernacle structures of which parts or depictions have been discovered in Egypt.[16] All of the components of the tabernacle, including upright boards held together by horizontal crossbars to make a rigid framework, over which layers of curtains were draped (Exod 26), could be disassembled and transported when the Israelite camp moved (Num 4).

3. Transcendence

As mentioned above, the absence of a material representation of YHWH in his "throne room" signified the reality of his immanent presence. At the same time, the way in which he was enthroned over the ark of the covenant manifested his transcendent nature. The ark was not shaped like a throne or even a footstool, and YHWH hovered in the air above and between the cherubim figures on the ark (Exod 25:22; Num 7:89).[17]

The fact that YHWH as a personal, volitional being was separate from the sanctuary, although he was present there, meant that he could come or go by himself. Thus, his glory filled the tabernacle (Exod 40:34–35) before the ritual consecration of the sanctuary (Lev 8), showing that his movements were not dependent on human activities. By contrast, ANE deities, represented by their idols, were installed in their new shrines through ritual processes carried out by humans.[18] If YHWH

---

15. On the complex of regular rituals performed inside the tabernacle, see Haran, *Temples and Temple-Service*, 208–10.

16. Kitchen, *On the Reliability*, 276–77. Also, some texts from Mari in Syria that date to about the eighteenth century BC speak of large public tents held up by wooden frames on bases (Fleming, "Mari's Large Public Tent," 486–98).

17. English translations refer to the golden lid/cover (*kapporet*) of the ark of the covenant as the "mercy seat" (Exod 25:17), but it was not shaped like a chair and it was not a place for YHWH to sit. Haran has suggested that the cherubim formed a kind of throne for YHWH with their outspread wings (Haran, *Temples and Temple-Service*, 251–53).

18. See, for example, "the Sumerian Cylinder B of the ruler Gudea, which describes initiation festivities when the god Ningirsu and his consort Baba, as represented by their idols, were settled into their new temple. Their entrance was accompanied by

could independently enter his shrine, he could also leave on his own if he wished. He did leave the temple built by Solomon shortly before it was destroyed, on account of the massive accumulation of egregious sins by his people (Ezek 9–11).

Several other features of the sanctuary also reflected YHWH's transcendent nature. First, winged cherubim figures on the ark (Exod 25:18–20; 37:7–9) and cherubim woven into the fabrics inside the tabernacle (26:1, 31; 36:8, 35) evoked otherworldly space because cherubim are mixed beings (cf. Ezek 1:5–14; 10:14–16) that are not among the natural inhabitants of planet earth.[19] In ANE iconography, composite creatures represented gods and demons.[20] For example, at Abu Simbel in the depiction of the smaller, square-shaped inner sanctum of the tent-shrine of Ramesses II, the cartouche representing the pharaoh's identity is flanked by two anthropomorphic (but winged) images of the god Horus facing each other, just as winged cherubim facing each other overshadowed the cover of YHWH's ark in the most holy room of the Israelite tabernacle (Exod 25:20).[21] However, despite the Egyptian association of the pharaoh with transcendence, he was really human, far inferior to the immortal divinity at the center of the Israelite camp. The mummy of Ramesses can be viewed in the Cairo Museum.

Second, it appears that horns (pl. of *qeren*) of altars in the outer sanctum (Exod 30:2–3) and the courtyard (27:2), i.e., projections from their upper corners, were associated with YHWH's divine power.

---

offerings, as well as purification and divination procedures. Gudea presented 'housewarming gifts' to the divine couple (cf. Num. 7), prepared a banquet for Ningirsu, and offered animal sacrifices" (Gane, "Leviticus," 1:298–99, referring to "The Cylinders of Gudea," trans. Averbeck, 2.155: 431–32).

19. Cf. Deut 22:9, where a mixed crop becomes "holy," and therefore is forfeited to the sanctuary (Milgrom, *Leviticus 17–22*, 1658–61, commenting on Lev 19:19). Mixed cloth (of wool and linen) was appropriate in some of the fabrics, including priestly garments, of the sanctuary (Exod 26, 28; 39:29), but it was forbidden for ordinary Israelites to wear such cloth (Lev 19:19; Deut 22:11). However, there was one exception: Num 15:38 requires Israelites to wear tassels on the corners of their garments, with a (wool) thread colored with expensive blue (or violet) dye on each tassel (otherwise probably linen). Garments with such blue threads were worn by the priests (Exod 28:5, 6, 8, 15, 31, 33), but the blue cords on tassels of ordinary Israelites affirmed their status as members of "a kingdom of priests and a holy nation" (Exod 19:6; see Milgrom, *Numbers*, 127, 411–14).

20. See, e.g., Gane, "Composite Beings," 2012.

21. Homan, "Divine Warrior," 29.

In the ancient Near East, the horns on the altar are emblems of the gods (Galling 1925). They are found on top of shrines (Obbink 1937) and the headdresses of the gods (Boehmer 1972–75). They signify the horns of a powerful animal (e.g., a bull or a ram) and are symbols of strength and force. Indeed, *qeren* in the Bible is invested with the same symbolism (1 Sam 2:1, 10; 2 Sam 22:3; Jer 48:25; Zech 2:4; Pss 75:5–6, 11; 89:18, 25; etc.).[22]

YHWH was shown to be transcendent at the altars because the incense (*qĕṭoret*) from the inner altar was directed to the immanent but transcendent deity (Exod 30:7–8) who hovered over the ark (see above), and sacrificial smoke burned (*hiphil* verb of the same root *q-ṭ-r*, "make smoke") on the outer altar ascended as a "soothing aroma" to the Lord up in heaven (e.g., Lev 1:9).

The ark and the altars were located along the central axis of the sanctuary,[23] and it was these objects that received applications of purging blood on the Day of Atonement (Exod 30:10; Lev 16:14–16, 18–19).[24] The connection between the three items linked the covenant stipulations with divine power in a way that seems to have signified YHWH's ability to justly hold his people accountable to the principles of his covenant, to which they were bound by the blood of the ritual through which the covenant was established (Exod 24:5–8). However, expiatory blood applied to these same objects throughout the year and on the Day of Atonement justly extended mercy to God's faulty people when they failed to live up to the standards of the covenant (Lev 4, 16).[25]

Third, unlike a human king, YHWH does not need human food (cf. Ps 50:12–13). The sacrificial "food" (e.g., Num 28:2) burned by a theophanically kindled and continually burning fire on the outer altar in the courtyard (Lev 6:5–6 [Eng. 12–13]; 9:24) went up to him in the form of smoke as a soothing aroma (e.g., 1:9). YHWH did not even

---

22. Milgrom, *Leviticus 1–16*, 234–36. Cf. the suggestion by Propp that the horns of the outer altar could be seen "as arrows pointing up, as forming the lower terminus of a conduit to Heaven. After the Altar's horns are purified with blood and consecrated with oil (29:36–37; Lev 8:15), the space they define belongs to God's realm, not Man's" (*Exodus 19–40*, 501).

23. For a diagram of the layout of the sanctuary, see, e.g., Dozeman, *Commentary on Exodus*, 608.

24. Also, blood sprinkled in front of the ark in the inner sanctum (Lev 16:14–15) and in front of the veil in the outer sanctum (compare the abbreviated reference in v. 16b with 4:6, 17) ritually purged these areas on the Day of Atonement (16:16a).

25. See Gane, *Cult and Character*.

symbolically consume the presentation offering of bread, called "bread of the Presence" (Exod 25:30), that was placed before him on the golden table in his "living room." Whereas other ANE peoples normally fed their gods twice per day, YHWH's bread was renewed only once per week on the Sabbath (Lev 24:8), the memorial of creation (cf. Exod 20:11; 31:17). Then he assigned the old bread to his priests, while he received only the frankincense that had been placed on the bread as a token portion (Lev 24:7, 9) and most likely was burned for him. Thus, the Israelites did not feed him. Rather, the bread acknowledged that YHWH's ongoing creative activity provided their food.[26]

Fourth, YHWH's lamps remained lit all night from evening until morning (Exod 27:21; Lev 24:3), signifying that, unlike a human monarch, "the guardian of Israel neither slumbers nor sleeps!" (Ps 121:4).

Fifth, two pieces of evidence regarding YHWH's creative power were kept in front of the ark: a jar containing a sample of manna, the food with which he miraculously sustained the Israelites in the wilderness (Exod 16:33–34), and Aaron's rod that sprouted with almond blossoms and brought forth almonds overnight, implicitly testifying to his watchfulness (see above) against rebellion concerning his choice of the high priest (Num 17:23, 25–26 [Eng. 8, 10–11]).

Sixth, the courtyard contained two items that were fitting for the shrine of a deity, rather than the palace of a human king: an altar for burning sacrifices (Exod 27:1–8) and a basin from which the priests were to draw water to purify their hands and feet before entering the tabernacle or officiating at the altar (30:17–21). Archaeological evidence reinforces the idea that such installations were appropriate for a shrine. Enclosed altars within forecourts of temple complexes dating to the Bronze and Iron Ages have been found in various places, including Arad in Judah and Kition on the island of Cyprus.[27] Egyptian temples had stone basins at their entrances, which priests used to purify themselves with water several times per day.[28]

---

26. Gane, "'Bread of the Presence,'" 179–203.
27. Haak, "Altars," 1:80.
28. Velde, "Theology, Priests, and Worship," 3:1733.

Conclusion

We have found that elements of the physical structure of YHWH's portable shrine displayed his sovereignty, immanence, and transcendence. Other ANE deities were also associated with these characteristics. For example, the Babylonians came to regard Marduk as king of the gods and their ultimate sovereign, before whom their human king was to be humbled every year during the New Year Festival of Spring.[29] ANE peoples revered immanent gods, especially their ancestors, in private cultic practices.[30] They also believed in great and transcendent cosmic gods who were served by priests in temples, but whose idols and rituals were rarely witnessed by common people.[31]

YHWH was unique. His immanence was so real that he could personally and directly exercise sovereignty, including law-giving, without the need of a human king. Moreover, his immanence and transcendence were simultaneous. Moses emphasized his immanence in Deuteronomy 4:7: "For what great nation is there that has a god so close at hand as is the LORD our God whenever we call upon Him?" On the other hand, Jeremiah 23:23–24 affirms his transcendence: "Am I only a God near at hand—says the LORD—And not a God far away? If a man enters a hiding place, Do I not see him?—says the LORD. For I fill both heaven and earth—declares the LORD."

YHWH was greater than the ANE gods in that he alone created and maintained the cosmos, and he was more transcendent in that he did not

---

29. On this deity, see Abusch, "Marduk," 543–49; for a readily accessible translation of the Akkadian text prescribing humiliation of the Babylonian king before (the idol of) Bēl = Marduk, see Sachs, "Temple Program," 334. For analysis (with translation) of the king's reconfirmation "rite of passage," see Gane, *Ritual Dynamic Structure*, 238–43.

30. On ANE ancestor cults in general, see Olyan, "Cult," 2:84. On family gods in Mesopotamia, see Stol, "Private Life," 1:488. On the Ugaritic cult of ancestors, see Xella, "Death and the Afterlife," 3:2065–66. Cf. Laban's household gods (Gen 31:19, 34–35).

31. Egyptian temple religion mostly consisted of performances witnessed by a few elite individuals: Spalinger, "Limitations of Egyptian Religion," 241–60. In Mesopotamia a major temple of a great deity, such as Enlil, Enki/Éa, Anu, Inanna, Aššur, or Marduk was "At a distance from the rest of the city, like a sacred neighborhood (they called it the 'city of the gods'), surrounded by tall and massive walls..." (Bottéro, *Religion in Ancient Mesopotamia*, 115). At Babylon it appears that the transcendence of the great deities Marduk, Adad, and Ishtar is implied by the fact that they were only indirectly represented by their attribute creatures on the publicly visible Ishtar Gate and Processional Way (as can be seen in the Pergamon Museum in Berlin).

consume human food. However, he was also near and accessible to all at his sanctuary, so Israelites did not need household gods in order to enjoy the security of divine presence.[32]

We have found rich theology in the physical structure of the Israelite wilderness sanctuary, without entering the subject of typology regarding Christ, who referred to his body as a temple (John 2:19–21). The New Testament speaks of him in terms reminiscent of several items found at the sanctuary, aside from the sacrificial victim (John 1:29; Heb 9:12–14) and the priest, who is now in God's temple in heaven (Heb 4–5, 7–8). These include "bread of life," referring to manna (John 6:48–51), "the light of the world" (9:5), the veil representing his flesh that was torn in order to provide people with access to God in heaven (Heb 10:19–20), and the place of Christ's sacrifice, i.e., the cross, as analogous to the altar (13:10–12). Furthermore, if Christ is divine (e.g., John 1:1, 14; 8:44; 8:58; 10:30) and God is love (1 John 4:8, 16) and God's law is based on love (Matt 22:37–40; Rom 13:8–10), the principles of the Ten Commandments inside the ark exemplified the character of Christ.

The Israelite sanctuary and subsequent temple are long gone, and New Testament Christianity has no holy space, temple, or priesthood on earth, aside from the "temple" constituted by the members of the church (1 Cor 3:16–17; 2 Cor 6:16; Eph 2:19–22; 1 Pet 2:5; cf. 1 Cor 6:19) and the priesthood of all believers (1 Pet 2:5, 9). However, the sovereign, immanent, transcendent deity whose attributes were reflected in the ancient Israelite shrine is still with us. According to the New Testament, he resides in heaven as the ineffable, immortal king of the universe (1 Tim 1:17; 6:15–16; Rev 4; 15:3) but remains more accessible than ever through Christ, our heavenly priest (Heb 4:14–16), and through his Holy Spirit (e.g., John 14:16–17, 26; 16:7–15).[33] Therefore, Christian faith and worship can humbly bow before him, look to him far above the gaze of telescopes, and cherish his near presence in our lives and hearts.

---

32. Ordinary men and women could bring their offerings to YHWH at the sanctuary (e.g., Lev. 1–7), although they were not allowed to officiate as priests or to enter the tabernacle (Num. 3:10, 38; 18:7).

33. Cf. Matt 18:20, where Jesus promised that "where two or three are gathered in my name, I am there among them" (NRSV).

Bibliography

Abusch, Tzvi. "Marduk." In *Dictionary of Deities and Demons in the Bible*, edited by Bob Becking, Pieter W. van der Horst and Karel van der Toorn, 543-49. Grand Rapids: Eerdmans, 1999.

Averbeck, Richard E. "The Cylinders of Gudea." In *The Context of Scripture*, edited by William Wolfgang Hallo et al., 417-32. Boston: Brill, 2003.

Bottéro, Jean. *Religion in Ancient Mesopotamia*. Translated by Teresa Lavendar Fagan. Chicago: University of Chicago Press, 2004.

Dozeman, Thomas B. *Commentary on Exodus*. Eerdmans Critical Commentary. Grand Rapids: Eerdmans, 2009.

Fleming, Daniel E. "Mari's Large Public Tent and the Priestly Tent Sanctuary." *Vetus Testamentum* 50, no. 4 (2000) 484-98.

Gane, Constance E. "Composite Beings in Neo-Babylonian Art." Ph.D. diss., University of California, Berkeley, 2012.

Gane, Roy E. "'Bread of the Presence' and Creator-in-Residence." *Vetus Testamentum* 42, no. 2 (1992) 179-203.

———. *Cult and Character: Purification Offerings, Day of Atonement, and Theodicy*. Winona Lake, IN: Eisenbrauns, 2005.

———. "Leviticus." In *Zondervan Illustrated Bible Backgrounds Commentary. O.T.: Genesis, Exodus, Leviticus, Numbers, Deuteronomy*, edited by John H. Walton, 284-337. Grand Rapids: Zondervan, 2009.

———. *Leviticus, Numbers*. NIV Application Commentary. Grand Rapids: Zondervan, 2004.

———. "Productive and Protected Ministry: Numbers 17:23 [English 17:8]." *Devotions on the Hebrew Bible: 54 Reflections to Inspire & Instruct*, edited by Milton Eng and Lee M. Fields, 30-32. Grand Rapids: Zondervan, 2015.

———. *Ritual Dynamic Structure*. Gorgias Dissertations. Piscataway, NJ: Gorgias, 2004.

Haak, Robert D. "Altars." In *The Oxford Encyclopedia of Archaeology in the Near East*, edited by Eric M. Meyers, 1:80-81. New York: Oxford University Press, 1996.

Haran, Menahem. *Temples and Temple-Service in Ancient Israel: An Inquiry into Biblical Cult Phenomena and the Historical Setting of the Priestly School*. Winona Lake, IN: Eisenbrauns, 1995.

Homan, Michael M. "The Divine Warrior in His Tent: A Military Model for Yahweh's Tabernacle." *Bible Review* 16 (2000) 22-33, 55.

———. *To Your Tents, O Israel!: The Terminology, Function, Form, and Symbolism of Tents in the Hebrew Bible and the Ancient Near East*. Leiden: Brill, 2002.

Keel, Othmar. *The Symbolism of the Biblical World: Ancient Near Eastern Iconography and the Book of Psalms*. Translated by Timothy J. Hallett. Winona Lake, IN: Eisenbrauns, 1997.

Kitchen, Kenneth A. *On the Reliability of the Old Testament*. Grand Rapids: Eerdmans, 2006.

Kitchen, Kenneth A., and Paul J. N. Lawrence. *Treaty, Law and Covenant in the Ancient Near East*. 3 vols. Wiesbaden: Harrassowitz, 2012.

Koehler, Ludwig, and Walter Baumgartner. *The Hebrew and Aramaic Lexicon of the Old Testament*. Translated by Mervyn Edwin John Richardson. Vol. 2. Leiden: Brill, 2001.

Mettinger, T. N. D. "Cherubim." In *Dictionary of Deities and Demons in the Bible*, edited by Bob Becking, Pieter W. van der Horst, and Karel van der Toorn, 189–92. Grand Rapids: Eerdmans, 1999.

Milgrom, Jacob. *Leviticus 1–16*. New York: Anchor Bible, 1998.

———. *Leviticus 17–22*. New York: Anchor Bible, 2000.

———. *Numbers: The Traditional Hebrew Text with the New JPS Translation*. The JPS Torah Commentary. Philadelphia: Jewish Publication Society, 1990.

Nielsen, Kjeld. *Incense in Ancient Israel*. Leiden: Brill, 1986.

Olyan, Saul M. "Cult." In *The Oxford Encyclopedia of Archaeology in the Near East*, edited by Eric M. Meyers, 2:79–86. New York: Oxford University Press, 1997.

Propp, William H. *Exodus 19–40: A New Translation with Introduction and Commentary*. New Haven, CT: Yale University Press, 2006.

Russell, John M. *Sennacherib's Palace without Rival at Nineveh*. Chicago: University of Chicago Press, 1992.

Sachs, Abraham. "Temple Program for the New Year's Festivals at Babylon." Translated by Abraham Sachs. In *Ancient Near Eastern Texts Relating to the Old Testament*, edited by J. B. Pritchard, 331–34. Princeton: Princeton University Press, 1969.

Spalinger, Anthony. "The Limitations of Formal Ancient Egyptian Religion." *Journal of Near Eastern Studies* 57, no. 4 (1998) 241–60.

Stol, Marten. "Private Life in Ancient Mesopotamia." In *Civilizations of the Ancient Near East*, edited by Jack M. Sasson, 1:485–501. Peabody, MA: Hendrickson, 2006.

Velde, Herman te. "Theology, Priests, and Worship in Ancient Egypt." In *Civilizations of the Ancient Near East*, edited by Jack M. Sasson, 1731–49. Peabody, MA: Hendrickson, 2000.

Walton, John H. *Ancient Israelite Literature in Its Cultural Context: A Survey of Parallels between Biblical and Ancient Near Eastern Texts*. Grand Rapids: Regency Reference Library, 1990.

Wells, Bruce. "Exodus." In *Zondervan Illustrated Bible Backgrounds Commentary: Genesis, Exodus, Leviticus, Numbers, Deuteronomy*, edited by John H. Walton, 160–283. Grand Rapids: Zondervan, 2009.

Xella, Paolo. "Death and the Afterlife in Canaanite and Hebrew Thought." In *Civilizations of the Ancient Near East*, edited by Jack M. Sasson, 3:2059–70. Peabody, MA: Hendrickson, 2000.

2

Sacred Space in Judaism after the Temple

Gary A. Rendsburg

It is almost impossible to overstate the singular importance of the Jerusalem Temple to ancient Judaism. Its predecessor, the tabernacle, dominates the latter half of the book of Exodus, while the priests who officiated there and the sacrifices which took place there are the subjects of much of Leviticus and portions of Numbers (see especially chs. 28–29).

As one reads through the rest of the Bible, especially from the time of Solomon onward, the temple looms large. The construction of the temple (1 Kgs 6–8) is the focal point of the description of Solomon's reign (1 Kgs 3–11).[1] Other portions of the book of Kings center on the temple as well. For example, when young Joash was spirited away by his aunt Jehosheba to escape certain slaughter at the hands of Athaliah, he was hidden in the temple for six years until he could rightfully be placed on the throne of Judah (2 Kgs 11). The selfsame king organized a major renovation and refurbishing of the temple (2 Kgs 12). At a later time, the temple served as the locus for Hezekiah's prayer (2 Kgs 19:14, with the words of the prayer recorded in vv. 15–34). Still later, more renovations of the temple were ordered by Josiah (2 Kgs 22:4–7), during the course of which a *sefer hattora* "scroll of the Torah" was found (2 Kgs 22:8). This crucial discovery, in turn, prompted Josiah to purge the temple of all the pagan elements and influences that had been introduced by his grandfather Manasseh

---

1. Radday, "Chaismus in Hebrew Biblical Narrative," 62–63; and Frisch, "Structure and Its Significance," 3–14.

and his father Amon (2 Kgs 22–23). Not surprisingly, when the book of Kings ends with the destruction of Jerusalem, the loss of Judahite independence, and the beginning of the Exile (2 Kgs 25), among the topics which receives the most specific attention is the burning of the temple and the looting of its appurtenances (2 Kgs 25:13–17).

The three major prophets are all connected to the temple. It was in the innermost sanctum of the temple that Isaiah first heard the call of God (Isa 6); it was at the gate to the temple that Jeremiah delivered one of his most famous speeches (Jer 7); while Ezekiel living in Babylonian Exile dedicated the last nine chapters of his book to a vision of the rebuilt temple (Ezek 40–48).

When the temple was rebuilt in 516 BCE, it once again played a prominent role in the life of the people, as reflected in biblical literature. The temple plays a central role in Haggai and Zechariah, in many Psalms (see, e.g., Ps 5:7; 23:6; 27:4; 29:9; 138:2; etc.),[2] and in Ezra–Nehemiah. Most prominently the temple dominates the retelling of Israel's history embodied in the book of Chronicles, in a much more significant way than is present in the earlier and parallel material in Samuel-Kings.[3]

Within post-biblical literature, we see the importance of the temple in the books of Maccabees, especially regarding its desecration by Antiochus IV and its rededication by the Maccabees (1 Macc 4:41–59; 2 Macc 10:1–4); while the book of Ben Sira (ch. 50) includes a glorious description of the role of the high priest. The Qumran community, with its priestly orientation, was very much devoted to the temple, as witnessed by the fact that the largest scroll at Qumran (by far) is the Temple Scroll (11QT)[4]—even as the community withdrew from Jerusalem and did not participate in the cult, due its disagreements with Sadducees and Pharisees alike over the proper administration thereof.[5]

---

2. Many of these Psalms, especially the lower-numbered ones, are pre-exilic compositions, but the use of Psalms increased with the passage of time, especially during the Second Temple period, and hence I mention them here. See my essay, Rendsburg, "Psalms as Hymns in the Temple of Jerusalem," 95–122.

3. Japhet, *I and II Chronicles*, 39–40; Williamson, "Temple in the Book of Chronicles," 15–31.

4. On the Temple Scroll, including its vision of a utopian and enormous temple, see Schiffman, *Reclaiming the Dead Sea Scrolls*, 257–71. Note, however, that Schiffman sees the Temple Scroll as less directly connected to the Qumran community, whereas I see a greater linkage between 11QT and the other Qumran sectarian writings.

5. For a general survey, see Goodman, "Qumran Sectarians and the Temple," 263–74.

And all of this emphasis occurs before the major reconstruction of the temple by Herod (21–14 BCE), which raised the prominence of the structure and the institution even more so, not only amongst Jews, but also amongst non-Jews.[6] The Herodian Temple is the setting for the Gospel accounts of Jesus in the temple. It is important to note that, contrary to some misguided views, Jesus was not anti-temple. Rather, he did what every other first-century CE Jew would have done: he journeyed to Jerusalem in advance of Passover to celebrate the festival there (John 2:13, etc.).[7] Alas, the Jerusalem Temple as expanded and beautified by Herod lasted less than a century, for the Romans sacked and burned the structure in 70 CE.

In light of this survey, which demonstrates the centrality of the Jerusalem Temple in the religion, culture, and mindset of the Jewish people—for approximately one thousand years (!)—one can imagine the loss (emotionally, religiously, etc.) felt upon its destruction. Indeed, one may justly ask the question: how could Judaism even carry on without the temple? And yet persist it did. While this is not the place for an extended discussion, suffice it to say that one of the most significant traits of the Jewish religion is its ability to adapt to changing times, places, and circumstances. The watershed marked by the destruction of Jerusalem and the devastation of the temple in 70 CE is clearly one of the most exemplary testimonies thereto.[8]

With the foregoing as introduction, included here to set the stage for what follows, we move to the subject adumbrated in the title of this essay: the issue of sacred space in Judaism *after* the destruction of the temple. To be sure, there is nothing that accedes to the level of "sacred space" akin to the temple, which belongs to a singular time and place, that is to say, the central structure in Jerusalem during the biblical and immediate

---

6. Our main source is Josephus, with further information forthcoming from the New Testament and from rabbinic recollections, especially in Mishnah tractate Middot, lit. "measurements." For a summary of the evidence, with liberal citation of specific passages from these sources, see Safrai and Avi-Yonah, "Temple," 19:612–16 (within the section entitled "Second Temple").

7. Charlesworth, "Jesus and the Temple," 145–81.

8. For further reading, see the essays collected in Schwartz and Weiss, *Was 70 CE a Watershed in Jewish History*. While traditionally the year 70 CE has been understood as a watershed year, as I myself have just indicated, the very fact that this book was published with this title demonstrates that some scholars have revisited the question. To cite just one essay in the volume relevant to the treatment herein, see Michael D. Swartz, "Liturgy, Poetry, and the Persistence of Sacrifice," 393–412.

post-biblical periods. Not even the emergent synagogue (more on this institution anon), the ever-increasing locus of Jewish ritual worship in the centuries immediately following the destruction of Jerusalem (and to this day), reached the level of sanctity ascribed to the temple. In sum, the temple is unique, full stop.

But the lack of the temple did not bring an end to its centrality in Jewish religion, culture, and mindset (to repeat the phrase from above). For while the temple ceased to exist, the *memory* of the temple persisted—and not in a minor way, but in manifold major ways.

We begin our survey with Rabbinic Judaism, if only because it is the best known and best recorded post-temple Jewish movement. Most scholars, myself included, understand the emergence of Rabbinic Judaism from the early Pharisee movement.[9] The earliest Rabbinic text is the Mishnah, dated to 200 CE, which serves as guidebook to Jewish law, custom, ritual, etc. The text was compiled by Rabbi Judah ha-Nasi ("the Prince"),[10] who organized the various subjects into six orders (Heb. *seder*), each of which in turn is divided into tractates (Heb. *maseket*) (between seven and twelve, depending on the order), for a total of sixty-three tractates. For guidance, see the appendix at the end of this essay.

Now the interesting thing about the Mishnah is that it is compiled at a distance of 130 years, perhaps four generations or so, after the destruction of the temple, and yet it includes so much information about

---

9. The subject requires a treatise, but for the nonce note the three following points. (1) Josephus, *Antiquities* 13.10.6, refers to the "traditions of the fathers" observed by the Pharisees, but not by the Sadducees, because they "are not written down in the law of Moses." This sounds remarkably similar to the later Rabbinic notion of the Oral Law. (2) Josephus, *Antiquities* 13.5.9, reports that the Pharisees took the middle ground on the question of free will vs. predetermination: "Now for the Pharisees, they say that some actions, but not all, are the work of fate, and some of them are in our own power, and they are liable to fate, but are not caused by fate." This middle ground appears in the famous dictum of Rabbi Aqiba, as recorded in Mishnah Avot 3:15: הכל צפוי והרשות נתונה *hak-kol ṣafuy wǝ-ha-rǝšut nǝtuna* "All is foreseen, but the authority [i.e., free will] is given." (3) In two passages Paul identified himself as a Pharisee (Acts 23:6, Phil 3:5), and in another passage (Acts 22:3) he informs us that he was a student of Gamaliel. The selfsame Gamaliel is identified as a Pharisee independently in another passage (Acts 5:34). On the Rabbinic side, note that the later Rabbis traced their legal teachings and religious outlook back to Gamaliel, who bears the title Rabban, and to Gamaliel's grandfather, Hillel. To my mind, these three pieces of evidence converge to demonstrate that the Pharisees of the pre–70 CE era emerged as the Rabbinic movement several generations after the destruction of the temple.

10. At least according to the traditional view. The Mishna itself makes no comment regarding authorship, redaction, compilation, etc.

the temple. At least one-third of the Mishnah is clearly related to temple ritual. The most obvious material is to be found in the fifth and sixth orders, Qodašim, lit. "holy things," related to sacrifices, and Ṭohorot, lit. "purities," which by and large appertain to the temple. Now the sacrifices had not been offered, to repeat, for 130 years; and the purity laws fell by the wayside without the temple as an anchor. First, the purity laws were less and less relevant, since the only real thing that a state of purity allowed one was entrance to the temple.[11] Second, the final act required for the formal transition from a state of impurity to a state of purity was a sacrifice (as outlined in Lev 12–15; Num 19), now impossible to perform without the temple.[12]

In light of these changes during the late-first century CE and throughout the second century CE, it is rather remarkable that so much of the Mishnah is devoted to temple matters. Furthermore, it is not just in the last two orders of the Mishnah, but in all manner of other tractates, especially in the order Mo'ed, lit. "festivals," where temple rituals are evoked and described. Thus, for example, Pesaḥim, "Passover," describes the Passover ritual not only as it existed in the post-temple world c. 200 CE, but also as it was observed in the temple; Yoma, "Yom Kippur," describes in great detail the Day of Atonement ritual as it existed in the Temple; Ḥagigah, "festival sacrifices," deals with the special offerings made in the temple on festival days; and Sheqalim, "shekels" recalls the temple accounting ritual.[13] Or, to cite an example from the first order Zera'im, lit. "seeds," which deals with agricultural laws, see Bikkurim, "first fruits," with its elaborate description of the bringing of the first fruits to the temple.[14] Here again I must reiterate that by the time of the compilation of the Mishnah, the temple had not been in existence for 130 years, or approximately four generations.

---

11. That said, we know that many Jews continued to cling to observance of the purity laws, even without the temple. See Miller, *At the Intersection of Texts and Material Finds*.

12. There are two exceptions to this procedure: removal of impurity after emission of semen, and removal of impurity caused by menstruation—for neither of these is a sacrifice required (see Lev 15:16–18; 15:19–24, respectively). The reason for this, most likely, is the regularity of sexual intercourse (in the case of the former) and the similar regularity of a woman's menstrual period (in the case of the latter), in contrast, for example, to more singular events such as childbirth, contact with the dead, etc.

13. For a comprehensive list of temple rituals embedded within the Mishnah, see Cohn, *Memory of the Temple*, 123–25 (appendix A).

14. Ibid., 4–7.

This point raises the question: why is so much of the Mishnah devoted to an edifice and an institution that no longer existed in Judaism? We may answer this question in three different ways, with none of the answers mutually exclusive. First, we may posit that Rabbi Judah felt the need to retain the cultic and ritual traditions for the time when the temple would be rebuilt. Jewish history and Jewish experience had taught the people that, in fact, the temple once before had been destroyed and rebuilt: destroyed by the Babylonians in 586 BCE; rebuilt following the decree of Cyrus the Great, the great Persian emperor, in 538 BCE; and then dedicated in 516 BCE, seventy years afterwards, thus inaugurating (what we now call) the Second Temple period. In light of this history, with a lesson that the Jews knew well, they had every reason to believe that the temple would be rebuilt yet again. True, by the year 200 CE, more time had passed than the historical rebuilding which followed the destruction of the First Temple, but the scenario outlined here would be one reason why Rabbi Judah included all this information about the temple and its rites in the Mishnah.

Second, without the temple standing, and without the ability to enact the sacrifices, as Jewish law and liturgy developed during this time period, the *memory* of the temple, just the memory alone, could serve to replace the actual ritual. One cannot execute the Day of Atonement ritual, the basics of which are outlined in Leviticus 16 and then expanded upon in the tractate of Yoma, but in the very least one can *virtually* perform the old temple rituals, by reciting what transpired in days of old.[15] In the words of Akiva Cohen, "The task undertaken by the redactors of the Mishnah was to fashion a way whereby the Jewish people could re-enter God's city and the temple courts."[16]

Third, as the rabbis of old stated, even the *study* of the sacrificial laws constituted a ritual act in itself. Obviously, there is some overlap here between this third point and the preceding second point. But to stress this point further, let me quote the actual passage, from the Babylonian Talmud, tractate Ta'anit 27b. There the rabbis actually place into the mouth of God the following statement, regarding those who study the ancient rituals: כאילו הקריבום לפני ואני מוחל להם על כל עונותיהם *kǝ-'illu*

---

15. Indeed, this ritual act remains part of traditional Judaism down to the present day, as the 'Avodah ("worship") service incorporated into the Musaf ("additional") service recited on Yom Kippur in the early afternoon. One may wish to consult the traditional Maḥzor (prayer book for the holidays) to peruse this portion of the liturgy.

16. Cohen, *Matthew and the Mishnah*, 404.

hiqrivum lifanay wǝ-'ani moẓel lahɛm ʿal kol ʿawonotehɛm "it is as if they offered them [i.e., the sacrifices] before me, and I absolve them of all their sins." Now, to be sure, this statement comes from a later time, say, two or three or even four centuries after the redaction of the Mishnah, but it goes a long way to understanding the rabbinic mindset.[17]

All of this, I trust, helps explain the inclusion of so much material concerning the temple in the Mishnah, a document compiled at some considerable remove from the year 70 CE. These numerous temple references notwithstanding, I also need to stress that in the entire Mishnah, a text which approaches 190,000 words (that is, about 60 percent the size of the Hebrew Bible), there are only three explicit statements about the rebuilding of the temple. Which is to say, while the Mishnah evokes and recalls and transmits the ancient temple rituals throughout, the actual rebuilding of the temple, with the concomitant restoration of the applicable rituals, is a topic barely mentioned.[18] The explanation for this is rather clear. The Rabbinic program led by Rabbi Judah, (most of) his predecessors and (all of) his successors, is very much a non-eschatological one. The reasons for this, in turn, are twofold.

First, while the Jewish community in the preceding centuries was captured by apocalyptic fervor, that fervor apparently informed the two revolts, the Great Revolt of 66–73 CE (even if we have less information about this), and the Bar-Kokhba Revolt of 132–135 CE (with more information forthcoming). Given the devastations caused by the two revolts, the Rabbinic movement steered clear of anything that might smack of nationalist aspirations, apocalyptic or otherwise, including the rebuilding of the temple.[19] Second, the emerging religion of Christianity had picked up the banner of apocalypticism, so that Judaism moved further away

---

17. Yet a fourth explanation is offered by Cohn, *Memory of the Temple*; indeed it serves as the main thesis of his book. According to Cohn, the rabbis attempted to gain control of the temple *post facto*, as it were, by demonstrating that their system of the temple rituals (as opposed to, for example, that of the Sadducees) was the 'correct' one, thereby according the rabbinic movement a sense of power and authority. See especially chapter 4, "Constructing Sacred Space" (pp. 73–89), with the most succinct statement on pp. 88–89.

18. For the three passages and analyses thereof, see Cohen, *Matthew and the Mishnah*, 413–15, 483.

19. Collins, "Apocalypse: Jewish Apocalypticism to the Rabbinic Period," 1.414–19, esp. p. 418, the section entitled "The Rabbis and Apocalypticism."

from such tendencies, as an element in the "parting of the two ways," if that term still has resonance.[20]

We now turn our attention to the synagogue.[21] The origins of the synagogue are to be found in the third century BCE, hence, while the temple still was standing. Many people are under the misconception that the temple was destroyed on such and such a date in the year 70 CE, and the next day the Jews built the first synagogue and voilà, the whole transition from temple to synagogue took place.[22] This is incorrect, however. The synagogue starts in the Diaspora, specifically in Egypt, in the middle of the third century BCE. From this point forward, for the next two and a half centuries, we have about a dozen dedicatory inscriptions of an institution known as the *proseuche*, literally "prayer" or "prayer-house," the forerunner of the synagogue.[23] Unfortunately, we do not know what these *proseuche* or early synagogue buildings looked like, for all of the stone inscriptions were found in secondary use.[24] Nonetheless, we can attest to the fact that the Jewish community of Ptolemaic Egypt created the institution of the synagogue for different kinds of ritual acts, including both prayer and the reading of the Torah. For at such a distance from Jerusalem, they could not visit the temple to offer sacrifices there (though they did send fiscal contributions, as we know from Philo and others), and thus parallel or replacement ritual acts developed.[25]

20. Gordon, "Jewish Reaction to Christian Borrowings," 685–90, esp. p. 687.

21. For all that follows, see Levine, *Ancient Synagogue*. I could cite this book on virtually every point to be raised in the ensuring treatment, though were I to do so, I would over-encumber this essay with too many repetitive footnotes. Accordingly, I cite the book below only occasionally, though as implied, for every subject regarding the synagogue raised herein, I direct the interested reader to Levine's *magnum opus* for further details. My page citations derive from the first edition, though see now also the second edition published in 2005.

22. I realize, of course, that I oversimplify here, which is to say, I oversimplify even the misconception.

23. The material, including images, is conveniently collected by Donald D. Binder at http://www.pohick.org/sts/egypt.html. For further details, see his co-authored book (which extends beyond Egypt) Runesson, Binder, and Olsson, *Ancient Synagogue from Its Origins to 200 C.E.* Again, for the most information, with even greater geographical and chronological scope, see Levine, *Ancient Synagogue*.

24. That is, the stones were reused in later construction projects.

25. Though we should mention the existence of a Jewish temple at Leontopolis, built by Onias IV, c. 150 BCE, after his exile from Jerusalem. Details are provided by Josephus, while the structure appears to have been found by the great Sir Flinders Petrie. For the former, see the references provided by Rosenberg, "Onias, Temple of," 15.432–33. The work of the latter is summarized in his book, *Hyksos and Israelite Cities*, 19–27.

In time, even as the temple stood, synagogues spread to other Jewish communities in the Diaspora. Two well-known examples are at Berenice in Cyrenaica (= modern-day Benghazi in eastern Libya) and at Ostia, located at the mouth of the Tiber River and which thus served as the main port of Rome (30 km [19 miles] upstream). A lengthy inscription found at the former site lists the donors who assisted in the repairs of the synagogue, dated to year 2 of Nero, that is, 55 CE, and hence we may posit the construction of this building sometime during the first century BCE. Incidentally, the inscription also refers both to the building and to the community as *synagoge* (as opposed to *proseuche*).[26]

At Ostia the preserved remains date mainly to the fourth century CE, but the excavations also revealed two earlier phases of the building, the first of which dates to the mid-first century CE.[27]

Yet another important Diaspora synagogue was found on the island of Delos, in the Aegean Sea. The structure dates to the second–first centuries BCE, though most likely this was a Samaritan synagogue, as opposed to a Jewish one.[28]

In time, the institution of the synagogue (a Diaspora creation, as noted above) spread to the land of Israel. Examples of excavated synagogues from the period while the temple still stood include Gamla, Masada, and Magdala.[29] Literary sources provide evidence for synagogues in other locations. The New Testament refers to synagogues in Capernaum (Mark 1:21) and Nazareth (Matt 13:54); while Josephus mentions synagogues in Tiberias (*Life*, 54 [280]), Dor (*Antiquities*, 19.6.3), and Caesarea (*War*, 2.14.4).[30]

This brief survey of the early synagogue does not do justice to the topic, but it sets the tone for the subject at hand. After the destruction of the temple in 70 CE, we see a burgeoning of synagogue buildings, both in

---

Though not everyone accepts Petrie's interpretation of the archaeological findings, for which see Hayward, "Jewish Temple at Leontopolis," 429–43, especially p. 431, n. 20 (with references).

26. For details, go to: http://www.pohick.org/sts/cyrenaica.html.
27. For details, go to: http://www.pohick.org/sts/ostia.html.
28. For details, go to: http://www.pohick.org/sts/delos.html.
29. For an important find from Magdala, see the coda at the conclusion of this essay.
30. Synagogues have been found in the excavations at Capernaum, Tiberias, and Caesarea, but these date to the later Byzantine period. Presumably they were built on the spots of the older synagogues dated to the first century CE.

the land of Israel and in the Diaspora.³¹ Most importantly for our present discussion, these later synagogue structures evoke the temple in manifold ways.

The most striking evidence, to my mind, is the artwork which adorns these synagogues. Such artwork takes different forms, and while we cannot do justice to this important topic in the space allotted here, we shall try nonetheless. The single artistic design which repeats again and again in these synagogues is the menorah, whose "original" stood in the inner sanctum of the temple.³² Thus, for example, one finds the menorah atop the columns at the Ostia Antica synagogue,³³ as a self-standing marble artifact (about one meter high) at the Sardis synagogue,³⁴ on the mosaic floors of the synagogues at Bet Alfa, Tiberias,³⁵ Sepphoris, Naʿaran, Susiya, and elsewhere,³⁶ and on the wall frescoes at the Dura Europos synagogue.³⁷ From such an array, and from other evidence,³⁸ we know that the menorah became the defining feature of Jewish art in late antiquity—indeed, one should say, the Jewish symbol par excellence.³⁹ Given the Menorah's central place in the Jerusalem Temple, one must imagine that the artistic representations of this important relic in synagogues both throughout the Diaspora and in the land of Israel helped Jews everywhere recall what once was.

Let us remain, for the moment, with the mosaic floors on the aforementioned Galilean synagogues: Bet Alfa, Tiberias, and Sepphoris. All

---

31. For synagogues in the land of Israel, see the map in Magness, "Heaven on Earth," 3. For synagogues in the Diaspora, see the map in Fine, *Sacred Realm*, vii.

32. The actual menorah, which presumably we should capitalize as "the Menorah" was taken away by the Roman soldiers who despoiled and destroyed the temple. It is displayed prominently on the Arch of Titus in Rome, constructed in 82 CE: https://en.wikipedia.org/wiki/Arch_of_Titus (with images).

33. https://en.wikipedia.org/wiki/Ostia_Synagogue (with image).

34. http://www.sardisexpedition.org/en/essays/about-synagogue (see especially figs. 33–34).

35. Scholars typically refer to this structure as the Hammat Tiberias synagogue, because it was built right next to the hot springs (Heb. ḥamma) of Tiberias. For simplicity's sake, however, I will call it simply the Tiberias synagogue.

36. For images of the *menorot* on the floors of the Tiberias and Sepphoris synagogues, see below, figure 1 and figure 2.

37. http://users.stlcc.edu/mfuller/DuraSynagogue.html (with image).

38. See Fine, *Menorah*.

39. The six-pointed *magen dawid*, lit. "shield of David," though often called the Star of David, did not develop as a specifically Jewish symbol until the Middle Ages.

three mosaic floors include an upper register, which was closest to the visual focal point of the synagogue, that is, the spot where the Ark (which housed the Torah scrolls) stood.[40] The central feature in the upper register is the depiction of the Ark; while on each flank of the Ark is a large menorah. Filling in the remaining space, especially on the Tiberias and Sepphoris synagogue floors, are visual reminders of the temple and its rituals.[41] In figure 1 below, with the upper register of the Tiberias synagogue floor, one sees three objects associated with the temple, again on either flank of the Ark: the *lulavim*, or palm fronds, used in the celebration of Sukkot (Feast of Booths), for which see Lev 23:40; the *maḥtot*, or incense shovels, for which see Exod 27:3; 38:3, along with the key role that these objects play in the story of Korah's rebellion in Num 16–17; and the *šofarot*, or shofar-horns. These last items are not associated with the temple rituals *per se* in the Bible (unless one accounts Ps 150:3), but rabbinic tradition records the use of the shofar horn for various ritual acts, especially on Rosh ha-Shana, the New Year festival (see, for example, Mishnah tractate Rosh ha-Shana, especially ch. 3). Any congregant gazing at these images, especially the incense shovels, would be transported to the temple of old, now destroyed, but still alive within the communal memory.

---

40. For the Leviticus scroll found at the corresponding spot in the Ein Gedi synagogue (burnt c. 700 CE, but with the text now revealed through a CT-scan), see Segal, et al., "Early Leviticus Scroll from En-Gedi," 1–30.

41. Some of the items are present in the upper register of the Bet Alfa synagogue floor as well, but the largest items there, after the two lampstands are two lions and two birds, with the temple accoutrements much smaller. For images, go to: http://synagogues.kinneret.ac.il/synagogues/beth-alpha/.

Figure 1: A portion of the mosaic stone floor
at the Tiberias synagogue, c. 500 C.E. (photo by author)

In figure 2 below, with a large portion of the Sepphoris synagogue floor visible, one sees even more of the temple rituals. While the images alone would suffice in identifying the various objects, we are aided by the Hebrew and Greek labels which accompany each item. Thus we see such items and read such Hebrew words as *solet* "fine flour," *šemen* "oil," and *ḥaṣoṣrot* "trumpets" (all in the bottom left square), the large table with the twelve loaves of bread (in the bottom center square), and the basket of first fruits, with accompanying Greek inscription (in the bottom right square, only partially visible in figure 2)—in addition to the two large *mənorot* in the upper register (with the one to the right much better preserved).[42]

[42]. For further details on the ritual objects, see Hachlili, *Ancient Mosaic Pavements*, 28–30. One does not typically think of trumpets in conjunction with the cult, though see Num 10:10. The use of the trumpets appears to have increased with time, as witnessed by the fact that sixteen of the twenty-seven occurrences of the word *ḥaṣoṣra* "trumpet" in the Bible occur in the book of Chronicles. They also are mentioned, alongside the shofar, in m. Rosh ha-Shana 3:3–4. Finally, note the inclusion of the trumpets along with other temple treasures taken as booty by the Romans, as depicted

Figure 2: A portion of the mosaic stone floor
at the Sepphoris synagogue, c. 400 C.E. (photo by author)

The date of this mosaic floor is at least several centuries after the destruction of the temple in 70 CE, and yet here are Jews still recalling the temple cult in a building devoted to a wholly different set of ritual practices (prayer, Torah reading, etc.).

These two examples of Galilean synagogues demonstrate to serve the point, though I hasten to add that many other synagogues in the region (and elsewhere) evoke memories of the temple in similar fashion and with similar artwork (Bet Alfa, etc.). I also wish to stress that one should not automatically conclude that these synagogues are connected to rabbinic Judaism. For while today we associate the two words "rabbi" and "synagogue" very closely,[43] the rabbinic "control" of the synagogue may not have been established by the Byzantine period. Rather, these synagogues simply may be establishments of the Jewish community generally. This would explain, for example, why some of these structures include exquisite representations of Helios and the zodiac in the center of the mosaic floors, in clear violation of the rabbinic interpretation of the

---

on the bas relief on the Arch of Titus.

43. For example, in a word association game, were I to say "rabbi," you might say "synagogue," and vice versa.

prohibition against images (*pesel*) and likenesses (*təmuna*) in Exod 20:4 || Deut 5:8.[44] The best preserved examples of this artwork are to be found at Bet Alfa, Tiberias, and Sepphoris (see figure 3), the same synagogues under discussion here, where they appear alongside the evocations of the temple appurtenances.

Figure 3: A portion of the mosaic stone floor at the Sepphoris synagogue, c. 400 C.E., depicting Helios in the center circle and the twelve signs of the zodiac in the outer circle (photo by author)

Eventually, the rabbinic influence over the synagogue did take hold, as witnessed best of all at Rehov, where the mosaic floor is comprised entirely of citations of rabbinic literature (Tosefta, Talmud of the Land of Israel, etc.),[45] but one should not simply assume the presence of rabbinic Judaism in the Roman- and Byzantine-era synagogues. By and large, the rabbis were in the *bet midraš* "study hall," and not necessarily in the *bet kəneset* "synagogue."[46] Judaism post-70 CE remained as variegated as Judaism in late Second Temple times, with rabbinic Judaism as one stream,

---

44. See Mishnah tractate ʿAvodah Zarah, lit. "foreign worship," especially ch. 3, and the Talmudic discussions thereon (in both the Talmud of the Land of Israel and the Babylonian Talmud).

45. For further information, go to http://synagogues.kinneret.ac.il/synagogues/rehob/.

46. This may explain why there is no tractate in the Mishnah devoted to the synagogue. For a list of occurrences of the term *bet kəneset* "synagogue" in the Mishnah and related literature, see Meyers, "Problem of the Scarcity of Synagogues," 448.

but clearly there were non-rabbinic streams as well.[47] If anything, one may wish to countenance priestly influence over the synagogues under discussion here,[48] a proposal which would explain, for example, the presence of reminders of the temple in synagogue mosaic floors. Or perhaps, and this may be the preferred approach, these synagogue buildings served the general Jewish community, comprised of the people who adhered to what scholars call Common Judaism.

Regardless of who prayed, gathered, and worshipped in these synagogue buildings, let us return now to our main focus—for it is not just a matter of the artwork on the floors and on other parts of synagogue buildings, but also what transpired in the worship service. We learn from the Mishnah and from later Jewish texts, and indeed from Jewish liturgy down to the present day, that many ritual acts associated with the temple were transferred to the developing liturgy in the synagogue in a post-temple world.

For the priestly blessing, whose source is Num 6:22–27, see m. Sotah 7:6, m. Tamid 5:1.[49] For the blowing of the shofar, whose source is Num 29:1, see m. Rosh ha-Shana, chs. 3–4.[50] For the lulav, whose source is Lev 23:40, see m. Sukkah 3:12, m. Rosh ha-Shana 4:3.[51] In fact, we read in these passages of a very conscious reminder of the temple ritual: "Beforetime the *lulav* was carried seven days in the temple, but in the provinces one day only. After the Temple was destroyed, Rabban Yoḥanan ben Zakkai ordained that in the provinces it should be carried seven days in memory of the Temple."[52]

One also may point to the use of the *ner tamid* "perpetual lamp," even if this item represents an extension of the biblical source. According to Exod 27:20–21; Lev 24:1–4; the Menorah was to burn through the night, *me-ɛrev ɐd boqer*, "from evening until morning" (Exod 27:21; Lev

47. Goodman, "Sadducees and Essenes after 70 CE," 347–56.

48. See Magness, "Heaven on Earth," 1–52; and Magness, "Priests and Purity in the Dura-Europos Synagogue," 421–33.

49. For a possible biblical reference, see 2 Chr 30:27. It is true that the Mishna passages here cited do not identify the locus of the priestly blessing in post-temple times, though later sources clearly indicate the synagogue as the venue for this practice.

50. See especially m. Rosh ha-Shana 3:7 for mention of the sounding of the shofar in the synagogue.

51. See m. Sukkah 3:13 for mention of the *lulav* ritual within the synagogue liturgy.

52. Adapted from the translation of Danby, *Mishnah*, 177, 192. Note that the rabbinic authority quoted here, Yoḥanan ben Zakkai, lived during the Great Revolt and, according to tradition, witnessed the destruction of the temple.

24:3), on a regular basis. By late Second Temple times, however, the lamp was understood to be one that burns perpetually, as noted, for example, by Josephus, *Contra Apion*, 1.199.[53] For rabbinic recollections of this item in the temple, see, for example, m. Tamid 3:9; 6:1. This item, too, found its way into the synagogue, as evidenced by both figural and architectural evidence (especially in the Nevoraya synagogue),[54] and it remains a fixture in synagogue design down to the present day.

An additional, and to some extent more important, liturgical act which shifted from temple to synagogue, is the recitation of psalms, including both the daily psalms and the Hallel series (Pss 113–18) recited on festivals.[55] The Mishnah recalls their use in the temple rituals: for the former, see the list (one for each day of the week) in m. Tamid 7:4; for the latter, see m. Pesaḥim 5:7 (as well as m. Sukkah 3:9, though only Ps 118 is mentioned there). These, too, become a key feature of the synagogue liturgy, as indicated in various Talmudic references.[56]

Before we move to the next major theme, let us refer one more time to the Mishnah. While the memory of the temple may be seen in numerous places (see above for examples), we also should call attention to the very opening of the Mishnah. M. Berakhot 1:1 asks, "From when may one recite the *Shemaʿ* prayer in the evening?" Which is to say, how dark must it be before one can actually recite the evening prayer? When the sun is ready to dip below the horizon (in which case there is still some visible daylight)? When there is total darkness? At some (defined or undefined) point in between? The answer which the rabbis provide is actually somewhat surprising: "from the time when the priests would enter [i.e., the temple] to eat their *tĕruma*-offering?" Now, this is a useful answer *if and only if* one is able to recall at what time the priests would

---

53. Whether this change in the burning of the lamp was due to the semantic shift of the word *tamid* from "regularly" (Exod 27:20; Lev 24:2–3) to "perpetually" (as in Rabbinic Hebrew), or whether the meaning of the word shifted based on the practice of burning the lamp in the temple perpetually, is unclear. Either way, the practice developed, and hence the temple included the *ner tamid* "perpetual lamp" as one of its key appurtenances. Note, incidentally, that in the relevant biblical passages, the ṭĕʿamim indicate that *ner* "lamp" and *tamid* "regularly" do not constitute the combination of noun + adjective. Rather, the equivalent of a comma should follow the noun, so that Exod 27:20; Lev 24:2 should be rendered "for the lighting of the lamp, regularly" (and similarly in Lev 24:3).

54. Levine, *Ancient Synagogue*, 223–24, 332–33.

55. See Rendsburg, "Psalms as Hymns in the Temple of Jerusalem."

56. See "Hallel," 8.279–80.

enter the temple to partake of the *tĕruma*-offering (see Num 18:8–32 for the biblical basis of the rabbinic discussion). The question is: at a chronological remove of about 130 years, from 70 CE, the date of the destruction of the temple, to c. 200 CE, the approximate date of the redaction of the Mishnah, did anyone really know the precise moment in the late afternoon or early evening when this daily occurrence had transpired?[57] At a distance of almost two thousand years, no one today knows how to judge this question, but somehow this formerly daily priestly ritual continued to serve as a time marker for Rabbi Judah and his colleagues as a means to determine when the evening *Shema'* could be recited. This is, to be sure, a very fine point of Mishnaic law, though it speaks volumes to the subject at hand, the manner in which the memory of the temple and its rituals continued to reverberate amongst Jews for generations afterwards.

We now turn to an element of synagogue architecture, though first let us once more recall the temple. Most visitors to the temple entered via a set of triple gates at the southern end of the large complex (outside of which many *miqwa'ot* "ritual baths" have been found). These gates led to an underground passageway, under the Stoa, which eventually granted visitors access to the large plaza which surrounded the temple. Of the three gates, the middle one was larger, with smaller ones on either side (see figure 4).[58]

---

57. I rendered the participle above with modal force, "would enter," but truth be told, the participle typically refers to the present tense in Rabbinic Hebrew, in which case the passage should be rendered "from the time when the priests enter [i.e., the temple] to eat their *tĕruma*-offering." This is an even more striking reading, since in the year c. 200 CE the remembered ritual took place in the ever increasingly distant past, and yet m. Berakhot 1:1 refers to the practice as occuring in the present. For the grammar, see Pérez Fernández, *Introductory Grammar of Rabbinic Hebrew*, 108, 133–35. And indeed this is how Pérez Fernández renders the passage, "From the moment the priests enter to eat their offerings" (p. 99). For additional treatment, see Cohn, *Making of the Rabbis*, 6–8, 62 (the latter within the context of general verb usage, pp. 60–65).

58. The sealed triple gate entranceway, with its three gates of identical size, visible today in the southern wall, dates to the Umayyad period, and is thus not relevant to the present discussion.

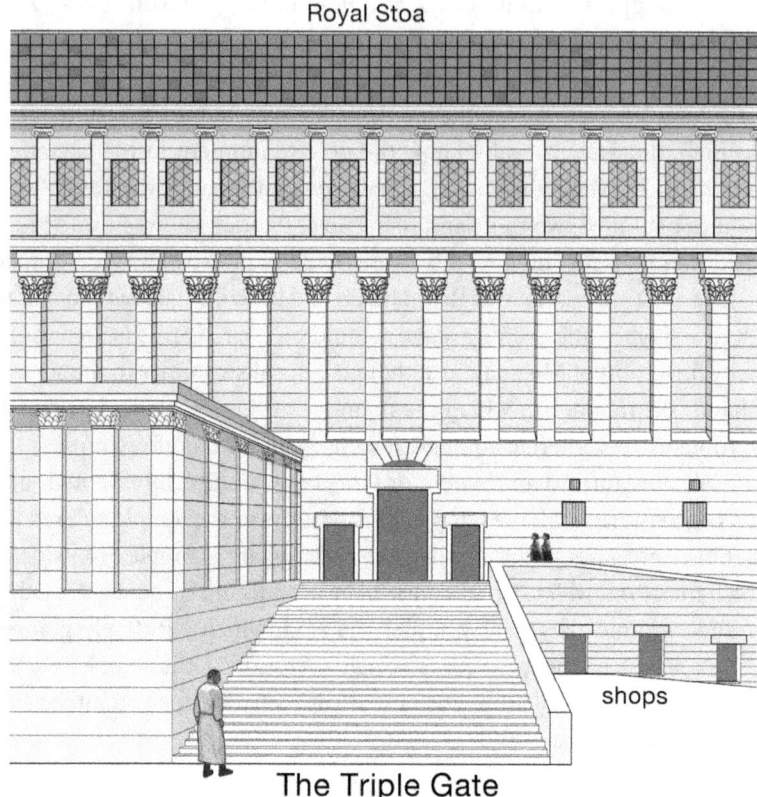

Figure 4: Rendering of the Triple Gates, at the southern end of the Jerusalem Temple complex, after its great expansion by King Herod (© Ritmeyer Archaeological Design)

Similarly, in order to proceed from the large plaza into the temple itself, one passed through a set of three gates. Again, the middle gate was larger, with smaller ones on either side (see figure 5, at the very bottom).[59]

---

59. The reconstructions by Leen Ritmeyer and by all others who have produced similar models are based mainly on Josephus, *Antiquities* (15.11.5) (near the very end of book 15), and on Mishnah tractate Middot, lit., "measurements."

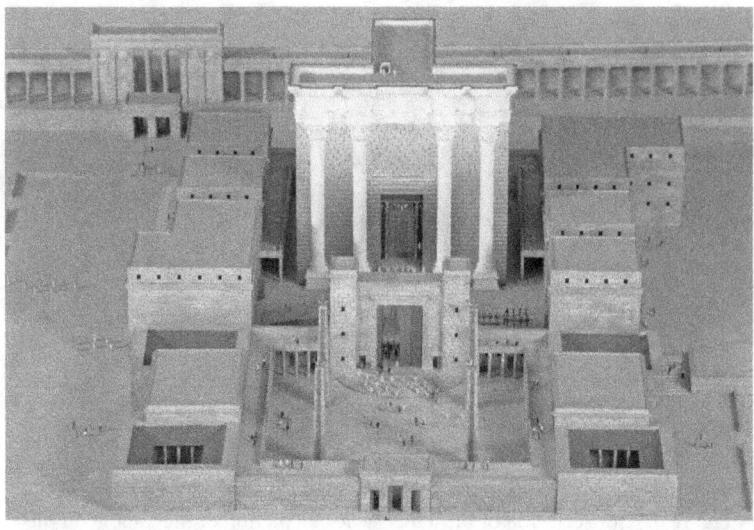

Figure 5: Rendering of the temple courts, after the great construction project by King Herod, with the triple gate entranceway seen at the bottom of this image (© Ritmeyer Archaeological Design)

Once more, at a distance of several centuries, the Jews recalled these two sets of triple gates either by depicting them in the wall frescoes at Dura Europos or more commonly by erecting synagogue façades with entranceways comprised of triple gates, with the middle one larger than the two flanking ones.

At Dura Europos we have two portrayals of the temple, one to the upper left of the Torah niche and one to the upper right thereof (see figure 6 and figure 7). In both of these vignettes, the triple gates are visible, with the middle one larger than the other two. In the former panel, one also sees visitors to the temple bringing various sacrificial animals (bovines, etc.), along with a depiction of Aaron the high priest, with his name in Greek written above. In the latter panel, one sees the temple only, with just the architecture, devoid of human activity.[60]

---

60. As an aside, note further that in the former scene (figure 6) the three gates have rounded tops; while in the latter scene (figure 7) the large middle gate has no design above it, with the two smaller flanking ones bearing triangular tops. Either different sets of gates are portrayed (see above, the discussion surrounding figure 4 and figure 5), or possibly different artists are responsible for the two panels. This observation constitutes a minor and tangential point, but one worth noting nonetheless.

Figure 6: "Consecration of the Tabernacle." Depiction of the temple on the Dura Europos synagogue wall frescoes, to the upper left of the Torah shrine (Yale University Art Gallery, Dura Europos Collection)

Figure 7: "Temple of Solomon, Jerusalem." Depiction of the temple on the Dura Europos synagogue wall frescoes, to the upper right of the Torah shrine (Yale University Art Gallery, Dura Europos Collection)

The triple gates are seen in synagogue architecture as well. In a number of cases, the entire front façade has been preserved, so that we can see the triple gates *in situ*. In other instances, we can reconstruct the presence of triple gates based on thresholds and other archaeological remains at the entranceways to the synagogue buildings.⁶¹ The best preserved façade is at the Bar'am synagogue in the far north of Israel, close to the present-day Israeli-Lebanese border (see figure 8).

Figure 8: Bar'am synagogue, front façade, c. 300 C.E. (photo by author)

Though such can be seen elsewhere as well, including, quite impressively, at the Capernaum synagogue.⁶² Again, by the time these synagogue buildings were constructed, in the early Byzantine period, and as they persisted into the late Byzantine period, one must assume that those who passed through these portals understood their significance. The temple was no longer, but evocations thereof were to be found in "minor sacred spaces" such as the synagogues which served the local Jewish communities.⁶³

61. For details, see Hachlili, *Ancient Synagogues*, 131–33. These pages include table IV–1 (b), which lists all synagogues and the kind of entranceway each one has (triple gate, single gate, etc.), along with the ensuing discussion.

62. See especially the aerial views available at http://synagogues.kinneret.ac.il/synagogues/capernaum/—even if, in these images, the large central portal is difficult to ascertain, since the view of it is blocked by the large palm tree (!) standing just outside the building.

63. The term "minor sacred spaces" is my rendering of *miqdaš mə'aṭ* "a minor

The triple gates are found in one other important location in the land of Israel, namely, the necropolis at Bet Sheʻarim, situated in the Lower Galilee, which prospered during the third and fourth centuries CE. According to rabbinic tradition, Rabbi Judah himself was buried at Bet Sheʻarim (y. Kil'ayim 9:4 [32b]; y. Ketubbot 12:3 [35a]; Qohelet Rabba 7:12), so that the site developed over the course of the ensuing centuries as a burial ground for thousands of Jews. The necropolis is a series of several dozen caves, cut into the mountainside, into which were placed the deceased, either in sarcophagi or in tombs hewn into the rock itself. Jews not only from the land of Israel, but from as far away as Antioch in the north and Yemen (Ḥimyar) in the south were buried there. Presumably these (mainly wealthy?) individuals arranged for the conveyance of their deceased bodies and their subsequent burials in Bet Sheʻarim while yet alive. Here, too, the main catacomb recalls the triple gates of the temple, with the central gate larger than the two side ones (see figure 9). As such, the "holy space" of the necropolis conjured up memories of the temple, even at a distance of several centuries, by people who obviously experienced the temple only as an *objet de mémoire*.

Figure 9: The entrance to the main catacomb at Bet Sheʻarim, with the central gate larger than the two on either side (photo by author)

---

sanctuary." The term appears in Ezek 11:16, and is then used in rabbinic texts (e.g., b. Megillah 29a) to refer to the synagogue.

One final element relevant to our discussion is the presence of lists of the twenty-four priestly courses, based on the details given in 1 Chr 24:3–19, long after the destruction of the temple. According to this biblical passage, various priestly families rotated in weekly shifts for service in the temple. To be more accurate, the Chronicles passage does not mention the duration of each shift, but the weekly rotation may be deduced from later sources. Josephus, *Antiquities* (8.14.7) mentions this explicitly; while rabbinic sources such as m. Taʿanit 4:2; m. Sukkah 5:8; t. Sukkah 4:11 imply such. So, what happened when the temple was destroyed in 70 CE?

One might think that this kind of "record-keeping" may have fallen by the wayside, since it had no more practical use in the everyday lives of post-temple Jews. Remarkably, however, various Jewish communities recalled the names of the twenty-four priestly families, and in different ways. Three locations in the land of Israel—Caesarea, Ashkelon, and Kissufim—have yielded inscriptions which record the list of the twenty-four priestly courses. And while all three epigraphs are in a fragmentary state of preservation, based on the repetitive nature of the wording of these lists, we are quite confident in their total reconstruction. For example, in the Caesarea inscription, made of gray marble, we have only three small fragments, but as a whole they include the beginning and the end of the word *mišmeret* "guard, watch, course, rotation," a numeral, and the names of known priestly families (see figure 10 and figure 11 below).[64] Presumably, "these fragments once formed tablets which were affixed to the walls of synagogues in the places in which they were found."[65]

---

64. For the *editio princeps*, see Avi-Yonah, "List of Priestly Courses from Caesarea," 137–39.

65. Thus Miller, *Studies in the History and Traditions of Sepphoris*, 125, n. 360.

38 SACRED SPACE, SACRED THREAD

Figure 10: Two of the three fragments of the Caesarea inscription of the 24 priestly courses (courtesy of the Israel Exploration Society)

```
משמרת ראשונה יהויריב מסרבי מחן
משמרת שניה ידעיה עמוק צפורים
משמרת שלישית חזרים משומה
משמרת רביעית שערים עיתלו
משמרת חמישית מלכיה בית לחם
משמרת ששות בימין יודפת
משמרת שביעית הקוץ עילבו
משמרת שמינית אבי הכפר עזיזה
משמרת תשיעית ישוע ערב אל
משמרת עשירית שכניה כבול
משמרת אחת עשרה אלישיב כהן קנה
משמרת שתים עשרה יקים פשחור עפת
משמרת שלוש עשרה חופה בית מעון
משמרת ארבע עשרה ישבאב אליקפיא שחין
משמרת חמש עשרה בלגה מעריה בל גזיית
משמרת שש עשרה אמר כפר נמריה
משמרת שבע עשרה חזיר מממליח
משמרת שמונה עשרה הפיצץ
משמרת תשע עשרה פתחיה אכלה ערב
משמרת עשרים יחזקאל מגדל נוניא
משמרת עשרים ואחד יכין כפר יוחנה
משמרת עשרים ושתים גמול בית חוביה
משמרת עשרים ושלוש דליהו גנתון צלמין
משמרת עשרים וארבע מעזיהו אריח
```

Figure 11: Line drawing of the "complete" Caesarea inscription of the 24 priestly courses, reconstructed from the three extant fragments (courtesy of the Israel Exploration Society)

One might think that it was only in synagogues in the land of Israel, given their relative proximity to the temple of yore, where such documentation was retained. It was quite a striking discovery, accordingly, when Walter W. Müller, working in far-off Yemen (specifically at Bayt Ḥāḍir, 15 km east of Ṣanʿāʾ) in 1970, discovered a similar registry of the priestly courses.[66] This plaque, moreover, was found relatively intact (see figures 12 and 13), making it the largest extant example of this type of Hebrew inscription. The inscription includes thirteen lines of text, recording eleven individual priestly courses, numbered as no. 4 through no. 14. Furthermore, of the eleven names recorded, nine are known from 1 Chr 24. While it is difficult to date a text such as this one, with very little comparative material available, Rainer Degen, who published the inscription, suggested the fifth or sixth century CE.[67] Regardless, this inscription serves as remarkable evidence for the continuity of Jewish tradition in this regard, not only across time but also across space.[68]

66. The plaque was found in secondary use, in the village mosque, actually. Presumably, its original home was a nearby synagogue, c. fifteen hundred years ago.

67. For the *editio princeps*, see Degen, "Ketovet mi-Teman ʿal 24 Mišmerot ha-Kohanim," 302–3. See also the follow-up survey by Urbach, "Mišmarot u-Maʿamadot," 304–27. See now most recently Gorea, "Les classes sacerdotales," 297–329.

68. For the reader unfamiliar with the Jewish community in Yemen at such an early period, see the superb syntheses of the relatively rich (and relatively surprising!) documentation from the pen of Christian Robin: Robin, "Le judaïsme de Ḥimyar"; and

Figure 12: The Hebrew inscription of the priestly courses found at Bayt Ḥāḍir, Yemen (© Christian Robin, used with kind permission)

Figure 13: Line drawing by Maria Gorea, based on Robin's photo
(© Maria Gorea used with kind permission)

Robin, "Ḥimyar et Israël." More recently see the collection of essays in Robin, ed., *Le Judaïsme de l'Arabie Antique* (one of which is cited in the previous note).

Finally, I note that such lists of priestly courses served as the basis for intricate liturgical poems (known collectively as *piyyuṭ*) written by Jewish poets such as Eleazar Qillir (c. 570–c. 640). These poems, which were recited in the synagogue, in some cases regularly on the Sabbath, are one more indication of how the memory of the temple—where these priestly families once had served—remained alive for half a millennium and then some.[69]

This essay has surveyed a variety of data—from the Mishnah, from synagogues (both in the Land of Israel and in the Diaspora), from the necropolis at Bet Sheʿarim, from the realm of art and architecture, and from the realm of ritual and liturgy—all of which points to a sustained effort to keep the memory of the temple alive. No "sacred space" replaced that of the temple. The synagogue may have been considered a "minor sanctuary" in some circles (see n. 63), and attributions of sanctity to the synagogue may have grown over time, especially as the temple became more and more of a distant memory—but in the end, and to repeat, no "sacred space" ever truly replaced the temple.[70] Nonetheless, and quite remarkably, the temple, or at least the memory thereof, lived on in the minds of Jews in manifold ways, for a half-millennium and well beyond.[71]

---

69. See further Sperber, "Mishmarot and Maʿamadot," 14:318–19.

70. Levine, *Ancient Synagogue*, 597–98.

71. I am grateful to my former students Joshua Blachorsky (New York University) and Charles Loder (Southern Baptist Theological Seminary) for their comments on an earlier draft of this article, and to the former in particular for several bibliographic references.

Coda: The Magdala Stone

During the preparation of the oral presentation of this paper, news reports reached scholars concerning the discovery of the Magdala stone, found in the synagogue at Magdala, on the shore of the Sea of Galilee, dated to the first century CE.[72] There is still some debate concerning the function of this large stone object, but the artwork which adorns its sides is unmistakable: a menorah, two jugs of olive oil, and what appear to be grain offerings. These images all evoke the temple and its rituals—and yet this object was created while the temple still was standing, in the first century CE, at least according to the archaeological context of the building and the smaller finds.

Isabel Kershner's report in the *New York Times* is apt:

> Experts have long believed that in the period before Herod's Temple was destroyed in A.D. 70, synagogues were used as a general place of assembly and learning, something like a neighborhood community center. The more formal conception of a synagogue as a sacred space reserved for religious ritual was thought to have developed later, in the Jewish Diaspora after the Temple had been destroyed. But the Magdala Stone was found in the center of the old synagogue, and Ms. Talgam [sc. Rina Talgam, Professor of Art History at the Hebrew University] said it might have been intended to give the space an aura of holiness "like a lesser temple" even while Herod's Temple still existed.[73]

Possibly, the Jews of Magdala already felt a distance from the Jerusalem temple, not in time, since the temple was still standing, but in space, given the location of the former in the Galilee and the latter in the south

---

72. The stone was discovered in 2009, and in fact was announced to the scholarly world at that time through various outlets (including the Agade listserv). To the best of my knowledge, though, its existence did not become widely known until 2015. (Or at least my words here include a self-admission, since I for one did not become aware of the stone, or at least its significance, until six years after its discovery.) For a press report, see Isabel Kershner, "A Carved Stone Block Upends Assumptions about Ancient Judaism," *New York Times*, December 8, 2015, available at https://www.nytimes.com/2015/12/09/world/middleeast/magdala-stone-israel-judaism.html. The stone was mentioned by Corbett, "New Synagogue Excavations In Israel and Beyond," 24–36, though as one of a number of finds in a survey article. An article dedicated to the Magdala synagogue, with an especial focus on the Magdala Stone, appeared only very recently: Zapata-Meza and Sanz-Rincón, "Excavating Mary Magdalene's Hometown," 37–42.

73. See the article cited in the previous footnote.

of the country,[74] or in character, given the controversy surrounding the control of the temple throughout this period.[75]

In sum, the main conclusions of my essay remain, but this curious find from the excavations at Magdala certainly provides fodder for some further evaluation and for some continued discussion.

---

74. Even if the distance is only c. 155 km.

75. I refer here to differences of opinion between the Sadducees and the Pharisees concerning the purity laws, how to proceed with the sacrificial rituals, etc.; the radical step taken by the Essenes (Qumran community, etc.) not to participate in the temple rites; and presumably other issues for which we have less evidence.

Appendix: The orders and tractates of the Mishnah (c. 200 CE), and the presence or absence of discussion in the two Talmudim

Order	Mishnah Tractate *(with number of chapters and topic)*	Talmud of the Land of Israel	Babylonian Talmud
Zera'im	*Agricultural Laws*		
	1. Berakot (9)—Benedictions	X	X
	2. Pe'ah (8)—Gleanings of the Field	X	–
	3. Demai (7)—Doubtfully Tithed Produce	X	–
	4. Kil'ayim (9)—Forbidden Mixtures	X	–
	5. Shevi'it (10)—Sabbatical Year	X	–
	6. Terumot (11)—Priestly Portions	X	–
	7. Ma'aserot (5)—Tithes for Levites and the Poor	X	–
	8. Ma'aser Sheni (5)—Second Tithe	X	–
	9. Ḥallah (4)—Dough Offering	X	–
	10. 'Orlah (3)—Fruit of Young Trees	X	–
	11. Bikkurim (3)—First Fruits	X	–
Mo'ed	*Festivals and Sacred Times*		
	1. Shabbat (24)—Sabbath	X	X
	2. 'Eruvin (10)—Sabbath limits	X	X
	3. Pesaḥim (10)—Passover	X	X
	4. Sheqalim (8)—Half-Shekel Offering	X	–
	5. Yoma (8)—Yom Kippur (Day of Atonement)	X	X
	6. Sukkah (5)—Festival of Sukkot	X	X
	7. Beṣah (Yom Tov) (5)—Festival laws	X	X

	8. Rosh ha-Shanah (4)—New Year Festival	X	X
	9. Ta'anit (4)—Fast Days	X	X
	10. Megillah (4)—Purim	X	X
	11. Mo'ed Qatan (3)—Intermediate Days of Festivals	X	X
	12. Ḥagigah (3)—Festival Sacrifices	X	X
Nashim	*Women*		
	1. Yevamot (16)—Levirate Marriage	X	X
	2. Ketubbot (13)—Marriage contracts	X	X
	3. Nedarim (11)—Vows	X	X
	4. Nazir (9)—Nazirites	X	X
	5. Giṭṭin (9)—Divorce	X	X
	6. Soṭah (9)—Suspected Adulteress	X	X
	7. Qiddushin (4)—Marriage	X	X
Neziqin	*Torts / Damages / Civil Law*		
	1. Bava Qama (10)—Damages	X	X
	2. Bava Meṣi'a (10)—Civil law	X	X
	3. Bava Batra (10)—Property law	X	X
	4. Sanhedrin (11)—Courts	X	X
	5. Makkot (3)—Punishment of flogging	X	X
	6. Shevu'ot (8)—Oaths	X	X
	7. 'Eduyyot (8)—Attested Legal Teachings	–	–
	8. 'Avodah Zarah (5)—Idolatry	X	X
	9. 'Avot (5)—Sayings of the Fathers	–	–
	10. Horayot (3)—Erroneous Court Decisions	X	X

Qodašim	Sacrifices		
	1. Zebaḥim (14)—Animal Sacrifices	–	X
	2. Menaḥot (13)—Meal Offerings	–	X
	3. Ḥullin (12)—Slaughter of Profane Animals	–	X
	4. Bekorot (9)—Firstborn Animals	–	X
	5. ʿArakhin (9)—Vows of Valuation	–	X
	6. Temurah (7)—Substitution of Offerings	–	X
	7. Keritot (6)—Penalty of Extirpation	–	X
	8. Meʿilah (6)—Misappropriation of sacred offerings	–	X
	9. Tamid (7)—Daily Sacrifices	–	X
	10. Middot (5)—Dimensions of the Temple	–	–
	11. Qinnim (3)—Bird Offerings	–	–
Ṭoharot	Purities		
	1. Kelim (30)—Impurity of Vessels	–	–
	2. ʾOhalot (14)—Impurity of Tents	–	–
	3. Negaʿim (14)—Scale-disease	–	–
	4. Parah (12)—The Red Heifer	–	–
	5. Toharot (10)—Ritual Purification	–	–
	6. Miqvaʾot (10)—Ritual baths	–	–
	7. Niddah (10)—Menstrual Impurity	X	X
	8. Makshirin (6)—Liquids susceptible to Impurity	–	–
	9. Zavim (5)—Genital fluxes	–	–
	10. Ṭevul Yom (4) –Immersion before Sunset	–	–
	11. Yadayim (4)—Impurity of the Hands	–	–
	12. ʿUqṣin (3)—Impurity of some Plant Parts	–	

Bibliography

Avi-Yonah, Michael. "A List of Priestly Courses from Caesarea." *Israel Exploration Journal* 12 (1962) 137–39.
Charlesworth, James H. "Jesus and the Temple." In *Jesus and Temple: Textual and Archaeological Explorations*, edited by James H. Charlesworth, 145–81. Minneapolis: Fortress, 2014.
Cohen, Akiva. *Matthew and the Mishnah: Redefining Identity and Ethos in the Shadow of the Second Temple's Destruction*. Wissenschaftliche Untersuchungen zum Neuen Testament 2.418. Tübingen: Mohr Siebeck, 2016.
Cohn, Naftali S. *The Memory of the Temple and the Making of the Rabbis*. Philadelphia: University of Pennsylvania Press, 2013.
Collins, John J. "Apocalypse: Jewish Apocalypticism to the Rabbinic Period." In *Encyclopedia of Religion*, vol. 1, 685–90. 2nd ed. Detroit: Macmillan, 2005.
Corbett, Glenn J. "New Synagogue Excavations in Israel and Beyond." *Biblical Archaeology Review* 37, no. 4 (2011) 24–36.
Danby, Herbert. *The Mishnah*. London: Oxford University Press, 1933.
Degen, Rainer. "Ketovet mi-Teman ʿal 24 Mišmerot ha-Kohanim." *Tarbiz* 42 (1973) 302–3.
Fine, Steven. *The Menorah: From the Bible to Modern Israel*. Cambridge: Harvard University Press, 2016.
———, ed. *Sacred Realm: The Emergence of the Synagogue in the Ancient World*. New York: Oxford University Press, 1996.
Frisch, Amos. "Structure and Its Significance: The Narrative of Solomon's Reign (1 Kings 1–12:24)." *JSOT* 51 (1991) 3–14.
Goodman, Martin, "The Qumran Sectarians and the Temple." In *The Dead Sea Scrolls: Texts and Contexts*, edited by Charlotte Hempel, 263–74. Leiden: Brill, 2010.
———. "Sadducees and Essenes after 70 CE." In *Crossing the Boundaries: Essays in Biblical Interpretation in Honour of Michael D. Goulder*, edited by Stanley E. Porter, Paul Joyce, and David E. Orton, 347–56. Leiden: Brill, 1994.
Gordon, Cyrus H. "Jewish Reaction to Christian Borrowings." In *The Word of the Lord Shall Go Forth: Essays in Honor of David Noel Freedman in Celebration of His Sixtieth Birthday*, edited by Carol L. Meyers and M. O'Connor, 685–90. Winona Lake, IN: Eisenbrauns, 1983.
Gorea, Maria. "Les classes sacerdotales (*mišmarôt*) de l'inscription juive de Bayt Ḥāḍir (Yémen)." In *Le Judaïsme de l'Arabie Antique: Actes du Colloque de Jérusalem (février 2006)*, edited by Christian Julien Robin, 297–329. Turnhout: Brepols, 2015.
Hachlili, Rachel. *Ancient Mosaic Pavements: Themes, Issues, and Trends*. Leiden: Brill, 2009.
———. *Ancient Synagogues—Archaeology and Art: New Discoveries and Current Research*. Handbook of Oriental Studies / Handbuch der Orientalistik 1.105. Leiden: Brill, 2013.
"Hallel." In *Encyclopaedia Judaica*, 8.279–80. 2nd ed. Detroit: Macmillan, 2007.
Hayward, Robert. "The Jewish Temple at Leontopolis: A Reconsideration." *Journal of Jewish Studies* 33 (1982) 429–43.
Japhet, Sara. *I and II Chronicles: A Commentary*. The Old Testament Library. Louisville: Westminster John Knox, 1993.

Levine, Lee I. *The Ancient Synagogue: The First Thousand Years*. New Haven: Yale University Press, 2000.

Magness, Jodi. "Heaven on Earth: Helios and the Zodiac Cycle in Ancient Palestinian Synagogues." *Dumbarton Oaks Papers* 59 (2005) 1–52.

———. "Priests and Purity in the Dura-Europos Synagogue." In *"Follow the Wise": Studies in Jewish History and Culture in Honor of Lee I. Levine*, edited by Zeev Weiss and others, 421–33. Winona Lake, IN: Eisenbrauns, 2010.

Meyers, Eric M. "The Problem of the Scarcity of Synagogues from 70 to ca. 250 C.E.: The Case of Synagogue I at Nabratein (2nd–3rd Century C.E.)." In *"Follow the Wise": Studies in Jewish History and Culture in Honor of Lee I. Levine*, edited by Zeev Weiss and others, 435–48. Winona Lake, IN: Eisenbrauns, 2010.

Miller, Stuart S. *At the Intersection of Texts and Material Finds: Stepped Pools, Stone Vessels, and Ritual Purity among the Jews of Roman Galilee*. Göttingen: Vandenhoeck & Ruprecht, 2015.

———. *Studies in the History and Traditions of Sepphoris*. Leiden: Brill, 1984.

Pérez Fernández, Miguel. *An Introductory Grammar of Rabbinic Hebrew*. Leiden: Brill, 1999.

Petrie, W. M. Flinders. *Hyksos and Israelite Cities*. London: British School of Archaeology in Egypt, 1906.

Radday, Yehuda T. "Chaismus in Hebrew Biblical Narrative." In *Chiasmus in Antiquity: Structures, Analyses, Exegesis*, edited by John W. Welch, 50–117. Hildesheim: Gerstenberg, 1981.

Rendsburg, Gary A. "The Psalms as Hymns in the Temple of Jerusalem." In *Jesus and Temple: Textual and Archaeological Explorations*, edited by James H. Charlesworth, 95–122. Minneapolis: Fortress, 2014.

Robin, Christian Julien. "Ḥimyar et Israël." *Comptes rendus des séances de l'Académie des Inscriptions et Belles-Lettres* 148, no. 2 (2004) 831–908.

———. "Le judaïsme de Ḥimyar." *Arabia* 1 (2003) 97–172.

———, ed. *Le Judaïsme de l'Arabie Antique: Actes du Colloque de Jérusalem (février 2006)*. Turnhout: Brepols, 2015.

Rosenberg, Stephen G. "Onias, Temple of." In *Encyclopaedia Judaica*, 15.432–33. 2d ed. 2007.

Runesson, Anders, Donald D. Binder, and Birger Olsson. *The Ancient Synagogue from Its Origins to 200 C.E.: A Source Book*. Ancient Judaism and Early Christianity 72. Leiden: Brill, 2010.

Safrai, Shmuel, and Michael Avi-Yonah. "Temple." In *Encyclopaedia Judaica*, 19:612–16. 2nd ed. Detroit: Macmillan, 2007.

Schiffman, Lawrence H. *Reclaiming the Dead Sea Scrolls*. Philadelphia: Jewish Publication Society, 1994.

Schwartz, Daniel R., and Zeev Weiss, eds. *Was 70 CE a Watershed in Jewish History?* Leiden: Brill, 2012.

Segal, Michael, et al. "An Early Leviticus Scroll from En-Gedi: Preliminary Publication." With an appendix by Ada Yardeni. *Textus* 26 (2016) 1–30.

Sperber, Daniel. "Mishmarot and Ma'amadot." In *Encyclopaedia Judaica*, 14:318–19. 2nd ed. Detroit: Macmillan, 2007.

Urbach, Ephraim E. "Mišmarot u-Ma'amadot." *Tarbiz* 42 (1973) 304–27.

Williamson, H. G. M. "The Temple in the Book of Chronicles." In *Templum Amicitiae: Essays on the Second Temple Presented to Ernst Bammel*, edited by

William Horbury, 15–31. JSNTSupp 48. Sheffield: JSOT Press, 1991. Reprinted in H. G. M. Williamson, *Studies in Persian Period History and Historiography*, 150–61. Forschungen zum Alten Testament 38. Tübingen: Mohr Siebeck, 2004. Further reprinted as H. G. M. Williamson, *Studies in Persian Period History and Historiography*, 150–61. Eugene, OR: Wipf and Stock, 2010.

Zapata-Meza, Marcela, and Rosaura Sanz-Rincón. "Excavating Mary Magdalene's Hometown." *Biblical Archaeology Review* 43, no. 3 (2017) 37–42.

3

Navigating the Aqueous and Fluvial Imagery of the Liquid Temple

Ross E. Winkle

Introduction

In Rev 22:1, the author, John, describes an aspect of the visionary, eschatological New Jerusalem in which "the river of the water of life" flows from "the throne of God and of the Lamb."[1] He has earlier made it clear in 21:22 that he did not see any physical temple in the New Jerusalem, because the Lord God Almighty and the Lamb are its temple. Thus, in John's vision of the New Jerusalem, water flows from the divine "temple" that is God and the Lamb. This resonates not only with myths from the ancient Near East associating flowing water with the gods and their thrones, but also with other biblical texts depicting what one might describe as a "liquid temple" or "liquid sanctuary."[2]

Of all of the liquids utilized in and associated with the biblical sanctuary—such as sacrificial blood, oil for lamps, anointing oil, and libations—water is one of the most fundamental. Besides Rev 22:1, a number

---

1. Unless otherwise indicated, all biblical quotations are taken from the New Revised Standard Version (NRSV).

2. For the purposes of this paper, I will use the term "sanctuary" when referring in general to the Israelite tabernacle, Solomon's Temple, the Second Temple, and the heavenly temple.

of biblical texts explicitly refer to water both associated with and flowing from the temple. Furthermore, other texts imply such by referring to trees flourishing in the temple, which would be implicitly irrigated or nourished by a water source. Since it is arguably the case that no river literally flowed from the sanctuary, such texts must consequently be seen as symbolic. I intend to illustrate how this aqueous (or, watery) imagery and more specifically fluvial imagery (i.e., imagery related to a flowing river) is presented in relation to the "liquid temple" and understood to represent such concepts as wisdom; law and instruction; cosmology; life, fertility, and healing; and Spirit.

YHWH as the Source of Water

In the Hebrew Bible, YHWH is described as a fountain of flowing (or, "living") water in two significant texts in Jeremiah.[3] In chapter 2, YHWH states that his people have rejected him and changed their allegiance from him, the *kābōd* or "Glory" (YHWH's presence), which was understood to reside in the temple,[4] to other gods, in particular, "the Useless One," a play on the name Baal (Jer 2:11; cf. 2:17–18 and 1:16).[5] In 2:13 YHWH specifically laments: "my people have committed two evils: they have forsaken me, the fountain of living water, and dug out cisterns for themselves, cracked cisterns that can hold no water."

One finds this striking description of YHWH as the fountain of living water, rejected by YHWH's people, once more in Jer 17:13, this time on the lips of Jeremiah himself. While the verse begins with an address to YHWH as "the hope of Israel" (ESV), the Hebrew here could also be translated instead as, "the pool of Israel."[6] This latter possibility makes sense in the context of rebuking those who have forsaken YHWH, the fountain of living water. The use of this particular aqueous metaphor here follows Jeremiah earlier in the same chapter observing that the one who rejects and abandons YHWH "is like a shrub in the desert" and "shall dwell in the parched places of the wilderness, in an uninhabited salt land"

---

3. For an examination of water imagery associated with God in the Hebrew Bible beyond that of fluvial imagery, see Ben Zvi, "Thinking of Water, 11–28.

4. E.g., Exod 15:17; 1 Sam 4:4; 1 Kgs 8:11–13; 2 Chr 7:1; Ps 26:8; 27:4; Isa 6:1–4; Ezek 43:6–7; Matt 23:21.

5. See the discussion in Thompson, *Book of Jeremiah*, 170.

6. See the discussion in Holladay, *Jeremiah 1*, 502, and cf. p. 433 on a similar usage in Jer 14:8. See also Ben Zvi, "Thinking of Water," 14–15.

(17:6, ESV). Jeremiah then contrasts this person with the one who trusts in YHWH, the fountain of living water, since the latter "shall be like a tree planted by water, sending out its roots by the stream"; such a "tree" who trusts in YHWH "shall not fear when heat comes, and its leaves shall stay green; in the year of drought it is not anxious, and it does not cease to bear fruit" (17:8).

What makes Jer 17:13's reference to YHWH as a fountain of living water more interesting is that the immediately prior verse refers to the "glorious throne" (or, "throne of glory"), the "place of our sanctuary" (17:12, ESV). This is a clear reference to the temple, where the glory of YHWH resided.[7] It is from this temple context that YHWH is described as a fountain of living water. This suggests that the motif of the divine fountain of living water was understood to flow from the temple of YHWH.

Both Jer 2:13 and 17:13, depicting YHWH as a fountain of living water, illuminate another related text in Jeremiah. In light of Jeremiah's persecution (cf. 17:20–21), the prophet complains in 15:18 about his endless pain, incurable wound, and lack of healing by questioning whether YHWH will be like a "deceitful brook" to him. Instead of being a fountain of living water, Jeremiah feels that God has instead become a dried up brook, a stream that goes dry in the intense summer heat and cannot be depended upon for providing essential, necessary, and refreshing water. But his experience has, in reality, become that of the "shrub in the desert" mentioned later in 17:6. It is he, Jeremiah, who needs to repent of his bitterness, his lack of trust in YHWH, and his sense that he has been abandoned by him (cf. 15:19–21). And so, 17:5–8 essentially resonates with Jeremiah's own earlier repentance and subsequent experience of YHWH as a refreshing and life-giving fountain.[8]

Jeremiah's literary references to YHWH as a fountain of living water are not unusual for his time and culture. In the ancient Near East, the motif of a deity from whom streams flow is well-known.[9] For example, Akkadian representations of the water god Ea (or, Enki in Sumerian mythology) depict the god with two streams or rivers apparently emanating or flowing from his shoulders.[10] While sometimes the depiction is of the

---

7. On this referring to the heavenly sanctuary instead of the earthly one, see Holladay, *Jeremiah 1*, 501.

8. See Thompson, *Book of Jeremiah*, 420–21.

9. Cf., e.g., Fontaine, "Visual Metaphors," 196.

10. For example, see the Akkadian "Greenstone Seal of Adda" in the British

god holding a jar with two or four streams flowing from it, in other depictions the streams emanate from the god himself.[11] In another example of this motif, both sides of the lower panel of a two-paneled fresco from the Old Babylonian throne room of King Zimri-Lim of Mari depict a complex scene featuring two goddesses, each with a vase from which flows a four-fold stream, and each four-fold stream connected together in the middle by another stream. Fish swim up the streams towards the goddesses on each side of the lower panel.[12] One could exhibit a number of other examples, both literary and iconographic, of the same motif of gods or goddesses associated with streaming water.[13]

Since YHWH is described as a fountain of living water in the Hebrew Bible, one would expect to see other references to water—in particular, flowing or fluvial water—associated with the sanctuary of YHWH. And this is clearly what one discovers.

Water in the Sanctuary

The concept of an *aqueous* sanctuary in the biblical text is primarily known from the references to the Mosaic tabernacle basin or laver (located between the Tent of Meeting and the bronze altar of sacrifice), and the massive analogue in Solomon's Temple described alternatively as "the sea" (*hayyām*), "the molten sea" (*hayyām mûṣāq*), or "the bronze sea" (*hayyām hannĕḥōšet*), mounted on twelve bronze oxen facing the four cardinal directions, and located on the southeast corner of the courtyard in the temple complex.[14] Unlike the Mosaic Tabernacle, Solomon also constructed ten additional, smaller bronze water-basins on moveable stands, half of them placed on the north side of the courtyard and half on the south (1 Kgs 7:27–40, 43, 45; 2 Kgs 25:13–16; 2 Chr 4:6, 14; Jer 52:17–20). The purpose of the Mosaic tabernacle laver was for washing

---

Museum.

11. Fontaine, "Visual Metaphors," 196.

12. Parrot, "Les Peintures," 336, fig. 8; cf. Barrelet, "Une peinture," 16, fig. 4. See the discussion in Batto ("Divine Sovereign," 158–59) and Bodi ("Double Current," 27–29).

13. See, e.g., ibid., 27–31; and Clifford, *Cosmic Mountain*, 35–57.

14. For the tabernacle laver, see Exod 30:17–21, 28; 31:9; 35:16; 38:8; 39:39; 40:7, 11–12, 30–32; Lev 8:11. For Solomon's gigantic laver, see 1 Kgs 7:25, 39, 44; 2 Kgs 16:17; 2 Chr 4:3–4, 6, 10 ("the sea"); 1 Kgs 7:23–24 and 2 Chr 4:2 ("the molten sea"); and 2 Kgs 25:13, 1 Chr 18:8, and Jer 52:17 ("the bronze sea"). For ancient Near Eastern parallels, see the discussion in Bloch-Smith, "'Who Is the King of Glory?'" 19–20.

the hands and the feet of the priests before they entered the Tent of Meeting or came near to the altar to make an offering.[15] As for Solomon's "sea" and additional ten water-basins, their biblical purpose is sketchy at best, with only a brief note that the priests washed in the "sea" and the water-basins were used for washing the burnt offerings (2 Chr 4:6).[16]

In terms of physical water in the earthly sanctuary, these large and smaller lavers or water-basins were the most conspicuous. Later Jewish authors also understood sea imagery in several physical aspects of the temple cult. Philo of Alexandria (c. 25 BCE–c. 50 CE) understood the purple dye utilized in the sanctuary fabrics and the high priest's robes to symbolize water, since the dye was derived from a sea snail (*Prelim. Studies* 1.117; cf. *Moses* 2.88).[17] The historian Josephus (37 BCE–c. 100 CE) understood the holy place of the sanctuary to represent both land and sea (*Ant.* 3.123). He also saw the purple color embroidered into the temple veil as representing the sea (*Ant.* 3.183; *War* 5.213). He noted that this color (along with gold, scarlet, and hyacinth) was part of the high priest's sash (*Ant.* 3.154; *War* 5.213, 232), and he believed that the sash as a whole represented the ocean (*Ant.* 3.185).

Other biblical references to the heavenly sanctuary utilized similar kinds of aqueous imagery. For instance, in Rev 4:6, John sees what appears like a "sea of glass, like crystal" situated in front of the throne of God.[18] Later in 15:2 John sees again what appears to be a "sea of glass" in heaven, but this time he describes it as "mixed with fire." These few examples demonstrate that liquid imagery was understood to be associated with physical aspects of the temple and its cult.

---

15. The priests were warned that if they did not wash first, they would die (Exod 30:20–21).

16. For detailed discussions on "the Sea," cf. Hurowitz, "YHWH's Exalted House," 78–82; and Kang, "'Molten Sea,'" 101–3 and the literature cited therein. Kang suggests that the Hebrew terminology should not be understood as "the Molten Sea"—that is, the Sea of Bronze—but rather as "the Sea has been constrained!"; he views this alluding to YHWH's defeat of and victory over the mythological Sea (ibid.).

17. On this color as well as on blue and scarlet, see Winkle, "'Clothes Make the (One Like a Son of) Man,'" 93, n. 50. The "purple" is reddish or Tyrian purple, while the "blue" is hyacinth or bluish purple.

18. For this occurring in a temple setting, cf. the throne associated with the temple in Rev 7:15 and 16:17 and references to the temple in heaven in 11:19; 14:17; 15:5–8; and 16:1.

Water Flowing from the Sanctuary

The concept of a *fluvial* sanctuary is known from several biblical texts that explicitly or implicitly describe streams or rivers flowing from the earthly sanctuary and its heavenly analogue. In one of the most influential of these texts, Ezek 47:1–12, Ezekiel explicitly describes water at first gurgling or trickling out, as if from a jar or a vase,[19] towards the east from the south side of the altar within the visionary temple complex. That gurgling or trickling flow of water becomes progressively deeper and deeper until it is higher than one's waist, and one can consequently swim in the deepening river. The river flows east from the temple towards the Jordan Valley and enters the Dead Sea, where it becomes fresh or "healed" (47:8, 9). Everything—in particular, a variety of fish—lives where the fresh, healing water flows; the marshes and swamps, however, remain salty. All kinds of trees grow along the riverbank where the water flows from the temple, and they provide fruit every month as food and leaves for healing. In this utopian, visionary portrayal, the river from the temple thus brings life, healing, and fertility to virtually everything it touches.[20]

The trickling water that becomes a great river brings us back to Solomon's "sea" and associated water-basins. The gigantic size of the "sea" was one of the dominant features of the courtyard of the Solomonic Temple.[21] One can thus appreciate why later Jewish interpreters understood the courtyard and other physical aspects of the temple to represent the primeval waters or sea.[22] Among various interpretations advanced more recently, Elizabeth Bloch-Smith has suggested that the "sea" symbolizes the waters emerging from Eden as described in Gen 2:10.[23] Victor Avigdor Hurowitz, however, suggests that the inner-biblical meaning of the "sea" is hinted at in Ezekiel's description of the trickling water from the temple that becomes a great river.[24] Because Ezekiel's vision includes no "sea" or associated water-basins, and because the location of the source of

---

19. With regards to the gurgling or trickling water, see Bodi, "Double Current," 25; and cf. Bodi, "Ezekiel," 495–96; and Parrot, "Les Fouilles de Mari Troisième campagne," 54–84, pl. XIII.

20. For a recent analysis of fluvial and arboreal similarities between Ezekiel's account and Babylonian iconography, see Bodi, "Double Current," 22–37.

21. Barker, *Gate of Heaven*, 65.

22. Josephus, *Ant.* 3.123, 181; cf. *b. Sukkah* 51b.

23. Bloch-Smith, "'Who Is the King of Glory?,'" 27.

24. Hurowitz, "YHWH's Exalted House," 80–82.

the trickling water from the temple is apparently in the exact place where the "sea" had stood in Solomon's Temple, he suggests that the deepening river replaced the "sea" and the water-basins and represented the fertility, healing, and life that Ezekiel's river did.[25] Such an interpretation provides cohesiveness between both aqueous and fluvial water imagery associated with the sanctuary.

A second explicit biblical reference to water flowing from the sanctuary occurs in Joel 3:18 [MT 4:18]. Here, God promises the nation of Judah that "in that day" of its glorious future "the mountains shall drip sweet wine, the hills shall flow with milk, and all the stream beds of Judah shall flow with water." However, that was not all: not only would the former occur, but "a fountain shall come forth from the house of the LORD and water the Wadi Shittim" or Valley of Acacias. Here one finds another example of an eschatological description of fluvial imagery associated with the "liquid temple."

Other biblical texts, while only implicit, also support this motif of water flowing from the sanctuary. Psalm 36:7–9 describes humans dwelling in the shadow of God's wings. There they feast on the abundance of his house and drink from the stream or river of his "abundant provisions"[26] or delights.[27] While this text may simply be referring to God's protection and provision, the combination of "wings" and God's "house" and a "stream" or "river" resonates with other texts that describe fluvial flow from the sanctuary.[28] In Ps 46:4 [MT 46:5] the psalmist declares that a river exists whose streams bring gladness to the city of God. The assumption here is that this refers to Jerusalem, despite the fact that there was no river in Jerusalem.[29] As such, the sanctuary would also be implicitly the source of that symbolic river. Finally, Zech 14:8 prophesies that living waters will flow out from Jerusalem—half to the eastern sea (i.e., the Dead Sea), and half to the western sea (i.e., the Mediterranean), both in summer as well as in winter. Again, the reference to the sanctuary is only

---

25. Cf. Jordan, *Through New Eyes*, 249.

26. So Smith, "Like Deities," 7. He, as others have done, earlier compares this usage to ancient Near Eastern references to abundance and fertility as a result of rain cycles produced by their gods (ibid., 4–5).

27. The Hebrew word for "delights" is the plural of the same word translated in Genesis 2 as "Eden."

28. See Craigie (*Psalms 1–50*, 292) and Dahood (*Psalms I*, 221–22) and cf. Barker (*King of the Jews*, 267).

29. Wilson, *Psalms—Volume I*, 717, especially notes 9 and 10.

implicit. But the fact that half of the waters here flow towards the Dead Sea resonates with Ezekiel's vision where the waters flowed from the temple towards the Dead Sea (47:1–12).[30] All these texts assume a fluvial motif of water flowing from the historical or eschatological sanctuary.

Another set of texts provides an unusual perspective on the implicit understanding of water flowing from, or rather, irrigating the sanctuary and its environs. In Ps 52:8 the psalmist describes his faithfulness to God by asserting "I am like a green olive tree in the house of God." Similarly, Ps 92:12–14 asserts, "The righteous flourish like the palm tree, and grow like a cedar in Lebanon. They are planted in the house of the LORD; they flourish in the courts of our God. In old age they still produce fruit; they are always green and full of sap." Such texts compare faithful humans to trees in the temple. But these human "trees" flourish and produce fruit because they are nourished by water[31]—water that flows from the sanctuary (cf. Ps 1:3[32]).

While there was no physical river of water flowing from the Mosaic tabernacle or Jerusalem sanctuary,[33] it is clear that literature about the sanctuary did have a place for a flowing river. Since it is a literary construct rather than a physical, historical reality, such water flowing from the sanctuary could be termed, in the words of Francis Landy, a "fluvial fantasy."[34] But of what was such fantastic, flowing fluid a symbol?

---

30. Note that in a cosmic scene in Dan 7:10, a lava-like fiery river surges forward from the heavenly throne of the Ancient of Days. The text clearly describes the scene as one of judgment, and it is likely that the fiery nature of the flow from the throne underscores that theme. On the combination of fire with the theme of judgment, cf., e.g., Ps 50:3–4; Isa 4:4; 66:12; Heb 10:27; and 2 Pet 3:7. As for Daniel 7 sanctuary imagery, cf. Fletcher-Louis, "High Priest as Divine Mediator," 174 (Dan 7 "is ultimately Temple centered"); Lacocque, *Book of Daniel*, 124–25 ("The vision in chapter 7 has the Temple as its framework"); and Sweeney, "End of Eschatology," 138 ("the visions of Daniel 7–12 are permeated with priestly imagery, symbolism, and concepts").

31. Cf. the discussion in Barker, *Creation*, 257–58.

32. Gillingham ("Zion Tradition," 333) agrees with Creach ("'Like a Tree Planted by the Temple Stream,'" 31–46) that the reference here to the tree planted by water, providing fruit in season, may well be describing the righteous person in the temple.

33. E.g., as Hurowitz notes, there is no natural river in Jerusalem, and the Gihon spring, while nearby, was not on the temple grounds ("YHWH's Exalted House," 82).

34. Landy, "Fluvial Fantasies," 437–55.

Flowing Water, Flowing Symbol

Certain Second Temple Jewish writers understood that there was water imagery associated with various aspects of the sanctuary. Not only did they view various physical elements of the sanctuary cult symbolizing flowing water in the sanctuary, but they also understood the reverse: literary references to water flowing from the sanctuary were themselves symbols of other important concepts and themes.

For instance, Ben Sira described Wisdom, ministering first in the "holy tent" and then "resting" in the temple of the beloved city, Jerusalem, as the Law or Torah, and he does so by utilizing the fluvial imagery of the Pishon, Tigris, Euphrates, Jordan, Nile, and Gihon rivers (24:10–11, 23–27), reminiscent of the four rivers (Pishon, Gihon, Tigris, Euphrates) emerging from the primeval Garden of Eden (Gen 2:10–14).[35] In the same chapter Ben Sira himself also describes his instruction and teaching of those seeking wisdom in terms of fluvial imagery, comparing himself to a canal of the river Wisdom that waters a garden and becomes a river and then a sea (Sir 24:30–33).[36]

Another example is the cosmological exegesis of Philo. In contradistinction to the Hebrew Bible, which indicated that the pomegranate figures attached to the hem of the foot-length, hyacinthine robe of the high priest were made out of hyacinth, purple, and scarlet material (Exod 28:33–34; 39:24–26 [LXX 36:31–33]), he instead indicated that these were golden in fabrication (*Moses* 2.110). But what is of interest here is that he understood these golden pomegranates to be symbolic of water (*Moses* 2.118–21, 133; *Spec. Laws* 1.93–94)[37] based on linguistic considerations: the Greek word for pomegranate, *rhoïskos*, was etymologically derived from the "flowing" (*rhúsis*) of water (*Moses* 2.119; *Spec. Laws* 1.93). This connection between "pomegranate" and "flowing" is linguistically possible: *rhóa*, a word related to *rhoïskos* and also meaning "pomegranate," may have derived from the term *rhoûs*, which means "stream."[38] Philo also understood that the hyacinthine robe, symbolizing the element of

---

35. On the cosmic and sacral significance of Eden, see, e.g., Beale, *Temple*, 66–80; Morales, *Tabernacle Pre-Figured*, 76–91; and Stordalen, *Echoes of Eden*.

36. For discussion, see Skehan and Di Lella, *Wisdom of Ben Sira*, 337–38.

37. Cf. Steyn, "Elements of the Universe," 2–5. The Bible does not indicate what meaning the pomegranates had, contrary to C. Houtman, who refers to Prov 25:11 to conclude that they symbolize the Word of God ("Pomegranates," 225 [cf. p. 227]).

38. Beekes, "*rhóa*," in *Etymological Dictionary of Greek*, 2.1289.

the air, was the chariot from which was suspended both the earth, symbolized by floral imagery on the hem of the robe, and water, symbolized by the pomegranates (*Moses* 2.121).

But working in a different direction, Josephus appears to have also provided an interpretation of the pomegranates based on his understanding of the hyacinthine robe representing the sky or firmament (*Ant.* 3.184). Consequently, he understood that, while the golden bells attached to the hyacinthine robe represented thunder, the interspersed pomegranates instead represented lightning (*Ant.* 3.184; *War* 5.231).

We know that Josephus knew who Philo was and was aware of at least some of Philo's writings.[39] Josephus probably shared a common exegetical tradition with Philo about the cosmological meaning of the sanctuary cult, but it is possible that he subscribed to a separate exegetical tradition in which the pomegranate was associated with lightning because of linguistic reasons related to the Semitic storm god Rammān, who was associated with thunder, lightning, and rain. This particular Semitic god's Hebrew consonantal spelling is the same as the Hebrew word for pomegranate.[40]

Alternatively, Josephus may have subscribed to an exegetical tradition like Philo in which the pomegranate (*rhoïskos* or *rhóa*) was linguistically associated with a verb meaning "flow, run like water, stream" (*rhéō*). The phenomena of lightning (*astrapē*)—which Josephus had stated was what the pomegranates symbolized—is similar to that of a thunderbolt (*keraunós*). In another text Philo describes thunderbolts that fell or "streamed or "flowed like water" from heaven (*keraunoì rhuéntes eks ouranoû* [*Moses* 2:56]). This would make Josephus' interpretation of the pomegranates symbolizing lightning closer to Philo's pomegranates symbolizing flowing water, since both water and thunderbolts (similar to lightning) could be described as "flowing."

---

39. Sterling, "'Man of the Highest Repute,'" 101–13; Sterling concludes that Philo's works "easily eclipsed" those of Josephus "in exegetical and philosophical sophistication" (p. 113).

40. Cf., e.g., 2 Kgs 5:18 and Joel 1:12. Whether the latter association was a purposeful parody by the Hebrew scribe to denigrate the foreign god is certainly possible. See Cohn, "Form and Perspective," 178; Gray, *I and II Kings*, 507–8; Maier, "Hadadrimmon," 3:13. Note that LXX Zech 12:11 translated the reference to the weeping for Hadad-rimmon in the plain of Megiddo into mourning for the "pomegranate grove" (*rhoōn*) cut down on the plain. On this, see the discussion in Thompson, "Lamentation for Christ," 686.

When one examines the New Testament writings, the imagery of water flowing from the sanctuary, as understood by Christians, had largely coalesced around the theology of life through the Spirit, whether Spirit of God or Spirit of Jesus. One contributing factor was the explicit and implicit association of the Spirit with water in such texts as Isa 32:14–15 and 44:3–4, where the water "poured out" on the ground and the resultant streams refreshing the earth parallel the Spirit "poured out" on God's people.[41] Interpreting the water flowing out of the "liquid temple" as the Spirit would be natural. Thus, one observes Acts describing Jesus "pouring out" the Spirit from heaven on the Day of Pentecost (2:17–18, 33; 10:45; cf. Titus 3:6). Paul's references to drinking the "liquid" Spirit (1 Cor 12:13; Eph 5:18–20; cf. 1 Cor 10:1–4), as well as his reference to Christians producing the "fruit of the Spirit" (Gal 5:22), that is, fruit produced by "human" trees that are nourished by the "liquid" Spirit, are also illuminating in this regard.

The pervasive and striking water imagery in the gospel of John (e.g., 4:4–15; 6:35; 19:34),[42] along with John's emphasis on Jesus being the new temple (cf. 1:14; 2:19–21), yields the streams or rivers[43] flowing from the temple understood as the Spirit flowing from Jesus. Thus, in John 7:37–39, when Jesus, on the last day of the Feast of Tabernacles, a feast that involved striking water rituals in the temple, invites the crowds to drink from him, he refers to the rivers of living waters that would consequently flow. But John then explicitly states that these rivers that flow refer to the Spirit. These rivers arguably flow from Jesus, the temple,[44] and yet in probable Johannine ambiguity can also be understood to be flowing out from the believer.[45]

And in the book of Revelation, John's inaugural vision entails a description of the one like a son of man dressed in a high priestly robe and sash (1:12–13). A seven-part further description then ensues (1:14–16).

---

41. See Beale, *Book of Revelation*, 1105, who also lists such texts as Ezek 36:25–27; John 3:5; 4:10–24; Pesiq. Rab. 1.2; and Odes Sol. 6:7–18.

42. For extensive discussions of this thematic imagery, see, e.g., Crutcher, *That He Might Be Revealed*; Jones, *Symbol of Water*; Ng, *Water Symbolism in John*; and Um, *Theme of Temple Christology*.

43. Bodi is one who suggests that the plural here in John derives from the dual Hebrew term for "rivers" in Ezek 47:9 ("Double Current," 25–26, 36; cf. Bodi, "Der altorientalische Hintergrund," 152).

44. On the difficulties in John 7:37–39, again, the literature is vast. See, e.g., Carson, *Gospel According to John*, 321–29; and Greene, "Integrating Interpretations," 333–53.

45. On this, see Brodie, *Gospel According to John*, 318–19.

John describes the voice of the one dressed in this high priestly robe and sash as sounding like "many waters" (1:15)—an allusion to Ezek 43:2, which described the return of the glory of God from the east, the glory sounding like "many waters" (ESV).[46] The noisy, roaring reference to his voice is the exact center and the only audible aspect of this detailed, seven-part description.[47] As the visionary narrative flows into chapters 2–3, the voice of "many waters" becomes the voice of the Spirit of Jesus[48] that speaks (2:7, 11, 17, 29; 3:6, 13, 22). In a sanctuary setting, the "many waters" flow from the mouth of the high priestly Jesus in messages of love, encouragement, warning, and rebuke to the seven churches of Asia Minor—encompassing both the refreshing river of life and the river of fire and judgment (cf. Dan 7:10). Thus, in John's inaugural vision and subsequent messages to the seven churches, the motif of flowing water in a sanctuary setting is associated with—and is a symbol of—the Spirit.

Revelation 7:17 describes Jesus, the Lamb, guiding the "great multitude" of God's people to fountains (or, springs) of living water. The eternal culmination of the flowing river is envisioned in John's description of the New Jerusalem, where the Alpha and Omega promises that he will give water from the fountain (or, spring) of living water as a gift (21:6; cf. 22:17). The New Jerusalem itself is where the river of living water flows from the throne of God and the Lamb, providing water to the paradisiacal tree of life that produces fruit each month and has leaves that heal the nations (22:1–2), a clear allusion to Ezekiel 47.[49] The river of living water, flowing from the temple that is God and the Lamb, would make coherent sense as a liquid symbol of the Spirit, flowing from the temple and bringing life, healing, and blessing to all.[50]

---

46. Cf. LXX Ezek 43:2. Cf. also Ezek 1:24, where the sound of the wings of the four living creatures is like the sound of many waters, which there is also compared to the voice of YHWH, or the sound of a tumult (or rainstorm), or that of an army.

47. Cf. Diop, "Jesus Christ in the Midst of His People," 42, who takes these verses as a chiastic structure.

48. It is Jesus, since the "one like a son of man" in 1:13 indicates that he was dead but is alive (1:18).

49. This alludes to the liquid imagery in Ezek 47:1–12, Joel 4:18, Zech 14:8, and Gen 2:10 (cf. Beale, *Book of Revelation*, 1103).

50. Cf. Beale, *Book of Revelation*, 1104; and Macaskill, "Paradise in the New Testament," 77–78. Macaskill argues that the throne appears in association with the Spirit in Rev 1:4, 4:5, and 5:6, and since the Spirit is not dissociated from the throne in these passages, it must be seen before the throne and proceeding from it in Rev 22:1–2; the river of living water fulfills this role (ibid., 78). Macaskill also notes that the resulting

In so many of these New Testament portrayals, the overall imagery finds coherence in the water, fountains, springs, and rivers streaming, flowing, gurgling, and gushing from the sanctuary, bringing nourishment, life, freshness, healing, blessing, and abundance.

Conclusion

The consciousness of today's world to things ecological and environmental is high. In particular, we in California over the last few years have become much more attuned to the necessity of preserving water, since it is so critical to our physical life. In the ancient world, the necessity of water was arguably more urgent because of such things as the lack of modern technology, fast transportation, and engineered water supplies and systems. One of the fundamental and critical meanings of water thus became the sustenance of life for all living things, and this image became a foundational aspect of temple theology.

Just as contemporary efforts to maintain the purity and supply of water, though not easy, are both necessary and rewarding, navigating the aqueous and fluvial imagery of the "liquid temple" is not easy, but it is necessary for an appreciation of temple theology as well as for spiritual vitality. Just as water sustains animate life in our world today, rehydrating and refreshing our lives both individually and together, so a renewed interest in, understanding of, and appreciation for the imagery of both aqueous and fluvial water in association with sacred spaces like the biblical sanctuary would also be refreshing. In biblical terms, the river(s) would flow, the desolate wilderness would bloom and blossom, the fruitless trees would repeatedly bear fruit, and people would not only be refreshed, but healed.[51] We can irrigate and rehydrate our understanding of and appreciation for the truths conveyed by the sanctuary, emphasizing that temple theology includes the trickling, gurgling, streaming, flowing, surging, cascading, splashing, and gushing work of God in bringing new life, radical healing, flourishing nourishment, and rich blessing to those who drink its thirst-quenching waters.

"life that is enjoyed by the occupants of the New Jerusalem is in no way separable from the presence of God. Nor is it in any way separable from the atoning work of Jesus, since it proceeds from the throne of the Lamb" (ibid., 77).

51. Cf., e.g., Isa 35:1–2 and Ezek 47:1–12.

Bibliography

The Anchor Bible Dictionary. 6 vols. Edited by David Noel Freedman. New York: Doubleday, 1992.
Barker, Margaret. *Creation: A Biblical Vision for the Environment*. London: T. & T. Clark International, 2010.
———. *The Gate of Heaven: The History and Symbolism of the Temple in Jerusalem*. 1991. Reprint, Sheffield, UK: Sheffield Phoenix, 2008.
———. *King of the Jews: Temple Theology in John's Gospel*. London: SPCK, 2014.
Barrelet, Marie-Thérèse. "Une peinture de la cour 106 du palais Mari." In *Studia Mariana*, edited by A. Parrot, 9–35. Leiden: Brill, 1950.
Batto, Bernard F. "The Divine Sovereign: The Image of God in the Priestly Creation Account." In *David and Zion: Biblical Studies in Honor of J. J. M. Roberts*, edited by Bernard F. Batto and Kathryn L. Roberts, 143–86. Winona Lakes, IN: Eisenbrauns, 2004.
Beale, G. K. *The Book of Revelation: A Commentary on the Greek Text*. New International Greek Testament Commentary. Grand Rapids: Eerdmans, 1999.
———. *The Temple and the Church's Mission: A Biblical Theology of the Dwelling Place of God*. New Studies in Biblical Theology 17. Downers Grove, IL: InterVarsity, 2004.
Beekes, Robert, with the assistance of Lucien van Beek. "rhóa." In *Etymological Dictionary of Greek*, 2:1289. Leiden: Brill, 2010.
Ben Zvi, Ehud. "Thinking of Water in Late Persian/Early Hellenistic Judah: An Exploration." In *Thinking of Water in the Early Second Temple Period*, edited by Ehud Ben Zvi and Christoph Levin, 11–28. Beihefte zur Zeitschrift für die alttestamentliche Wissenschaft 461. Berlin: De Gruyter, 2014.
Bloch-Smith, Elizabeth. "'Who Is the King of Glory?' Solomon's Temple and Its Symbolism." In *Scripture and Other Artifacts: Essays on the Bible and Archaeology in Honor of Philip J. King*, edited by Michael D. Coogan et al., 18–31. Louisville: Westminster John Knox, 1994.
Bodi, Daniel. "Der altorientalische Hintergrund des Themas der 'Ströme lebendigen Wassers' in Joh 7,38." In *Johannes-Studien: Interdisziplinäre Zugänge zum Johannes-Evangelium: Freundesgabe für Jean Zumstein*, edited by Martin Rose, 137–58. Université de Neuchâtel Publications de la Faculté de théologie 6. Zürich: Theologischer Verlag, 1991.
———. "The Double Current and the Tree of Healing in Ezekiel 47:1–12 in Light of Babylonian Iconography and Texts." *Die Welt des Orients* 45 (2015) 22–37.
———. "Ezekiel." In *Zondervan Illustrated Bible Backgrounds Commentary: Volume 4: Isaiah, Jeremiah, Lamentations, Ezekiel, Daniel*, edited by John H. Walton, 400–517. Grand Rapids: Zondervan, 2009.
Brodie, Thomas L. *The Gospel According to John: A Literary and Theological Commentary*. Oxford: Oxford University Press, 1993.
Carson, D. A. *The Gospel According to John*. The Pillar New Testament Commentary. Grand Rapids: Eerdmans, 1991.
Clifford, Richard J. *The Cosmic Mountain in Canaan and the Old Testament*. Harvard Semitic Monographs 4. Cambridge: Harvard University Press, 1972.
Cohn, Robert. "Form and Perspective in 2 Kings V." *Vetus Testamentum* 33 (1983) 171–84.
Craigie, Peter. *Psalms 1–50*. Word Biblical Commentary 19. Waco, TX: Word, 1983.

Creach, Jerome F. D. "'Like a Tree Planted by the Temple Stream': The Portrait of the Righteous in Psalm 1.3." *Catholic Biblical Quarterly* 61 (1999) 31–46.

Crutcher, Rhonda G. *That He Might Be Revealed: Water Imagery and the Identity of Jesus in the Gospel of John*. Eugene, OR: Pickwick, 2015.

Dahood, Mitchell. *Psalms I: 1–50: Introduction, Translation, and Notes*. Anchor Bible 16. Garden City, NY: Doubleday, 1965, 1966.

Diop, Ganoune. "Jesus Christ in the Midst of His People: A Study of Revelation 1:9–22." *Journal of the Adventist Theological Society* 8 (1997) 40–58.

Fletcher-Louis, Crispin H. T. "The High Priest as Divine Mediator in the Hebrew Bible: Dan 7:13 as a Test Case." *Society of Biblical Literature Seminar Papers* 36 (1997) 161–93.

Fontaine, Carole R. "Visual Metaphors and Proverbs 5:15–20: Some Archaeological Reflections on Gendered Iconography." In *Seeking Out the Wisdom of the Ancients: Essays Offered to Honor Michael V. Fox on the Occasion of His Sixty-Fifth Birthday*, edited by Ronald L. Troxel et al., 185–202. Winona Lakes, IN: Eisenbrauns, 2005.

Gillingham, Susan. "The Zion Tradition and the Editing of the Hebrew Psalter." In *Temple and Worship in Biblical Israel: Proceedings of the Oxford Old Testament Seminar*, edited by John Day, 308–41. London: T. & T. Clark, 2007.

Gray, John. *I and II Kings: A Commentary*. 2nd ed. The Old Testament Library. Philadelphia: Westminster, 1970.

Greene, Joseph R. "Integrating Interpretations of John 7:37–39 into the Temple Theme: The Spirit as Efflux from the New Temple." *Neotestimentica* 47 (2013) 333–53.

"Greenstone Seal of Adda." https://www.bmimages.com/preview.asp?image=00032574 001& imagex=2&searchnum=0003.

Holladay, William L. *Jeremiah I: A Commentary on the Book of the Prophet Jeremiah: Chapters 1–25*. Edited by Paul D. Hanson. Hermeneia—a Critical and Historical Commentary on the Bible. Philadelphia: Fortress, 1986.

Houtman, C. "Of the Pomegranates and the Golden Bells of the High Priest's Mantle." *Vetus Testamentum* 40 (1990) 223–29.

Hurowitz, Victor Avigdor. "YHWH's Exalted House—Aspects of the Design and Symbolism of Solomon's Temple." In *Temple and Worship in Biblical Israel: Proceedings of the Oxford Old Testament Seminar*, edited by John Day, 63–110. London: T. & T. Clark, 2007.

Jones, Larry Paul. *The Symbol of Water in the Gospel of John*. Journal for the Study of the New Testament Supplement Series 145. Sheffield, UK: Sheffield Academic Press, 1997.

Jordan, James B. *Through New Eyes: Developing a Biblical View of the World*. Brentwood, TN: Wolgemuth & Hyatt, 1988.

Kang, Seung Il. "The 'Molten Sea,' or Is It?" *Biblica* 89 (2008) 101–3.

Lacocque, André. *The Book of Daniel*. Translated by David Pellauer. Edited by André Lacocque. Atlanta: John Knox, 1979.

Landy, Francis. "Fluvial Fantasies." In *Thinking of Water in the Early Second Temple Period*, edited by Ehud Ben Zvi and Christoph Levin, 437–55. Beihefte zur Zeitschrift für die alttestamentliche Wissenschaft 461. Berlin: De Gruyter, 2014.

Macaskill, Grant. "Paradise in the New Testament." In *Paradise in Antiquity: Jewish and Christian Views*, edited by Markus Bockmuehl and Guy G. Stroumsa, 64–81. Cambridge: Cambridge University Press, 2010.

Maier, Walter A., III. "Hadadrimmon." In *Anchor Bible Dictionary* 3:13.

Morales, L. Michael. *The Tabernacle Pre-Figured: Cosmic Mountain Ideology in Genesis and Exodus*. Biblical Tools and Studies 15. Leuven: Peeters, 2012.

Ng, Wai-yee. *Water Symbolism in John: An Eschatological Interpretation*. Studies in Biblical Literature 15. New York: Lang, 2001.

Parrot, André. "Les Fouilles de Mari Troisième campagne (Hiver 1935–36)." *Syria* 18 (1937) 54–84.

———. "Les Peintures du Palais de Mari." *Syria* 18 (1937) 325–54.

Skehan, Patrick W., and Alexander A. Di Lella. *The Wisdom of Ben Sira: A New Translation with Notes; Introduction and Commentary*. Anchor Bible 39. Garden City, NY: Doubleday, 1987.

Smith, Mark S. "Like Deities, Like Temples (Like People)." In *Temple and Worship in Biblical Israel: Proceedings of the Oxford Old Testament Seminar*, edited by John Day, 3–27. London: T. & T. Clark, 2007.

Sterling, Gregory E. "'A Man of the Highest Repute': Did Josephus Know the Writings of Philo?" *Studia Philonica Annual* 25 (2013) 101–13.

Steyn, Gert. "Elements of the Universe in Philo's *De Vita Mosis*: Cosmological Theology or Theological Cosmology?" *In die Skriflig / In Luce Verbi* 47, no. 2 (2013). http://dx.doi.org/10.4102/ids.v47i2.699.

Stordalen, Terje. *Echoes of Eden: Genesis 2–3 and Symbolism of the Eden Garden in Biblical Hebrew Literature*. Contributions to Biblical Exegesis and Theology 25. Leuven: Peeters, 2000.

Sweeney, Marvin A. "The End of Eschatology in Daniel? Theological and Socio-Political Ramifications of the Changing Contexts of Interpretation." *Biblical Interpretation* 9 (2001) 123–40.

Thompson, J. A. *The Book of Jeremiah*. The New International Commentary on the Old Testament. Grand Rapids: Eerdmans, 1980.

Thompson, Leonard L. "Lamentation for Christ as a Hero: Revelation 1:7." *Journal of Biblical Literature* 119 (2000) 683–703.

Um, Stephen T. *The Theme of Temple Christology in John's Gospel*. Library of New Testament Studies 312. London: T. & T. Clark, 2006.

Wilson, Gerald H. *Psalms—Volume 1*. NIV Application Commentary. Grand Rapids: Zondervan, 2002.

Winkle, Ross E. "'Clothes Make the (One Like a Son of) Man': Dress Imagery in Revelation 1 as an Indicator of High Priestly Status." PhD diss., Andrews University, 2012.

4

From Tree to Temple Town
The Sacred Urbanism of Hindu India

Vinayak Bharne[1]

The magnificent Meenakshi Temple in Madurai may appear at first glance like a built-at-once complex, but a closer examination reveals quite the opposite. It is, in fact, a piecemeal cohesion of multiple buildings and open spaces, beginning with an anonymous stone *lingam* (phallic symbol of Shiva) in around 1600 BC, and the subsequent commemoration of that sacred spot over centuries of communal worship, patronage, and craftsmanship. In this sense, the entire temple town of Madurai as its stands today represents the teleological end of an ancient lineage of grass-roots urbanism powerful enough to bear the makings of an entire city.

Three millennia since Madurai's inception, such patterns continue to exert a dominant influence on Indian urbanity. Innumerable rural habitats evolve around anonymous sacred insignia and shrines, and the influx of village migrants into cities brings, among other things, a sacred substratum into the public and private dimensions of Indian urbanity. Indian cities have become gigantic "faithscapes," sprinkled with a thousand

---

1. This essay is an abridged and modified version of a longer article titled "Holy Metamorphosis! The Incremental Urbanism of Hindu India." It was also published as a chapter titled "Anointed Cities: The Incremental Urbanism of Hindu India," in Bharne, *Emerging Asian City: Concomitant Urbanities and Urbanisms*.

nameless spots of Hindu devotion that transcend all legal norms and nurture a parallel urbanism associated with Hindu shrines. What is the place of these elusive, illegal sacred encroachments? As alternative paradigms on place-making and populist informality, do they surface other, contradictory dialogues on the future of Indian cities?

Anonymous Beginnings: The Venerated Tree

As the antediluvian allegories of Hindu India, trees have since Vedic times connoted the idea of supernatural abodes—where things happen as part of larger cosmic orders and under whose branches lies a place of enlightenment. Not surprisingly then, many Hindu temples have begun as anointed trees. Shading a smeared stone or a diminutive portrait of divinity, marked with flags and banners, or its trunk dressed like the goddess herself, a *devasthana* ("place of the deities") has appeared mysteriously under its branches, whether along a city street or remote in a rural field.[2] As the venerated abode of a *gramadevata* (local deity), the anointed tree is worshipped through diurnal and seasonal rituals directly under its sacred canopy.

Over centuries of Hinduism's evolution, select tree species have been endowed with divine associations and mythic meanings. The peepal tree, for instance, also known as *ashvattha* in Sanskrit, represents the divine Hindu Trinity or *trimurti*: the roots being Brahma, the trunk Vishnu, and the leaves Shiva. Some believe that Krishna died under this tree, and according to the Skanda Purana, cutting down a peepal tree is therefore a sin. The Vat, Bargad, or banyan tree is another of the most venerated trees in India, invariably planted in front of temples and mentioned in several scriptures as a tree of immortality.

Thousands of such venerated trees presently dot Indian cities, as both the centers of various invisible cults, as well as the meeting places of microcommunities. When a positive change happens, gifts are endowed to these biological abodes, gradually eliciting their transformation into a shrine. When such a tree dies, the spot remains sacred, believed to be vibrant with the energies of the innumerable rituals that became the focus

---

2. The word *devasthana* derives from two Sanskrit words: *deva* (God) and *sthana* (place) and is used here to communicate the idea of the shrine under the tree. There are several regional linguistic variations of this word across the Indian geography.

of community worship. In these venerated trees, then, lie seeds of larger hallowed places to come (figure 15).

Figure 15: A lingam (phallic symbol of Shiva) anoints a wayside tree in Connought Place, New Delhi (photo by author)

Marking Sacredness: The Wayside Shrine

As parallel components of this sacred urbanism, wayside shrines are born anywhere and everywhere, shrouding all sources of their inception. They may be appendages to buildings, companions to street trees, or autonomous objects floating in urban space. In form, they range from the abstract to the literal: Some are diminutive semantic icons, such as a small lingam or a statuette; others have the formal rudiments of a temple, as a niche or chamber with a pyramidal roof. And some are ad hoc accumulations of any or all of these types, as if displaying the various stages of a shrine's evolution in the same place.

Interestingly, for all their semiotic association, these shrines do not follow the canonized rules of a Hindu temple. Their orientation to the cardinal directions is ad hoc, as opposed to the strict east-west alignment of formal temples, facing any and every way, as if no canon mattered at all. And unlike the managed hygienic environment of city temples, most are open to all people and wandering animals alike. But that said, Ranjit

Hoskote, in his essay "Look Out! Darshana Ahead," has also observed how shrines in Mumbai's suburbs have, in fact, followed "a standard evolutionary graph: first the platform, then the parapet; in due course, an archway, this additive process culminating in the consecration of a miniature temple, rendered in grey-veined marble, complete with grille-guarded, white-tiled sanctum, bells, saffron pennant, and that vital basis of the shrine's financial model, a collection box."[3] This observation affirms a predictable, formal pattern behind a wayside shrine's evolution, from modest sacred spots to identifiable places with rudimentary structures and caretakers, marking the beginnings of miniature temples.

The Rudimentary Temple as Microcosm

A rudimentary temple is larger than a wayside shrine, but not so dominant as to become an urban marker. Whether an accumulation of multiple shrines under ad hoc canopies, or a single built structure, it is different from a formal temple in that it does not bear any "authentic" canon of traditional Indian temple design. Even so, it is typically endowed through local communal sponsorship affording minimal infrastructure, such as electricity and water, and an assigned priest or caretaker.

The Popileshwar Kali Mandir of New Delhi, for instance, is located near Connought Circus within the city's bustling central business district, on a vacant lot beneath a mature peepul tree. With no frontage to any surrounding street, it serves as a quiet retreat behind the district's daily wholesale flower bazaar. Some ten odd statuettes and symbols of various deities sit atop a platform surrounding the tree trunk. A metal board bears the shrine name and advertises the temple's scope of religious services—"the mitigation of problems through various prescribed daily prayers (pujas), weddings, and other celebratory rituals." Every day around seven o'clock, a priest in saffron garb arrives to officiate the shrine's proceedings (figure 16).

---

3. See Hoskote Ranjit, "Look Out! Darshana Ahead," *The Hindu*, January 4, 2004, magazine section.

Figure 16: Popileshwar temple, Connought Place, New Delhi (photo by author)

How did the Popileshwar temple come to be? Per a wandering fakir, Mastanji, the peepul tree was a sacred spot since the seventies. An idol of Mahakali was installed under the tree circa 1982, followed by a Durga (another incarnation of Parvati) idol around 1994, and two years later by idols of Ram (an incarnation of Vishnu) and Hanuman (the monkey god), with the shed built in 1998.[4] Today, the temple has a staff of six priests and a maintenance lady, 100–150 visitors a day, and is the local setting for celebrating important Hindu festivals like Diwali and Navratri. An elusive urban space of a thousand square feet surrounding a tree has become a microcosm of Hindu worship, as well as a local urban community center, typifying innumerable such hidden places within the Indian metropolis.

Birthing the Franchised Temple

The transformation of a shrine or rudimentary temple into a franchised sculptural building is evidence not only of its growing reputation, but of changing the status-quo from illegitimacy to recognized ownership. Modest or grand, it is vividly transformed from an object of populist kitsch to one embodying the prescribed canons of identifiable temple form, or, conversely, a conspicuous formal presence. Some temples formalize the

---

4. Based on documentation by Vinayak Bharne done in July 2007.

open space around them, but most are ingenious siting solutions within limited spatial confines; some even retain and incorporate the original anointed tree as part of their design.

Some temples boast new identities. The Sankat Mochan Temple, completed in New Delhi in 2007, began as a wayside spot with a small vessel of *dhuna* (sacred ash) dedicated to Shiva and Hanuman (the monkey god) idol anointed by a local man. Today, the temple features a 108-foot-high red Hanuman statue that took thirteen years to complete. Enacting an episode from the Ramayana epic, Hanuman shows the presence of Vishnu's incarnation Rama and the goddess Sita in his chest by tearing it apart;[5] through an automatic electronic system; his arms open and a trolley holding the two idols come out of his heart. The building is a local icon, both for the statue and the Shiva dhuna, with claims that wishes made will be fulfilled.

The sacred metamorphosis does not stop here. Across India, numerous sacred place types have evolved over centuries from such modest beginnings. They may be regionally diverse, each representing interim stages of a larger evolutionary process, but they are unified in their modest and often anonymous beginnings as trees or shrines nurtured through continuous communal will.

In several parts of India, the growth of a temple occurs through an enclosing fence or wall creating a formalized setting for sacred ritual. As seen in the Shantadurga and Mangesh Temples in the coastal region of Goa, such enclosures can morph over time into enclosed compounds, accommodating multiple shrines and living quarters. The history of the Shantadurga Temple must also have had such anonymous beginnings. But it is known that circa 1715, Naro Ram Mantri, a minister in the cabinet of a Maratha clan ruler, convinced that his wealth and stature were the goddess's gifts, decided to transform the modest shed enshrining the deity into a grand temple.[6] Today, as the centers of their respective villages, these sacred compounds have gathered other informal commodities, from flower vendors to craft stands that have now formed a permanent kinship with the domains. There are presently more than six hundred thousand such villages in India, excluding its towns and cities, each with

---

5. This is an important episode from the Indian epic Ramayana, and symbolizes the unswerving devotion of Hanuman to Rama and his wife Sita.

6. This has been documented by Dr. Pandurang Pisurlekar. For more, see Malgaonkar, *Inside Goa*, 135.

its own individual *gramadevatas*. As exemplars of ecologically balanced habitats, they will perhaps find maturity as larger sacred complexes and towns, separated and connected by dirt roads or perhaps by railroads, to the anathemas of unregulated sprawl and industrialization.

Such sacred complexes and towns exist across India, but their most dramatic form is in the Dravidian prototypes of Tamil Nadu. The Arunachaleshwara Temple in Tiruvannamalai for instance is not a single temple, but a large sacred complex, almost a campus of sorts, characterized by an enclosed precinct with *prakaras* (concentric rectangular stone fences) and *gopurams* (sacred gateways).[7] The *prakaras* may seem today little more than formal symbols, yet they were historically not only protective elements, but also political ones. Reversing the fortified town's precedent, they did away with the peripheral wall. The town surrounding the sacred campus could now open into nature, assured of a fortified core for safety. Meanwhile, the *gopurams* were more than local markers, orienting the temple at the nexus of two worlds: the sacred and the profane. They offered, like the gates of a medieval European town, the first greeting to the distant pilgrim and the local devotee: at once a custom-house for trade transactions with the temple, and a triumphal arch with its gigantic turrets as a regional means of communication with other cities (figure 17).

Figure 17: The Arunachaleshwara Temple, Tiruvannamalai, Tamil Nadu (photo by author)

7. There is speculation that the word *gopuram* comes from *go* probably referring to cows or *go shala* meaning cowshed and *puram* meaning city, neighborhood or residence. Ancient temples in India had separate quarters inside the temple precincts to house cow-sheds. Often these cowsheds were built abutting the temple tower giving it the unique name of *gopuram*—the "residence of cows."

The origins of one of the most famous Dravidian temple complexes, the Meenakshi temple in Madurai is mentioned in the ancient Puranic scriptures. But the beginnings of the sacred complex we see today are attributed to the thirteenth century, when the south Indian king Kulasekara Pandyan had a sanctuary built at the spot. In time, two shrines emerged, for Shiva and his consort, Meenakshi, each within its own enclosure. With increasing patronage, the two enclosures were merged within a larger compound at the center of the surrounding hamlet. In the seventeenth century, Pandyan's successor, Tirumala Nayaka, improved its defenses and fortifications and built its large gathering hall (Pudumandapam). Circa 1800 CE, the temple town came under the hold of the British East India Company, and, surviving the colonial rule, was eventually designated as the Madurai District in 1984, which centered on the magnificent renovated sacred fortress we see today (figure 9).[8] Thus, contrary to their built-at-once appearances, these sacred campuses are, in fact, summations of centuries of piecemeal growth, fueled by the devotion of both commoners and chieftains (figure 18).

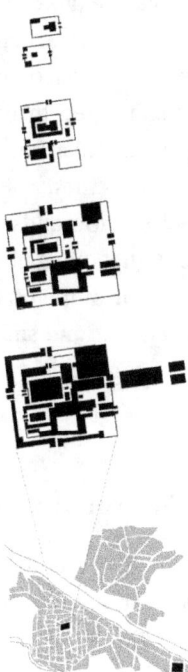

Figure 18: Possible evolution of Meenakshi Temple (drawing by author)

8. For more on the Meenakshi Temple, see Rao, *of Tamil Nadu*, 111–24.

Srirangam in the Tiruchirapalli District of Tamil Nadu embodies the most complete transformation from a Dravidian temple complex into a sacred town. Between the river Cauvery and its tributary, Coleroon, stands the Ranganatha Swami Temple, centered within four concentric rectangular enclosures. The four concentric *prakaras* of the Ranganatha temple expand into three outer layers, together forming a 156-acre town fabric. Each of the seven concentric walls has a *gopuram* in all four cardinal directions, decreasing in size towards the sacred vortex. Between every two walls is a parallel street, with activities becoming increasingly holier as one moves within—the innermost ring contains shrines and prayer halls, the second ring the priest's dwellings and flower and fruit stalls, all the way to the outermost ring with the least sacred activity of normal businesses.

There is another place type where hundreds of evolving anointed spots have congealed into the gigantic "faithscape" of what we now call pilgrimage cities. It differs from other sacred habitats not so much through its size or form, but more through their concentrated spiritual associations with sacred lore or myth, giving it a highly coveted destination status. In the city of Ujjain for instance, folklore talks about the existence of a primordial forest called Mahakal *van* (forest) where the Hindu God Shiva is supposed to have performed penance. Fueled by its strategic location along trade routes, an anonymous lingam grew through the successive royal patronage into a walled city's spiritual fulcrum, the Mahakal Temple. In Varanasi, another of Hinduism holiest cities, a similar sacred cartography is simultaneously evolving, with thousands of temples: towering spires, elusive shrines, innumerable ghats, lingams and *kunds* (sacred water tanks). They form the "stations" of numerous pilgrimage circuits, each marked by a finite number of temples and shrines thereby forming a simultaneously cosmogonic and geographic spatial model, symbolically linking divinity and humanity.

Planning the Anointed Metropolis

There is, then, a tradition of Hindu urbanism that generates entire cities from elusive sacred beginnings, and this pattern continues to this day. What does this suggest for the future of the Indian city? Can and should the ubiquity of sacred trees and shrines be included within the conduits of Indian urban planning? Can parts of the Indian city be understood as evolving communities around maturing holy nuclei, whose future patterns may not be entirely unpredictable? Do the mysterious inceptions, growth, and resilience of these shrines challenge the linear reading of zoning, land use, land, and land value?

For all their populist paranoia, wayside shrines are illegal encroachments on the public domain, blatantly violating zoning ordinances and by-laws, and it is not that they have always escaped their infractions. In Mumbai, for instance, in October 2003, the municipal authorities, undeterred by citizen protest, launched a campaign to demolish street shrines. Several illegal shrines and temples vanished, leaving behind traces of their trees or paving. Yet their continuing veneration as sacred 'ruins' hardly negates their possible reincarnations through the same religiosity that fueled their once obscure, yet currently accredited, city temple counterparts.

Hardly a bourgeois utopia, the demographic associated with (but not limited to) this urbanism largely comprises rural migrants, slum dwellers, and denizens of the pavement. However, far from being a burden on the urban economy, this, in fact, supplies the economy with a vast labor pool for the "unpleasant" jobs that organized labor evades. Wayside shrines embody their intuitive manifestations, unlicensed religious entrepreneurship, and uncanny ability to elude law and authority. Do the millions of wayside shrines and their continuing evolution, then, suggest a sort of parallel "building industry," where the ingenious skills of the city's floating populace—masons, brick-layers, construction workers, gardeners—can contribute to a significant employment base for the urban economy within a facilitating socio-political context?

For many of these denizens, anointed trees and shrines are places of sacred as well as mundane use—analogous to the *chaupal* (central village platform) that serves as an open to sky community hall. This spontaneous usage of the urban void can therefore be read as part of an intuitive rural wisdom with significant economic advantages. Many of these migrants live in shacks less than five square meters, appropriating the adjoining urban space to eat, sleep, and socialize, and shrines are an intrinsic part of this pattern. They may be illegal encroachments on the public domain, but they are also the prominent meeting places of a disenfranchised people that are simply claiming their place in the Indian city.

On this thin line between inclusion and tolerance, then, are the seeds of a non-utopian sacred urbanism, celebrating and building on everyday ordinary life with little pre-tense of a perfectible future. Thus, against the backdrop of accredited city temples, we cannot afford to forget the significance of the hidden order of the thousands of revered trees and wayside shrines. Size does not matter; what matters are the locations of these sacred dots powerful enough to bypass socio-economic legitimacy and exert powerful influences on an emerging urbanity. Today's trees and shrines will become tomorrow's centers and monuments, for in them are the hopes and spiritual aspirations of the millions of underserved that are as much a part of the Indian city as anyone else. They need to be identified, accepted, and celebrated as essential elements of the Indian urban landscape.

Bibliography

Bharne, Vinayak. "Anointed Cities: The Incremental Urbanism of Hindu India." In *The Emerging Asian City: Concomitant Urbanities and Urbanisms*, edited by Vinayak Bharne, 19–26. London: Routledge, 2013.

———. "Holy Metamorphosis! The Incremental Urbanism of Hindu India." *Marg* 63 (March 2012) 30–43.

Bharne, Vinayak, and Krusche Krupali. *Rediscovering the Hindu Temple: The Sacred Architecture and Urbanism of India*. London: Cambridge Scholars, 2013.

Hardy Adam. *Indian Temple Architecture: Form and Transformation: The Karṇāṭa Drāviṇa Tradition, 7th to 13th Centuries*. Indira Gandhi National Centre for the Arts series. New Delhi: Abhinav, 1995.

Malgaonkar, Manohar. *Inside Goa*. Panaji: Government of Goa, Daman & Diu, 1982,

Kramrisch, Stella, and Burnier Raymond. *The Hindu Temple*. Delhi: Motilal Banarsidass, 1976.

Rao, A. V. Shankaranarayana. *Temples of Tamilnadu*. Vol. 3 of Heritage Series. Bangalore: Vasan, 2005.

5

Seeing Scents
Space and Sensory Experience in a Hindu Temple

James McHugh[1]

Texts on rites of worship and on temple rituals from pre-modern South Asia[2] contain many formulae such as the following: "Having devotedly besmeared a figure of Viṣṇu with saffron, aloeswood, sandalwood, and camphor, oh Lord of Kings! one may dwell in heaven for ten million

---

1. I would like to thank the two anonymous reviewers for their extremely valuable and detailed comments on this article. I am also grateful to the useful discussions at the Religion and Material Culture working group supported by the Center for Religion and Civic Culture at the University of Southern California and headed by Ann Marie Yasin and Anne Porter. The Office of the Provost and the Grant Program for Advancing Scholarship in the Humanities and Social Sciences at the University of Southern California provided generous support for my travel and research in India in summer 2010. I presented this article in the weekly seminar at the Society for the Humanities at Cornell in Spring 2011 and all the fellows of the Society gave me very valuable comments. At Tirupati Dr. A. V. Ramana Dikshitulu was extremely kind to meet me and discuss the use of aromatics in the temple there. I would also like to thank Dr. Mohan Babu, Lakshmi Manchu, and Dean Varun Soni of USC for helping me to prepare for my research in India. Finally I would never have come to understand the nature of the phenomenology of smell and perfume without the constant help and advice of perfumer Christophe Laudamiel. I am entirely responsible for any shortcomings.

2. No doubt similar formulae occur in texts from other religious traditions.

kalpas." I shall discuss this particular formula in detail below, but I begin here by raising the question as to how scholars are to consider such texts—texts that describe material things, and, in particular, perfumes or "smell-artifacts." What, if anything, can we gain from reflecting on how the perfume described in this text—a fragrant golden paste—might have actually looked and smelled? Can somehow translating such a text into an actual or imaginary material object provide us with a more complex starting point for a culturally nuanced phenomenology of ritual? Can the occurrence of this formula in a certain type of religious text tell us anything about the perfume in question, about the people who would have used it, or even about the god to whom it was supposed to be offered?

Materials valued for their aromatic properties, such as sandalwood paste and incense, have long been an indispensable part of the adornment and worship of sacred images in many South Asian religious traditions. Yet, whilst scholars of South Asian history and religion have recently turned their attention to the importance of adornment,[3] the nature and significance of ornament with aromatic materials remains largely unexplored. The study of these particular materials poses some special and interesting problems, and a focus on the material properties of aromatic materials reveals that perceptions of this type of material might have been distinctly varied according to peoples' proximity to an adorned image, as well as according to their knowledge and experience of these often costly and rare aromatics. A cloud of odor is invisible and one therefore might tend to think of perfumes as particularly ethereal phenomena, yet the most important aromatics traditionally used in South Asia are valued not only for their odor, but also for their visual, tactile, and other sensible qualities. In some South Asian philosophical accounts of matter and the senses, odor is the special quality of the element "earth": where there is a smell there are earth particles, and thus, perhaps surprisingly to some, smell of all the senses is intrinsically associated with concrete, multisensory matter. Leaving aside indigenous sense theory, the perfumes used in many medieval and modern South Asian religious contexts were indeed quite visible and, moreover, *darśan* of an adorned image might produce an empathic, imaginary smell (or touch) experience of perfumes that were not actually smelled. Scholars of aromatic materials in South

---

3. Ali, *Courtly Culture and Political Life*; Dehejia, *Body Adorned*. Most recently the excellent work of Cynthia Packert on the visual ornamentation in the worship of Kṛṣṇa reflects on highly focused case studies in contemporary Hinduism. Packert, *Art of Loving Krishna*.

Asian religions thus need to consider their visual and tactile qualities; conversely, scholars of the visual should consider that some of the things people saw (and see) when viewing an adorned icon are what we would normally call perfumes in English.

Unlike visual culture, the nature of aromatics and smelling in South Asian religions is, as I have noted, an almost entirely unexplored topic. Even beyond the context of South Asian religions, there is no significant tradition of the hermeneutics of perfumes, and thus before we can begin to understand these materials we need to spend some time reflecting on matters of methodology, and on how a material valued for its smell might lie at the crossroads of larger social forces in distinctive and possibly surprising ways. There are many aspects of religious perfumes that one might consider in that respect: their economic values, imagined exotic origins, conventional affective and erotic powers, their role in literature, and their traditional medicinal usages. In this article, however, I wish to set forth some reflections on the material aspects of aromatics—the fact that these perfumes and incenses were lumps of stuff—and I suggest that this rather mundane fact might help us to consider these materials, and thus South Asian religious and social practices, in new ways. For example, in studying traditional perfumes, if we focus our attention on the material properties of these substances we realize that in some cases people could only *see* these from a distance, and *not* smell them. In a temple where the adorned icon was separated from many people taking *darśan*, this would probably create inequalities in terms of who had access to the full range of sensory qualities of such adornments. Of course, this observation also highlights that the investigation of perfumes in South Asian religions—both historical and contemporary—demands that the scholar pay attention, not only to the materiality of the aromatics, but also to the historical act of sensing these materials. Thus, in this article we need to think about both the study of material culture and the study of the senses.[4]

---

4. Smith provides a very useful survey of recent work on the senses, together with some valuable reflections on methodology and future prospects. See Smith, *Sensing the Past*.

In this article I will be referring to some of the excellent recent work by Daniel Miller on material culture, in particular Miller, *Materiality*; and Miller, *Stuff*. Boivin provides a thoughtful survey of certain trends in the study of material culture that emphasize above all the properties of matter. See Boivin, *Material Cultures, Material Minds*.

A Divine Perfume

It is quite likely that, amongst the types of artifacts that engage the senses, perfumes are the least familiar to many readers. The perfumes used in traditional South Asian religious rituals are possibly even less familiar. Therefore, I will begin by discussing an example of one such perfume. We can then refer to this exemplary perfume in the subsequent discussion. The aromatic we will examine here is described in a medieval text, and this formula is quoted again in an early modern text. Using such a textual source (as opposed to an actual contemporary ritual perfume) will also highlight several issues involved in studying material culture as-represented-in-texts, as well as the problems of studying the history of the senses.

Formulae for making perfumes and incenses are quite common in texts that provide instructions for the performance of *pūjā* offerings. In the case of the varied Hindu religious traditions these include texts such as *Āgamas*[5] and *Purāṇas*. Of course, the tradition of making aromatic preparations was not limited to the realm of rites to worship gods and other revered beings, and such formulae are also found in many other sources, such as texts dealing with perfumery, divination, erotics, and medicine. My observations concerning the multi-sensory nature of aromatics will, of course, apply to these other contexts: there are just as many inequalities in terms of access to the smell of aromatics adorning a king in procession as there are in the case of an adorned image in a temple. And in the bedroom things are different again.

A variety of fragrant preparations are described in all these texts, both "sacred" and "profane," but a particularly rich source of information on the material preparations in Hindu traditions is an early seventeenth-century compendium of materials relating to *pūjā* rites: *The Elucidation of Pūjā* (*Pūjāprakāśa*) of Mitramiśra, part of an enormous digest on Hindu law (*dharmaśāstra*) and ritual called the *Vīramitrodaya*.[6] Along with many other topics, this text collects numerous formulae and practical instructions relating to perfumed pastes (*gandha*) and incenses (*dhūpa*), as well as materials on appropriate flowers for worship. This source is particularly useful for us here as it allows one quickly to examine and compare many examples of this sort of text. In *The Elucidation of Pūjā*

---

5. For a quick survey in English, see Rao, *Āgama Encyclopaedia, Vol. 7*.

6. Mitramiśra, *Vīramitrodaya*, vol. 4: *Pūjāprakāśa*. For a detailed discussion of this text, see Kane, *History of Dharmaśāstra*, 941–53.

the assembled passages dealing with these materials are also arranged in terms of the object of the offering, such that there are perfumed pastes (*gandha*) for the gods Viṣṇu, Śiva, Sūrya, and Dūrgā, along with incenses and other materials of worship. Already we can see there is quite a lot of variety in the world of South Asian perfumery: there are many different sources of formulae (e.g., ritual texts, medical texts), diverse types of preparation (e.g., fragrant waters, incenses), and numerous sectarian contexts (e.g., perfumes for Śiva, for Viṣṇu).

In this article, I wish above all to reflect on methods for studying these somewhat distinctive materials. I will not discuss incenses here as they have their own very distinctive spatial characteristics,[7] and instead I will concentrate on perfumes (*gandha*), and also perfume formulae. I will also limit myself to discussing just one example of a perfumed paste (*gandha*) intended to be offered to Viṣṇu. Although this is just one perfumed paste, a survey of the passages provided in *The Elucidation of Pūjā* reveals that many of these formulae are relatively similar, so what applies here broadly applies to many other such texts. The formula below is taken from the *Narasiṃha/Nṛsiṃha Purāṇa*, a text of uncertain date, possibly from between the ninth and thirteenth century CE.[8]

Although the contexts of such formulae are very important, especially in reflecting on such matters as the differences between perfumes in various sources, from different periods, intended for various gods, and other variables, it is not the purpose of this article to consider such questions,[9] but rather to establish some very general and rather basic methods for the study of such perfumes in relation to space and perception. My method is deliberately naïve, for I wish to expose and then develop some very basic and reasonable assumptions that scholars might make or might have made in studying this type of material, possibly also resolving certain arguments in the process. I chose this formula amongst the many that are to be found in *The Elucidation of Pūjā* as it is a quite exemplary perfumed-paste formula in simple Sanskrit. Nevertheless, the vast majority of formulae for *gandha*s would suit our purposes here:

---

7. The fragrance of incense is released by burning and takes the form of smoke, thus requiring special apparatus for producing this fragrance. Although far more diffusive than the fragrance of the perfumed pastes I describe here, nevertheless the concentrated fragrance of incense can be spatially directed towards an object by the use of certain types of censer.

8. Rocher, *Purāṇas*, 205–6.

9. I will be exploring such questions in future research.

> *kuṅkumāguruśrīkhaṇḍakarpūreṇācyutākṛtim /*
> *ālipya bhaktyā rājendra kalpakoṭiṁ vaset divi / /*[10]

Having devotedly besmeared a figure of Viṣṇu with saffron, aloeswood, sandalwood, and camphor, oh Lord of Kings! one may dwell in heaven for ten million *kalpas*[11]

This perfumed paste is a mixture of costly and often imported aromatic materials. Along with musk, which is absent here, the four named substances were the principal valued aromatics in early and medieval South Asian elite culture. No quantities are given here (though some texts specify exact proportions), nor is a method described, but presumably these are made into a paste with water and then smeared onto an image of the god Viṣṇu. How might we go about analyzing this perfumed paste and its role in religious practice?

The Materiality of Perfumes

Archaeologist Nicole Boivin has suggested that scholars might benefit from paying more attention to the sheer material properties of material culture, not merely reducing material culture to its symbolic or representational content. As she notes, "the material world acts on the social world in a real way, not just because of its ability to act as a carrier of ideas and concepts, but also because its very materiality exerts a force that in human hands becomes a social force."[12] In an example from her own work on South Indian Neolithic ashmounds, Boivin suggests that in order "to properly understand the ashmound rituals, archeologists will need to consider the noise, smell, heat, and brightness of the ashmound fires, and the way that the experience of these qualities would have impacted Neolithic peoples."[13] Similarly, Christopher Tilley has noted the importance of exploring the material properties of things, but this only in relation to people. Referring to a hypothetical stone excavated from Stonehenge, he notes: "I would like to interpret what qualities of this stone made it of such significance that it was brought so far: was it its

---

10. Mitramiśra, *Vīramitrodaya*, vol. 4: *Pūjāprakāśaḥ*, 39.
11. A *kalpa* is one thousand *yuga*s or 432 million human years.
12. Boivin, *Material Cultures, Material Minds*, 6.
13. Ibid., 96.

hardness, colour, spottedness, precise point of origin . . . ? In asking these questions I am concerned with the properties this stone has in relation to people."[14] This social significance of the stone is what he calls its "materiality." Even in emphasizing the social significance of the stone he is still interested in such aspects of the stone as the color, and hardness, and thus implicit here is an assumption about some basic human experiences of the stone that do rely on the brute properties of the stone. For example, human hands can touch stones like this, and people can see them, and if such stones are very big they will be difficult to carry. Some of these facts would seem to fall outside the realm of the socially conditioned but considering them is a necessary prelude to a better type of thicker description. I might also add that Marx provides what is perhaps the most remarkable discussion of the dialectic of the properties of materials and society (not to mention aesthetics) when he explains why the precious metals gold and silver possess natural properties that make them particularly suited to be used as money.[15]

If we apply this sort of approach to the present context, we ought to pay attention, not just to the symbolic implications of offering fragrant materials to gods, but also to the material aspects of this process. By doing so, we might come to think about the practices of offering aromatics in South Asian religions in different ways, even in a historical context in which we no longer have access to the actual practices. To begin with, let us consider the raw materials. The perfumed paste described above would have been made from quantities of aromatic stuff: richly perfumed, red filaments of saffron; misshapen pieces of resinous, dark-brown aloeswood; hard billets of light-brown sandalwood; small pieces of bright-white, volatile, and pungent camphor. In order to make these into a perfumed paste one would no doubt have used a grind-stone and water (as people in temples and at home in India sometimes still do today) and this process of rubbing the woods into a fine paste would have required quite a lot of physical effort. In the process of making such a paste, the wet grindstone would add the fragrance of cool damp stones, a similar smell to that produced when the first rains of the year fall on dry earth. The finished product would have been an intensely golden-brown, wet paste, with a fragrance both rich (from the sandalwood, saffron, and aloeswood), and pungent (from the camphor). Applied to the skin the

14. Tilley, "Materiality in Materials," 16–20.
15. Marx, *Contribution to the Critique of Political Economy*, 153–57.

paste would feel cool, although in the traditional understanding of the humoral qualities of these materials, it may have been understood to be quite balanced between cool and warm: sandal and camphor are traditionally understood as cool, whereas aloeswood and saffron are warming. Smeared onto a sacred icon of Viṣṇu this perfumed paste would have been both fragrant and colored, in addition to having the above mentioned "real" and conventional tactile qualities. Evidently such a perfume would have had a complex significance in relation to certain people.

Paying attention to the materiality of such things as this perfumed paste does not reveal some universal physical properties that require no further analysis in terms of their social and cultural implications in a given context. Rather, thinking about the brute material properties of things in the past (as well as the present) can help expand our awareness of the complexity of practices and situations involving these material things, possibly leading us to consider the implications of material culture in ever wider contexts. In short, the naive phenomenology we start out with will be simply better. And this is indeed what we shall see in the case of the perfume described above.

Intersensoriality and Ritual

This leads me to consider the senses, for if we have learned anything from thinking about the materiality of this preparation, it seems clear that this perfumed paste engages more than one sense. Historian Mark Smith has called attention to the need to study the senses together, to pay attention to intersensoriality,[16] something that the scholar of religions Lawrence Sullivan also noted in a famous paper in which he suggested scholars pay attention to synesthesia in ritual.[17] I find "intersensoriality" a far more useful (and clear) term than the more loaded and obscure term "synesthesia" for this type of discussion. The latter term—"synesthesia"—perhaps most often has the sense of "a phenomenon in which one type of stimulation evokes the sensation of another," namely seeing sounds as colored and so forth.[18] Yet even when Sullivan uses the term in a less specific sense to mean "unity of the senses" this usage seems to assume too

---

16. Smith, *Sensing the Past*, 125–28.
17. Sullivan, "Sound and Senses," 1–33.
18. Ibid., 6. For an excellent discussion of these issues, see also Howes, "Scent, Sound and Synaesthesia," 161–72.

much from the very start of the investigation. Namely, Sullivan's use of "synesthesia" implies a redundancy/unity of the various sensory modes in a ritual context. In using the word "synesthesia" in Sullivan's sense, one assumes from the start that a perfume cannot do anything that words or other media could not do quite adequately, and that there is nothing special about material culture.[19] In the case of this perfume, we can now see that there is a rather neat convergence between the study of material culture and the study of intersensoriality: if we focus on the materiality of stuff it becomes clear that a perfume is not just an odor but also a quantity of matter that affects more than one sense.[20]

If we think of this *gandha* as simply "perfume" we might be tempted to disregard the color and feel of this material. For us today, perfumes are invisible when applied and barely visible in the bottle. They are hardly tactile affairs, being based on highly refined ingredients and alcohol, and they leave barely any trace on the skin except for the fragrance. Nor do we experience their production: we buy them readymade and a bottle lasts for a long time. The perfumed paste above might well have been made afresh on a regular basis, but it would have been quite easy to compound, using techniques that would not require the expertise of professionals.[21] Above all such a *gandha* would have been a highly colored, opaque paste, and applying it would have involved the very sensuous act of smearing this rich, moist material on the body of a person or icon, something that would be understood to pleasure the sense of touch. And, of course, a religious image or person thus adorned would have been very visibly perfumed.

Recreating the Past?

What other methods might improve our understanding of the material culture of the past as recorded in texts? The reason I know what medieval South Asian perfumes are like—that they are highly-colored, tactile, and quite pungent—is that I have tried to make some myself. In his recent survey of historical writing on the senses, the historian Mark Smith

---

19. Sullivan, "Sound and Senses," 7–8.

20. Howes makes a very similar point on the convergence of materiality and intersensoriality. See Howes "Scent, Sound and Synaesthesia," 168–69.

21. Medieval South Asian texts on perfumery describe other preparations that are far more complex, requiring both special equipment and expertise. See McHugh, "Sandalwood and Carrion," ch. 3 and 4 for a discussion of such texts.

cautions against attempting to reconstruct the sensory experiences of the past: creating living, smelly museum environments, and so forth.[22] His point is that acts of sensing are not universal, and in trying to recreate the material and sensory environments of the past we risk ignoring the historically conditioned nature of acts of smelling, seeing, and so on in the past. Just as oil of wintergreen smells pleasantly like candy/chewing gum/root beer to Americans, and unpleasantly like old-fashioned medical ointments to the British, conditioned as they are by the common uses and associations of this material, so there is a great divide between our sense acts and those in the past.

I entirely agree with the point Smith makes, but I would like to suggest that there are circumstances where the reconstruction of the sensory experience of the past by means of the reconstruction of the material culture of the past can help us to understand some rather basic aspects of historical material practices and sense experiences. My reconstruction of this perfume is an example of this. In studying the history of perfumes in South Asia, I was aware that garlands had an evident visual appeal, but I had not paid attention to visible qualities of the pastes and other preparations until I made some. At that point I even began to notice a great many references to the colors of aromatics that I had previously ignored in my single-minded focus on the sense of smell in South Asia. This may be a simple point but it is an important one,[23] and we shall see below that the visibility of such adornments has some interesting possible implications for our understanding of certain acts of worship. Similarly, observing contemporary performances of Vedic sacrifices might be quite useful to scholars wishing to understand certain features of these complex rituals, regardless of questions of the authenticity of these rites.[24]

Beyond these very basic points about sensing materials, I would even argue that it is by no means impossible to attempt to "get inside" the sense acts of the past and then observe artifacts in new ways. The art historian Michael Baxandall very famously produced a meticulous

---

22. Smith, *Sensing the Past*, 118–25.

23. I should add that such reconstruction is not the only way in which one might come to such conclusions. Observations (fieldwork but not ethnography) of the practices of contemporary South Asian religions can likewise help historians to experience materiality in such a manner that is of use in subsequent theoretical analyses.

24. Colas and Tarabout summarize the arguments concerning the authenticity of the Vedic sacrifice documented by Frits Staal in 1975. Colas and Tarabout, *Rites Hindous*, 11–13.

and convincing account of the "period eye" of a certain class of fifteenth century Italian art patron.[25] If such thorough work can help us look at certain paintings in a more historically informed manner, what is to stop one trying to think about the "period nose" of medieval South Asia, and then to consider recreated aromatic preparations in the light of this? Of course, an important distinction between these two cases is that Baxandall does not have to recreate the paintings of the early Italian Renaissance, whereas in the case of these perfumes we would be trying to recreate both the historical perfume and the contemporaneous aesthetic sensibility or "cognitive style."

Visible Perfumes and Stratified Perceptions

Consistent with the multi-sensory nature of odorants is one well-known historical South Asian theory of smell and odors, namely the notion that smell is the special quality of the element earth, an idea associated with some early schools of thought that we might call Hindu.[26] According to this theory, the element earth, and things containing the element earth, can be perceived by all the senses: a clay pot can be heard, touched, seen, tasted, and smelled.[27] Thus anything that can be smelled can also by definition also be seen. Thought provoking as it may be, one does not have to accept early Indian theory of the elements and the senses to see that, in the case of many odorants, this is indeed the case: they are very multi-sensory materials. The cloud of odorous particles carried by the wind to our nose that we smell might indeed be invisible, but the source of that smell is visible, tangible, and so forth. In the case of perfumed pastes such as that described above, people could easily see them. And this latter observation leads us to the question of what this might tell us about the material culture of South Asian religions.

In early South Asian technical discussions of the senses, three different orders ("herarchies")[28] of the senses are commonly used and, as in

25. See Baxandall, *Painting and Experience in Fifteenth Century Italy*.

26. McHugh, "Classification of Smells," 374–419.

27. There were discussions regarding things made of earth that might not immediately seem to have an odor, such as stones which nevertheless reveal their odor when "cooked." McHugh, "Sandalwood and Carrion," 78–80.

28. I prefer not to use the term "hierarchy" here as it suggests a ranking according to importance, which is not necessarily the case in the South Asian orders, or "given sequences" of the senses.

the case of the theory of earth-as-odorous, the rationale for one of these orders can be quite helpful in thinking about this perfumed paste.[29] The three orders of the senses correspond to what we would call Hindu, Buddhist, and Jain religious traditions. The order found in many Buddhist sources is as follows: sight, hearing, smell, taste, and touch. One rationale given for this order in some Buddhist sources is that the senses are listed in this manner according to the distance at which they can perceive objects.[30] Thus one can see things at a greater distance than one can hear them. One can smell things at a lesser distance than these two senses; taste is located on the tongue and touch in the entire body. Some scholars of the senses might argue with the validity of this rationale, but at least it demonstrates one well-known, early South Asian understanding of the relationship between the senses and space. This rationale also differs from that of many contemporary North Americans and Europeans: when I ask my students to order the senses they typically do so according to how they understand their relative "importance." This spatial ordering of the senses, however, highlights the fact that very often one can see odorous objects from a greater distance than one can smell them.

This is not to say that we should only privilege indigenous categories in theorizing South Asian religion and culture, though I do not see any reason why we should not draw on this pool of ideas where useful.[31] Rather, this way of analyzing the senses can help us to see beyond the typical hierarchy of the senses used (or contested) in Western scholarship. Of course, it does not do any harm that this mode of analysis appears to have been evident to some South Asians who were interested in theorizing the senses: as Daniel Miller notes, "we try to recognize that in a given time and place there will be a link between the practical engagement with materiality and the beliefs or philosophy that emerged at that time."[32] To search for a total system might be quite misguided, but that does not mean that we should ignore any wider intellectual contexts. Indeed, a form of perception involving the cognitively constructed olfactory perception of

---

29. See McHugh "Classification of Smells," for a detailed discussed discussion of this subject.

30. Ibid., 404–6.

31. On the use (or neglect) of historical South Asian theories as an intellectual resource, see Chakrabarty, *Provincializing Europe*, 5–6.

32. Miller, *Materiality*, 15.

something seen but not smelled was even discussed by some South Asian philosophers.[33]

Although we might not necessarily define this latter type of experience as "perception," we can accept that people have the ability to imagine the smell of something such as a perfumed paste seen from afar but not actually smelled. So long, of course, that a person has smelled that odorant previously. This qualification adds yet another nuance to consider in the interpretation of aromatic materials in certain worship contexts in South Asian religions. Let us imagine an image adorned with a colored perfumed paste that is located in the inner sanctum of a temple, and thus somewhat removed from many worshippers. First, there is variety in the number of sensory qualities of that paste which different actors in worship can perceive: the priests in proximity to the image can touch and smell the paste, so too, presumably, can the image itself, to the extent that perception of some sort might be attributed to it—something I shall discuss below. On the other hand, people viewing the image from afar can only see the perfumed colored paste. In medieval South Asia some of those viewers might have been quite familiar with these pastes and they might wear similar preparations themselves. In addition to people wealthy enough to use such pastes,[34] perfumers, servants, and others dealing with these sorts of materials might be quite familiar with them. Others, perhaps poorer people, might have very little or no experience of such pastes, or they might only have experience of cheaper, substitute versions of these materials.[35] As with philosophical ideas on the nature of the senses, familiarity with these aromatic materials no doubt varied in any given community. Not only is there a spatial hierarchy of who can experience the range of sensory qualities of the perfume, but even amongst those who can only see it from afar, there would no doubt have been a great variety of responses. I should perhaps emphasize that this is all contingent on the worship space—where the icon is close and ac-

33. Explained by Phillips and Ramanuja Tatacharya as one type of extraordinary human perception: "direct perception through non-standard media that involve a special cognitive link, e.g., the fragrance of sandalwood through the agency of the visual organ assisted by previous experience of the fragrance." Phillips and Tatacharya, *Epistemology of Perception*, 332.

34. Aromatics were evidently very costly, being classed along with gemstones and precious textiles in many sources, such as the description of the treasury in the *Arthaśāstra* of Kauṭalya.

35. For a discussion of such artificial aromatics, in addition to the relative value of aromatics, see McHugh, "Sandalwood and Carrion," ch. 6.

cessible to worshippers, sensory experience of the adornments would be more widely shared.

In some cases the aromatics and other materials used in worship are, at least nowadays, shared with worshippers in the form of *prasāda*. In these cases, the sensory qualities of these adornments are not inaccessible to worshippers. These perceptions of materials received as *prasāda* are, however, by definition after-the-fact experiences and thus separated in time, if not space, from those of the image. Certainly, in the case of flowers and aromatics this passing of time diminishes their sensory intensity. Yet, perhaps more notable is the manner in which the above observation might contribute a small insight into one of the functions of taking *prasāda*. The receiving of *prasāda* has been very productively analyzed in terms of theories of the gift, transaction, and exchange.[36] If we think about the receipt of offerings and adornments of an icon in terms of senses and distance, we might consider that, in the case of religious institutions that separate the icon from the public, the offering of *prasāda* also allows the worshippers to sense the adornments and other materials offered to the icon in a manner that would be impossible were these materials not removed from the icon and brought to the worshipper. Even if these materials were originally brought by a worshipper, they should not have been previously tasted, smelled, and so on. In situ—next to or on the icon—these materials can only be *seen* by the worshipper, and thus receiving *prasāda* can sometimes permit a more rounded and multisensory experience of the adornments of the icon. Hence, *prasāda* might be understood from an etic point of view as, amongst many other things, a phenomenon that bridges the gap between vision and more proximate senses such as smell, and allows worshippers to share in a fuller sensory experience of *pūjā*.

Modern contexts in which the viewer is quite definitely separated from all but the visual aspects of the adorned icon are the viewing of poster art as well as the internet. For example, a common item such as a poster of the very well-known image of the Hindu god Veṅkaṭeśvara typically displays both numerous garlands and aromatics, and indeed these are arguably the most prominent aspects of such an image. Yet, unless such a poster be adorned with aromatics itself, it has no smell, and when such a poster is adorned with garlands and other aromatic materials these might be quite different to those represented visually in

---

36. For an excellent recent discussion of *prasāda*, see Pinkney, "Sacred Share."

the poster.[37] Religious websites might add sound to the experience, but exclude the other sensory modalities.

Smell-Darśan

What can all this tell us about intersensoriality in South Asian ritual, about multi-sensory materials, and above all about the act of *darśan*, perhaps the most important and studied act of perception in South Asian worship?[38] First, we have not yet really begun to talk of the symbolic or other significance of a perfumed paste here. Nevertheless, it seems there is plenty to say about aromatics before we even begin to consider how such perfumes might be the object of some variety of hermeneutics, as a religious text or image would be. Yet, with regard to *darśan* we are now in a better position to think in an engaged and detailed manner about the intersensorial aspects of South Asian forms of worship, supplementing an understanding of the visual with the other senses, especially with regard to aromatic materials. Daniel Miller suggests that "a material culture analysis has to listen to the explicit voices, but remain focused on messages that appear like invisible ink, emerging only under the wash of analysis."[39] Thus *darśan* as seeing not only implies the centrality of the visual in many South Asian religious traditions, but that it might also be a function of the spatial isolation of the consecrated icon from the majority of the worshippers in some important worship contexts. As some Buddhists were well aware, the sense that can perceive most effectively from a distance is the sense of sight. According to this hypothesis, although *darśan* is a mutual, relational act, the emphasis on this particular sensory mode (visual) of relating to the icon accommodates worship environments based on separation and distance, as well as others in which one has more intimate contact with the icon.[40] The materialized divinity is

---

37. Pinney discusses the adornment of chromolithographs: "The dressing of images takes the place of words. Instead of exegesis, instead of an outpouring of language—there is a poetics of materiality and corporeality around the images." Pinney, "Piercing the Skin of the Idol," 169.

38. For example see Eck, *Darśan*; Babb, "Glancing," 387–401.

39. Miller, *Stuff*, 85.

40. The structures of worship environments in South Asian Hindu, Jain, and Buddhist traditions are, and always have been, quite diverse with varying degrees of proximity and contact allowed to worshippers. My hypothesis applies most clearly to temple contexts where the icon in the inner sanctum is set quite far back from most

adorned with materials that have a multi-sensory appeal, yet it is not rare given the structure of many larger temples that at the moment of *darśan* many of these sensory qualities are quite out of reach of the worshipper and can only be (variously) imagined. Relating to religious images through seeing them—*darśan*—is thus a more universally available mode of sensory access to images than that available via the other senses. The structures of worship spaces might therefore be productively analyzed as exploiting the phenomenology of materials in order to regiment perceptions, not just positively, but also negatively, hierarchically, and quite possibly politically.[41] To give an example from a contemporary context, I have seen the icon of Kṛṣṇa at Udupi in South India adorned with thick, colored perfumed pastes, but at the time of viewing these adornments I was entirely unable to smell them owing to the distance of the icon, to which access is greatly restricted.[42] Perhaps one of the most famous images of a Hindu icon is that of Venkaṭeśvara in the temple at Tirumala in South India. This image typically bears a large and highly noticeable, white forehead-mark that actually consists of a considerable quantity of (borneol) camphor[43] molded onto the face of the image, divided in the center by a striking, bamboo-leaf shaped streak of dark musk (which is mixed with sandalwood paste).[44] Arguably this is one of the most famous and iconic adornments of any image worshipped in Hinduism today, and although a "perfume" it is most well known as a visual image. Richard Davis discusses another notable example of a colored perfume: "The preparation and application of a black fragrant balm (*kṛṣṇagandha*) is one

---

worshippers, though I would hope that scholars of religious architecture might find these general observations on the perception of aromatics useful when considering certain spaces. Interestingly, Packert notes that even the visual appreciation of ornament can be somewhat limited by the distances experienced by devotees in temples. Packert, *Art of Loving Krishna*, 46.

41. On a spatial hierarchy, reflecting a priestly point of view, that is implicit in the organization of temples as suggested by ritual manuals, see Colas, "Rites among Vaikhānasas and Related Matters," 26–27.

42. Also, the perfumes available at that temple as *prasāda* are quite dried out and have little scent.

43. "*paccakarpūra.*"

44. I am extremely grateful to Dr A. V. Ramana Dikshitulu, Pradhana Archaka and Agama Advisor, T. T. Devasthanams, Tirumala for explaining to me the composition and weekly preparation of the *namam* of Lord Venkateśvara in a personal interview, June 12, 2010.

of the central rites of the festival of Dancing Śiva. Smearing this balm, says *Kiraṇāgama*, is done in order to make Dancing Śiva black."[45]

Seeing is relational,[46] and in the case of a mutual gaze, reciprocal, but seeing is also perhaps the most "hands-off" form of contact one can have with a religious icon.[47] Why might this be the case? Although seeing inauspicious objects in a South Asian context is undesirable, and the evil eye is perhaps a form of contact that can have unfortunate effects, nevertheless seeing is arguably less likely to produce actual *ritual pollution* than touching, tasting, and also smelling in a Hindu context.[48]

In reflecting on *darśan* we have come to realize that people could (and can) see odorous things that they may or may not be able to smell depending on the context. Of course, *darśan* itself is a complex, variable phenomenon and the nature and interpretation of this act has varied over time and in different communities. Indeed, paying close attention to all the senses and modes of adornment in Hindu worship might help scholars to highlight and interpret this very diversity.[49] To give a striking recent example, the work of Amanda Huffer on the guru Amritanandamayi

---

45. Davis, *Priest's Guide for the Great Festival*, 129, n. 220.

46. Where the gaze of the deity and worshipper might be reciprocal in *darśan*, smelling and touch are not. Just as the worshipper might often be quite unable to smell the image of the deity, likewise the deity might not be able to smell the worshipper.

47. Although, in many Hindu philosophies seeing is understood to involve physical contact nevertheless this is not the case in Jain and Buddhist philosophies. For the former point see Eck, *Darśan*, 9. Also Babb, "Glancing," 396–97. For philosophical theories, see the thorough discussion in Preisendanz, "On *ātmendriyamanorthasannikarṣa* and the Nyāya-Vaiśeṣika Theory of Vision," 141–213. In particular, see pp. 146–48. If seeing-as-contact is to be considered in an analysis of the Hindu context of *darśan*, then arguably indigenous theories of seeing-as-not-involving-contact should be considered in these other religious contexts. As noted, however, with respect to my analysis of aromatics in terms of South Asian philosophical theories, we always need to be extremely cautious of assuming that philosophical and ritual theories always operate seamlessly as one coherent system.

48. As Gonda notes, in *The Law Code of Manu* 3:239 it is stated that the look of certain people and animals during the ritual feeding of Brahmins renders the materials seen "inefficacious." Gonda, *Eye and Gaze in the Veda*, 43; Olivelle, *Manu's Code of Law*, 120. This polluting gaze would therefore seem to have less power than the odor of a forbidden material, the smelling of which is indeed a sin (Manu 11:68), though a less major sin than eating or drinking something forbidden (Manu 11:55–57). On the evil eye, see Babb, "Glancing," 393–94.

49. As Packert notes, "*What* the devotee is looking at—the *object* of all this looking—is rarely discussed . . . *how* the deity looks is as important to the experience of *darshan* as the act of looking itself." *Art of Loving Krishna*, 13.

Ma (Amma), who gives hugs or *darśan* embraces to her followers, demonstrates very clearly how proximity to a revered being, in this case a person, is directly correlated with an emphasis on a particular sensory mode of interaction (touch).[50]

Any complete analysis of visuality in South Asian religions thus demands a study of the theory and technologies of other sensory modalities. Conversely, in reflecting on the significance of smells and aromatics, we also need to think of the significance of colors, temperatures, textures, flavors, and other sensory qualities of perfumes, in addition to the other factors mentioned at the very start of this article, such as the economic value and exotic origins of some aromatics. And I should perhaps emphasize again that the above use of the term "intersensoriality" does not in any way imply that some religious, altered-state of consciousness is involved here, in which people can see smells. What I am suggesting here is rather mundane, perhaps so mundane as to be easily overlooked: in seeing an adorned divinity (*darśan*), some of the things you see have significant sensory qualities beyond sight alone.[51]

Perfume and Agency

We have, however, left one rather important question unexplored here. We have considered the spatial and social variables to be considered when thinking about the manner in which the materiality of a perfumed paste might have been perceived by many people experiencing a *pūjā* ritual, but we have not considered how this affects the gods (or enlightened beings) worshipped. Comprehensive and nuanced studies of the sensory capacities of gods[52] and other beings worshipped (both as embodied-in-an-icon and not), would be of enormous use in understanding the finer details of the materials of worship, as would studies of the aesthetic preferences of beings who are the object of worship.[53] As I

---

50. Huffer, "Darshan in a Hotel Ballroom."

51. As Colas notes this was quite clear to the Vaikhanāsa Vaiṣṇavas who discussed both the differing sensory impacts of various worship materials as well as the multisensory impact of one single item of worship. Colas, *Viṣṇu, Ses Images et Ses Feux*, 303–4, 319.

52. On the sensibilities of religious images according to the Vaikhanāsa ritual school, see the interesting comments in ibid., 302–4.

53. The interesting question of the worship in Jainism of completely liberated beings, who by definition do not possess aesthetic sensibilities (or sensibilities of any

shall explain below, an account of these imagined aesthetic sensibilities is also essential to understanding how religious icons might be said to have agency in the context of rites of worship in South Asian religions. Such analyses in terms of imagined or represented sensibilities also link considerations of beliefs to the study of practice, matter, and the body. The use of aromatic preparations is common to many diverse religious traditions in South Asia, but concepts of the sensibilities of those beings offered aromatics must have varied widely. Therefore, although the form of the materials (i.e., sandalwood paste and so on) might be common to diverse traditions, the way these materials would have been (and are) interpreted by religious actors would have varied enormously. And this variety is not only from tradition to tradition: even within one tradition there would not just have been variety with regard to prior experience and understanding of aromatics, but there might also have been diversity with regard to beliefs about the sensibilities of the beings worshipped.

In the book *Art and Agency*, Alfred Gell created a powerful set of analytical tools for understanding and describing how artefacts work in society.[54] I shall provide here only the briefest summary of Gell's quite complex terminology. Gell wanted to create a theory of the art object/artifact that considered art objects as persons, particularly with regard to agency, this agency often only being perceived by those people interacting with an art object. He creates a very clear and useful form of notation to discuss such "art objects." This is the "art nexus," consisting of the index (e.g., an icon of Viṣṇu), the artist (e.g., the sculptor who made the icon), the recipient (e.g., people seeing and worshipping the icon), and the prototype (e.g., the god Viṣṇu). According to Gell, it is possible for any of these parts of the art nexus to be agent (the being or thing acting) or patient (the being or thing acted on) depending on the situation. In every case an index, normally somehow material or perceivable, will be involved, *through which* agency is exercised. Thus, agency is exercised through things. To give an example, from a point of view that emphasizes the patron of a work of art and somewhat effaces the role of the artist, one could say that the recipient is acting on the index (e.g., Louis XIV created the grounds at Versailles). Such a situation is in fact more complex, and actually the patron (recipient) really acts on the artist

---

variety), has been quite well addressed. For example, see Babb, *Absent Lord*; Humphrey and Laidlaw, *Archetypal Actions of Ritual*; and Cort, *Framing the Jina*.

54. Gell, *Art and Agency*.

who acts on the index.⁵⁵ A theory of art that emphasizes the creation of meaning in the reception of art might also be said to present the recipient as an agent. Whatever one might think of his theory as a whole, Gell's analysis nevertheless provides an extremely clear tool for describing a variety of situations involving artifacts both as we understand them, and also as they might have been understood by others who interacted with art objects in the past. As Gell demonstrates, referring to Diana Eck's work on *darśan*, this can be particularly helpful in thinking about the worship of images of gods.⁵⁶ Ultimately this framework clarifies who or what in any particular situation is being presented as an agent. Agency is here a function of the perspective of a given representation. For example, with the common royal causative in Sanskrit texts, and with Louis XIV creating the gardens, agency in doing and making things in the world is carefully and explicitly placed with the master, *not* the subjects. Gell helps us answer, not so much the questions "Where is the agency in a rite of adornment?" or "Does the purported agent exist?" but rather "Where does the tradition locate the agency in a rite of adornment and why so?"⁵⁷ Sensitive as it is to people's beliefs, his theory can be of use in attempts to state clearly indigenous theories concerning interaction with artifacts.⁵⁸

In addition to its use in understanding the worship of images, we can apply Gell's analysis of the complex agencies involved in a "work of art"/artifact to perfumes and other adornments. Indeed, considering how perfumes fit into Gell's scheme forces us to tackle the interesting question of how material artifacts of ornament and adornment—often so indispensible in a South Asian context⁵⁹—might be considered in terms

55. Such higher-order agency as this is represented in Sanskrit by causative verbs, so common in royal contexts.

56. Gell, *Art and Agency*, ch. 7.

57. Usefully this approach also allows us to bracket questions of the ontology of divine beings, something Chakrabarty discusses (Chakrabarty, *Provincializing Europe*, ch. 3). Here he notes, "Gods are as real as ideology is—that is to say they are both embedded in practice" (idem., 78). If we accept his point we still need to consider whether these real ideologies exist in the same way as stones, professors, gods, numbers, and one hundred dollars might be said to exist, tricky questions that have by no means been resolved *within* the apparently secular Western academy. For a good discussion of Chakrabarty's work that also emphasizes the significance of choices made in assigning agency in religious contexts, see Hollywood, "Gender, Agency, and the Divine in Religious Historiography," 514–28.

58. "For our purposes what is important are the beliefs people hold, not whether these beliefs are justified." Ibid., 34 n. 2.

59. For important reflections on ornament in South Asia, see Dehejia, *Body*

of agency. Typically, one might tend to think ornamental materials are simply material instruments used by worshippers to express their devotion, or other intentional attitude (i.e., the recipient acts on the index/icon *by means of* adornments). However, the agency of the being indexed in the icon (e.g., Viṣṇu) in relation to the form of the materials of worship is more elusive. Yet, it is by no means the case that in texts on worship, and in practice, devotees are given complete freedom of choice as to what materials they use to worship[60]—where do these restrictions come from?

Here we might usefully turn our attention away from the materiality of this perfume, and consider the fact that many of the formulae for such aromatics are embedded in texts that are somehow presented as revealed, either by a deity, or by a seer or other person highly qualified to speak about matters of worship. As with iconographic schemes found in such revealed religious texts, it seems possible that in some cases these texts are not supposed to be comprehensive instructions to be followed, and often the exact relation between theory and practice is not at all clear.[61] Rather, it seems such texts attempt to locate the ultimate agency for materials and forms of worship in the god or other authoritative source.[62] In such a case, the perfume-as-revealed is not merely an expression of human devotion. Rather such a perfume is presented in these texts as an adornment-instrument that is in fact the material expression of the agency of the god or his proxy. This adornment-instrument can, however, be offered *with* devotion by worshippers. And presumably the god dictates the form taken by the adornments in accordance with his or her personal preferences.[63] Or we might even say that for many devotees, the aesthetic

---

Adorned; 2009, Ali, *Courtly Culture*, 162–82; and Coomaraswamy, "Ornament," 1–19.

60. The materials collected in *The Elucidation of Pūjā* suggest that offerings of flowers were subject to particularly extensive regulation. A study of these materials for what they tell us both about flowers and gods in medieval South Asia would be very interesting, but given the complexity of this material such a discussion lies outside the scope of this article.

61. Pollock, "Theory of Practice and the Practice of Theory," 499–519.

62. Readers might be reminded of Pollock's famous discussion of the function of *śāstra* and the "mythic crystallizations of the postulate of shastric priority." Ibid., 512. Rather than focus on the importance of "transcendent *śāstra*," I am interested here in the implied agency-in-our-world of those beings who are often said to have originated such texts, or concerning whom other narrators are well qualified to speak. Such an analysis also highlights the (well-known) radical difference with respect to agency and intentionality between a text created by a god/qualified person, and the unauthored Vedas of Mīmāṃsā.

63. In her studies of ornamentation in temples today, Packert has noted the role

preferences of the god can actually be observed/sensed in the materials of worship, whose form is theoretically grounded in texts that are held to be revealed.[64] Such adornments and the texts prescribing them thus implicitly both reveal and construct the imagined aesthetic sensibilities of the beings offered the adornments.

Conclusion

The study of material culture is as important to the study of South Asian religious traditions (both past and present) as the study of texts. Meskell notes, in a discussion of the material culture of ancient Egypt, that "Bodies of artifacts ... implicate particular cosmologies where the role of materiality may have been central to peoples' relationships to each other and to the deities,"[65] something that clearly also applies to South Asia. Given the complex, multi-sensory nature of much Hindu (and Jain and Buddhist) ritual, scholars should not solely focus on the, admittedly very important, visual aspects of material worship. Although I just suggested that one should not rely on texts alone in the study of South Asian religions, nevertheless in the case of the historical study of aromatics we find ourselves in the peculiar position of studying material culture as described in texts—because, of course, no early medieval South Asian perfumes have survived. In studying other aspects of historical material culture this is not always the case: scholars of sculpture and architecture have access to both artifacts and texts. Ancient perfumes, however, are only ever available to us as represented in texts,[66] and studying this particular type of material culture therefore forces us to consider some

---

of priestly stewardship—and our texts could, of course, be codifications of these very sorts of practices that were responding to a variety of contexts. Packert, *Art of Loving Krishna*, ch. 1.

64. One might also productively compare the preferences of the gods revealed in the materials of worship with those described in more literary sources. As noted above, discussions of the flowers that should be used in worship are particularly detailed. Unlike perfumes and incenses, flowers are not what one would typically call artifacts (garlands, however, are). Nevertheless, the selection of a certain type of flower does put the selector in the role of agent, and the flower patient, using Gell's terminology. If the choice of a certain flower is presented as based on a revealed text, then in fact the person selecting the flower is only a proxy agent—ultimately the god (or expert seer) acts on the flower.

65. Meskell, "Objects in the Mirror Appear Closer Than They Are," 52.

66. The same applies to early music and food, to give two important examples.

methodological questions from the outset. When dealing with things-in-texts how might one go about reflecting on the materiality of these things? I have suggested that cautious reconstruction of the aromatics can help us to understand aspects of their *sheer materiality* that we might miss if we only ever read about these things. But we cannot assume that these texts actually provide practical instructions on how to make these things—the formula we considered above probably gives a good idea of what was in the perfumed paste, but there are very few details. Such a formula-as-text is equally, if not more, important in overtly attributing such a perfumed paste to a source more authorized to speak on behalf of the tastes of Viṣṇu than, for example, a priest making the perfume in a temple. Such a text not only authorizes and codifies the use of this perfumed paste, but it also appears to remove creative agency from us mere mortals. I also argued that the imagined aesthetic preferences of the gods are implicitly revealed in such texts.

As Eck notes, *darśan* is a multi-sensory affair,[67] yet this is not only because of the sounds and smells accompanying the visual experience. As already noted, some of the things people see adorning the icon are valued primarily for their non-visual qualities, such as fragrance (hence the paste is called a *gandha*), yet it is quite common in practice that these materials can only be perceived by the visual sense. This creates social discrepancies in both access and response—the icon and those near it have full access to these qualities, and amongst those who can only see it, their prior experience and knowledge of these materials will condition their responses. An examination of perfumes led us back to the importance of the visual, which therefore undeniably does hold a very central place in perception in Hinduism.[68]

Perfumed pastes (*gandha*) like the one we have considered here are, of course, still made and used in a great variety of religious contexts in South Asia today, but they are not removed from historical processes. People's acquaintance with and understanding of these materials has changed over time: for example nowadays camphor has been synthesized and is very cheap and not particularly prestigious. Musk, on the other hand, is now prohibitively expensive and very few people at the present

---

67. Eck, *Darśan*, 11–12.

68. Sarah Pink provides a clear discussion of the manner in which the study of the senses went though an "anti-visualism" phase, critical of "ocularcentrism." As Pink explains, many scholars, herself included, have now moved beyond this. Pink, *Doing Sensory Ethnography*, 11–15.

time would know what a musk forehead-mark (*kastūrītilaka*) as seen, or mentioned in a text, would smell like. But I will end with perhaps the most interesting outcome of this discussion, for we must also consider the possibility that such materials as this perfumed paste are not visibly conspicuous by a mere coincidence. It is very likely that one of the factors that led to the cultural importance of a material such as saffron, in addition to its rich perfume and preciousness, was its striking golden color. The centrality of the visual in South Asian culture thus no doubt led to the elevation in prestige of certain highly pigmented odorants—along with their odors—in the palette of South Asian aromatics. The perfume *had* to smell like this in order to *look good*. These materials generally had strong concentrated odors, often with fixative properties (i.e., their scents lasted long), they were rare, expensive, and their color permitted conspicuous display. A dialectic of the visual and olfactory thus took place: certain aromatics (e.g., musk, camphor, saffron) were especially valued because of their visual impact, and this in turn led to an increased olfactory prestige, which, again, led to their increased use and visual prominence. And these materials were often important items of global trade, with some species (e.g., certain trees that produce aloeswood) now endangered owing to over exploitation. Conversely, although modern Western alcohol-based perfumes are invisible on the skin, we can see them in the bottle. In this form, as a flacon to be marketed and displayed at home, the color of the fragrance also matters. Yet, where aromatics used to be valued for their strong colors, ironically, the phenomenon of fragrance-as-a-beautiful-glass-flacon sometimes creates the demand for a very clear, white liquid such that perfumers are required to use "decolorized" essential oils (including decolorized saffron) [69] and in the process we sometimes lose some of the quality of the fragrance.

Bibliography

Ali, Daud. *Courtly Culture and Political Life in Early Medieval India*. Cambridge: Cambridge University Press, 2004.
Babb, Lawrence A. *Absent Lord: Ascetics and Kings in a Jain Ritual Culture*. Berkeley: University of California Press, 1996.
———. "Glancing: Interaction in Hinduism." *Journal of Anthropological Research* 37, no. 4 (1981) 387–401.

69. I am grateful to perfumer Christophe Laudamiel for several discussions regarding decolorized oils.

Baxandall, Michael. *Painting and Experience in Fifteenth Century Italy*. 2nd ed. Oxford: Oxford University Press, 1988.

Boivin, Nicole. *Material Cultures, Material Minds: The Impact of Things on Human Thought, Society, and Evolution*. Cambridge: Cambridge University Press, 2008.

Chakrabarty, Dipesh. *Provincializing Europe: Postcolonial Thought and Historical Difference*. Reissue, with a new preface by the author. Princeton: Princeton University Press, 2008.

Colas, Gérard. "Rites among Vaikhanāsas and Related Matters: Some Methodological Issues." In *Words and Deeds: Hindu and Buddhist Rituals in South Asia* edited by Jörg Gengnagel, Ute Hüsken, and Srilata Raman, 23–44. Wiesbaden: Harrassowitz Verlag, 2005.

———. *Viṣṇu, Ses Images et Ses Feux: les metamorphoses du dieu chez les vaikhanāsa*. Paris: Presses de l'École Française d'Extrême-Orient, 1996.

Colas, Gérard, and Gilles Tarabout, eds. *Rites Hindous, Transferts et Transformations*. Paris: Éditions de l'École des Hautes Études en Sciences Sociales, 2006.

Coomaraswamy, Ananda K. "Ornament." *Art Bulletin* 21 (1939) 1–19.

Cort, John E. *Framing the Jina: Narratives of Icons and Idols in Jain History*. Oxford: Oxford University Press, 2010.

Davis, Richard H. *A Priest's Guide for the Great Festival: Aghoraśiva's Mahotsavavidhi*. Oxford: Oxford University Press, 2010.

Dehejia, Vidya. *The Body Adorned: Dissolving Boundaries between Sacred and Profane in India's Art*. New York: Columbia University Press, 2009.

Eck, Diana. *Darśan: Seeing the Divine Image in India*. 3rd ed. New York: Columbia University Press, 1998.

Gell, Alfred. *Art and Agency: An Anthropological Theory*. Oxford: Clarendon, 1998.

Gonda, J. *Eye and Gaze in the Veda*. Amsterdam: North-Holland, 1969.

Hollywood, Amy. "Gender, Agency, and the Divine in Religious Historiography." *Journal of Religion* 84, no. 4 (2004) 514–28.

Howes, David. "Scent, Sound and Synaesthesia: Intersensoriality and Material Culture Theory." In *Handbook of Material Culture*, edited by Christopher Tilley et al., 161–72. London: Sage, 2006.

Huffer, Amanda. "Darshan in a Hotel Ballroom: Amritanandamayi Ma's (Amma's) Communities of Devotees in the United States." PhD, University of Chicago, 2010.

Humphrey, Caroline, and James Laidlaw. *The Archetypal Actions of Ritual: A Theory of Ritual Illustrated by the Jain Rite of Worship*. Oxford: Clarendon, 1994.

Kane, P. V. *History of Dharmaśāstra*. Vol. 1, Part 2. Pune: Bhandarkar Oriental Research Institute, 1975.

Marx, Karl. *A Contribution to the Critique of Political Economy*. Edited by Maurice Dobb. Translated by S. W. Ryazanskaya. New York: International, 1970.

McHugh, James. "The Classification of Smells and the Order of the Senses in Indian Religious Traditions." *Numen: International Review for the History of Religions* 54, no. 4 (2007) 374–419.

———. "Sandalwood and Carrion: Smell in South Asian Culture and Religion." PhD diss., Harvard University, 2008.

Meskell, Lynn. "Objects in the Mirror Appear Closer Than They Are." In *Materiality*, edited by Daniel Miller, 51–71. Durham, NC: Duke University Press, 2005.

Miller, Daniel, ed. *Materiality*. Durham, NC: Duke University Press, 2005.

———. *Stuff*. Cambridge: Polity, 2010.

Mitramiśra. *Vīramitrodaya*. Vol. 4: *Pūjāprakāśa*. Chowkhamba Sanskrit Series 30. 1913. Reprint, Benares: Chowkhamba Sanskrit Book Depot, 1987.

Olivelle, Patrick. *Manu's Code of Law: A Critical Edition and Translation of the Mānava-Dharmaśāstra*. Oxford: Oxford University Press, 2005.

Packert, Cynthia. *The Art of Loving Krishna: Ornamentation and Devotion*. Bloomington, IN: Indiana University Press, 2010.

Phillips, Stephen H., and N. S. Ramanuja Tatacharya. *Epistemology of Perception: Gaṅgeśa's Tattvacintāmaṇi Jewel of Reflection on the Truth (about Epistemology), the Perception Chapter pratyakṣa-khaṇḍa, Transliterated Text, Translation, and Philosophical Commentary*. New York: American Institute of Buddhist Studies, 2004.

Pink, Sarah. *Doing Sensory Ethnography*. Los Angeles, London: Sage, 2009.

Pinkney, Andrea Marion. "The Sacred Share: Prasāda in South Asia." PhD diss. Columbia University, 2008.

Pinney, Christopher. "Piercing the Skin of the Idol." In *Beyond Aesthetics: Art and the Technologies of Enchantment*, edited by Christopher Pinney and Nicholas Thomas, 157–79. Oxford: Berg, 2001.

Pollock, Sheldon. "The Theory of Practice and the Practice of Theory in Indian Intellectual History." *Journal of the American Oriental Society* 105, no. 3 (1985) 499–519.

Preisendanz, Karin. "On ātmendriyamanorthasannikarṣa and the Nyāya-Vaiśeṣika Theory of Vision." *Berliner Indologische Studien* 4/5 (1989) 141–213.

Rao, S. K. Ramachandra. *The Āgama Encyclopaedia, Vol. 7: Preparations for Pūjā*. 2nd ed. Delhi: Sri Satguru, 2005.

Rocher, Ludo. *The Purāṇas. A History of Indian Literature*, vol. 2, fasc. 3. Wiesbaden: Otto Harrassowitz, 1986.

Smith, Mark M. *Sensing the Past: Seeing, Hearing, Smelling, Tasting, and Touching in History*. Berkeley: University of California Press, 2007.

Sullivan, Lawrence E. "Sound and Senses: Toward a Hermeneutics of Performance." *History of Religions* 26, no. 1 (1986) 1–33.

Tilley, Christopher. "Materiality in Materials." *Archaeological Dialogues* 14, no. 1 (2007) 16–20.

6

Religious Ritual and the Creation of Sacred Space

Alonzo L. Gaskill

The Commonality of Sacred Space

Among the most visible aspects of religion is sacred space.[1] Indeed, the concept of sacred space is foundational to many ancient and contemporary religious societies.[2] Among the Abrahamic traditions—Judaism, Christianity, and Islam—the concept of sacred space is prevalent and enduring. The Western ("Wailing") Wall, Mecca and Medina, and the Tomb of Christ are persistent places of pilgrimage. For practitioners, locations of veneration hold a place of profundity, sometimes for their religious and historical significance, but also because they offer hope for a bright future; a future which potentially brings again transcendental

---

1. "The English word 'sacredness' is derived from Latin, and is defined as restriction through pertaining to the gods. The concept of sacred implies restrictions and prohibitions on human behavior—if something is sacred then certain rules must be observed in relation to it, and this generally means that something that is said to be sacred, whether it be an object or site (or person), must be placed apart from everyday things or places, so that its special significance can be recognized, and rules regarding it obeyed." Hubert, "Sacred Beliefs," 11. Elsewhere we read that "the sacred has been identified as an uncanny, awesome, or powerful manifestation of reality, full of ultimate significance. . . . The sacred [is located] at the nexus of human practices." Chidester and Linenthal, "Introduction," 5.

2. See Davies, "Introduction: Raising the Issues," 1; King, "Religion," 12:288.

experiences akin to that which took place there in days past.[3] Each of the Abrahamic faiths has expectations of what God will do with, through, and for them if they hold out faithful to their deity—and sacred space is often perceived as playing a role in the fulfilling of God's promises.

There is often an opposition or tension that exists between sacred space—which, for the religious, is the only *real* space—and profane space, which surrounds the sacred on all sides.[4] For the faithful—or faith-filled[5]—sacred space often serves as a respite from the perceived fallen world; a place of protection, but also a place of communion with the divine.[6] The sacred is that which endures—that which is eternal; whereas the profane is fleeting, illusory, and unreliable. In sacred space, one finds one's bearings in the universe; one's orientation *toward* God and relationship *with* God.[7] Profane space, on the other hand, is traditionally perceived by the religious as the source of chaos and disorientation. It is where one loses one's way and forgets one's relationship to and with the divine.[8]

Reasons for Sacred Space

There are a variety of reasons why certain locations may be deemed "sacred." Sometimes it is because of what is believed to have already taken

---

3. See King, "Religion," 12:289.

4. See Eliade, *Sacred and the Profane*, 20. See King, "Religion," 12:289.

5. The distinction between "faithful" and "faith-filled" is subtle, but significant. Whereas faithful implies obedience to rules and expectations, faith-filled implies belief. One can be faithful without belief, faith-filled without obedience, or both.

6. One text noted, "sacred place is often the place where humans enter the realm of the gods or, conversely, the place where the gods are among humans. In either case, it becomes the place of the presence of divinity and therefore an image of the realm of divinity." Brereton, "Sacred Space," 12:532, see also 12:528; Ross, "Diversities of Divine Presence," 101, 102. Elsewhere we read, "God is viewed as actually dwelling in these [sacred] objects or places . . . and thus almost physically present in a specific place at a specific time. Thus, the sacredness of the space is due to God's presence there as opposed to God's being anywhere else." Kunin, "Judaism," 128. The rituals invoke God's presence, thus inviting His presence and allowing for communion. He does not come to the place aside from ritual acts of communion.

7. See Nibley, "What Is a Temple?" 357–58.

8. As one set of scholars put it, "the urban world of the twenty-first century is full of godless distractions that divert people's energies away from realizing their own capacity for holiness." North and North, "Introduction," 6; See also Morisy, "Seven Cairns," 117–33.

place there; for example, in Catholicism, the grotto at Lourdes (a site renowned for its miraculous healing properties[9]), or the Holy Sepulcher (the site presumed to be the place of Christ's burial) for Christians more generally.[10] At other times, space is held sacred because of what is expected to take place there; for example, the Mount of Olives, where Christ will place His feet at some point leading up to the second advent (Zech 14:1–4), or the Adam-ondi-Ahman valley (for Mormons).[11] Sometimes space is perceived as sacred because it belongs to the realm of belief, imagination, or hope; for example, purgatory or heaven.[12] Regardless, at the core of location veneration is the desire to connect with the divine;

---

9. Of Lourdes, one text points out that "when most people link cures with Catholicism they doubtless think first of Lourdes—the French shrine popularly credited with countless healing miracles since the middle of the [nineteenth] century. Today, Lourdes still attracts more supplicants—millions each year—than any other healing site in the world." Nickell, *Looking for a Miracle*, 145–46 (see pp. 145–53); see also Gesler, *Healing Places*, 65; Brereton, "Sacred Space," 12:530.

10. The Holy Sepulcher has been labeled as one of "Christianity's two most sacred sites"—the other being Calvary, the mount upon which Jesus was crucified. See Craughwell, *Saints Preserved*, 126–27. See also Webb, "Pilgrimage," 940. One scholar pointed out, "Some sacred spaces were designed to transport you, mystically, into other sacred spaces: round churches (the Temple Church in London or the Round Church in Cambridge) remind us of the Holy Sepulcher in Jerusalem . . . Pilgrims may not be able to get to the actual shrines themselves, but in prayer and imagination they can still enjoy its benefits and sense its holiness. Nor was this sense of 'sacred space by proxy' limited to the Catholic world: when chapels in Wales were named 'Bethel' and 'Ebenezer' and 'Horeb', worshipers were encouraged to see themselves as inhabiting these holy places." Tavinor, "Sacred Space and the Built Environment," 32. Elsewhere we read: "The place" which is deemed sacred "removes the physical distance between the worshiper and the event, and in doing so, it also mitigates the temporal distance between the time" when the miracle or sacred event happened "and the present. By thus collapsing space and time, it endows the event with an imposing reality." Brereton, "Sacred Space," 12:533.

11. In Mormon eschatology, prior to the second advent of Christ, there will be a large meeting in Daviess County, Missouri—a location known by Latter-day Saints as "Adam-ondi-Ahman" (or the "valley of God where Adam dwelt"). In LDS theology, prior to Jesus' return, there will be an appearance by Him "to selected members of his Church. He will come in private to his prophet and to the apostles then living. Those who have held keys and powers and authorities in all ages from Adam to the present will also be present. And further, all the faithful members of the Church then living and all the faithful saints of all the ages past will be present. It will be the greatest congregation of faithful saints ever assembled on planet earth. It will be a sacrament meeting. It will be a day of judgment for the faithful of all the ages." See McConkie, *Millennial Messiah*, 578–79 (see pp. 578–88). See also Matthews, "Adam-Ondi-Ahman," 27–35.

12. See Davies, "Christianity," 33.

to feel that one's God is more accessible because one has placed himself or herself within the precincts which constitute "sacred space." Thus, in times past when the transcendental occurred in some location, often the ancients would erect an altar or monument on the spot to commemorate the occasion and as a testament to their sense of the hallowed nature of the location in which the divine, in some way or another, revealed itself.[13] Such locations typically became places of pilgrimage for the faithful.[14] These sacred places serve as a "focusing lens" of sorts.[15] They are a constant reminder to pilgrims and patrons of a tradition's past, but also of its chosen status and anticipated future; a future which typically promises some form of redemption and elevation.

Of course, sacred space is not solely reserved for the location of the miraculous. As the historian of religion, Mircea Eliade, pointed out:

> Often there is no need for a theophany or hierophany properly speaking; some *sign* suffices to indicate the sacredness of a place. . . . [T]he *sign*, fraught with religious meaning, introduces an absolute element and puts an end to relativity and confusion. When no sign manifests itself, it is *provoked*. . . . This amounts to an evocation of sacred forms or figures for the immediate purpose of establishing an *orientation* in the homogeneity of space.[16]

In other words, where a "sacred location"—whatever that may be—cannot be directly attached to a hallowed historic event, the performance of sacred rites or rituals on such a spot is sufficient to establish its sacral nature. God, therefore, can be the creator of sacred space; *but so can humanity!* Thus, Eliade adds: "Since religious man cannot live except in an atmosphere impregnated with the sacred, we must expect to find a large number of techniques[17] for consecrating space. . . . The ritual by

---

13. See Davies, "Christianity," 33, 41–42, 44.

14. One scholar pointed out, "holy land and holy city seemed essentially Jewish concepts. Only when Christianity was publically triumphant could they be appropriated. . . . However, there is some evidence that already before the fourth century a few devout persons were making their way to Palestine in order to see the biblical sites, especially those associated with the life and death of Jesus." Webb, "Pilgrimage," 940. Thus, the concept of "sacred space"—and pilgrimage thereto—in Christianity may have grown out of Judaism, and its practice. For discussion of the hajj in Islam, see Glassé, *Concise Encyclopedia of Islam*, 313–17.

15. Brereton, "Sacred Space," 12:526, 533.

16. Eliade, *Sacred and the Profane*, 27, emphasis in original.

17. The "techniques" that would "consecrate space" could be formal ordinances, such as baptism or partaking of the Eucharist; or even liturgically low acts, such as the

which he constructs a sacred space is efficacious in the measure in which *it reproduces the work of the gods.*"[18] True it is; many go to their sacred space because they seek to do God's work—in whatever form that "work" takes in their particular tradition. Engagement in ritual acts—which are perceived by the practitioner as God's bidding—has an empowering and transformative effect upon the participant, as does the ritual clothing donned by the participant during such rites.[19] Humans innately seek the approval of the divine; and rituals and their accompanying sacred space give the patron a sense that they are partners with God—approved to do God's work on God's behalf.

Ritual as the Source of Sacred Space

While it is often assumed that a given place is holy because of what has taken place there, nevertheless, there is reason to assume that the exact opposite is sometimes the situation. In other words, in the case of a significant portion of sacred space, it is the ritual that takes place there which makes the location venerable, not the space itself. Highlighting this very point, the University of Durham's Douglas Davies pointed out: "Ritual often works in a way that adds many layers of meaning to objects used, to actions performed, and to the places where rites take place. . . . Holy

---

washing of the feet before entering a mosque or Krishna temple. Any ritual practice, regardless of how elaborate it is, has the potential to consecrate the space in which it is performed—particularly if that work or rite is perceived as pleasing God or being directed/required by God.

18. Eliade, *Sacred and the Profane*, 28, 29, emphasis in original. Similarly, Roman Catholic scholar Thomas Bokenkotter pointed out, "Worship . . . is a particularly human response to the overwhelming power and majesty radiant in the cosmos. . . . Worship, then, is deeply rooted in human nature itself. One might as well ask why people eat and drink, work and play, as ask why they pray and worship." Bokenkotter, *Dynamic Catholicism*, 162.

19. See for example, Hopko, *Orthodox Faith*, 25–27. Elsewhere in this same text, Hopko taught, "The Orthodox Church is quite firm in its insistence that liturgical vesting is essential to normal liturgical worship, experienced as the realization of communion with the glorious Kingdom of God." Ibid., 20. The "priestly clothing" often worn during rituals performed in space designated as "sacred" is frequently seen as a representation of "the garb of God and of the angels." Dressing in special clothing denotes a change in role, "from that of mortal to immortal, from ordinary human to priest or priestess, king or queen." Tvedtnes, "Priestly Clothing in Bible Times," 665, 666. "Priestly clothing, by its symbolic nature and pure whiteness, replaces the everyday garb which reminds us that we are in the world, thus bringing the wearer closer to heaven." Ibid., 677.

rites make sacred places."[20] Joel Brereton similarly noted: "The rituals that a people either practice at a place or direct toward it mark its sacredness and differentiate it from other defined spaces."[21] While this may seem counterintuitive to some, there seems ample evidence that rite and ritual set space apart as sacred.[22] Permit a brief elaboration on the point.

While space certainly exists independent of ritual, the ritualization of space is where the transition from the ordinary to the sanctified takes place.[23] Space—whether secular or sacred—becomes hallowed when it is endowed with sacral meaning. Prior to being endowed with sacrosanct significance, the holy is simply mundane. Thus, Chidester and Linenthal noted that "nothing is inherently sacred. Not full of meaning, *the sacred*, from this perspective, is an empty signifier. . . . As a situational term, therefore, *the sacred* is nothing more or less than a notional supplement to the ongoing cultural work of sacralizing space, time, persons, and social reactions. . . . The sacred is a by-product of this work of sacralization. . . . Place is sacralized as the result of the cultural labor of ritual."[24] For example, when one enters a Roman Catholic church and genuflects, one does so *not* because one has entered a sacred place, *but* because one has entered the presence of the consecrated Eucharist—which makes the space sacred.[25] It is not the church building (structure) that is holy, but what happens in that building (the ritual) that makes it sacred space.[26]

---

20. Davies, "Christianity," 44, 43. Similarly, Evan Zuesse pointed out "ritual definitively breaks up the homogeneity of space." It creates a sacred otherness out of otherwise mundane spheres. See Zuesse, "Ritual," 12:410.

21. Brereton, "Sacred Space," 12:526.

22. Chidester and Linenthal suggested "the formalized 'gestures of approach,' and the location and direction of embodied movement—all contribute towards producing the distinctive quality and character of sacred space." Chidester and Linenthal, "Introduction," 10. See also Weir, "Liminality, Sacred Space and the Diwan," 50.

23. Hugh Nibley suggested, "The purpose of . . . ordinances is to bridge the space between the world in which we now live . . . and that to which we aspire. . . . Therefore, the events of the temple were thought to take place in both terrestrial and telestial spheres, the world of the mysteries or ordinances." Nibley, "Meaning of the Temple," 29.

24. Chidester and Linenthal, "Introduction," 6, emphasis added. See also Bremborg, "Creating Sacred Space by Walking in Silence," 557.

25. Genuflection is the act of lowering oneself momentarily—typically on the right knee—to acknowledge the divine presence in the form of the consecrated Eucharist. It is customary to make the sign of the cross while kneeling.

26. One text notes: "This is a sign of adoration and greeting directed toward the divine presence of the Blessed Sacrament reserved in the tabernacle in the sanctuary.

One must "sacralize" the space by what one does *in* that space. The actions performed therein make the space holy because the space becomes the location of the sacred act or event. A similar example can be drawn from the world of the Latter-day Saints. Mormons make much of the sacred nature of their temples. However, it isn't the temple which makes their rites sacred; it is the rites that make the temple sacred.[27] Thus, on May 4, 1842, Joseph Smith administered the Mormon temple ordinances, known as the "endowment,"[28] in his red-brick store, in Nauvoo, Illinois—even though Latter-day Saints today would say that a dedicated temple is the *only* location upon the earth in which such rites can be performed.[29] Similarly, on July 21, 1849, Brigham Young—along with ten other men—climbed Ensign Peak (in Salt Lake City) in order to give Addison Pratt his "endowment."[30] The store was but a store, and the hill was but a hill—and they remain such today. However, because of what took place there, for a time each was "sacred space."[31]

In support of the view that the ritual creates the sacred, rather than the sacred creating the ritual, Mircea Eliade pointed out:

Today it is common that the Blessed Sacrament and the tabernacle be located in a special chapel separated from the sanctuary. Many parishioners still genuflect out of habit, even though the Blessed Sacrament is not present." Dues, *Catholic Customs and Traditions*, 183. See also *United States Catholic Catechism for Adults*, 223–24; McBrien, "Genuflection," 556. The same could be said of Judaism, wherein the Passover Seder is celebrated in the home. That ritualistic meal transforms the mortal abode into something sacred, as it "effects its enchantment by showing the individual that the everyday stands for something beyond." Neusner, *Enchantments of Judaism*, 76.

27. Latter-day Saints *do* dedicate their buildings (e.g., churches, temples, etc.), but the dedicatory prayer of such sites simply sets them apart for holy activities to be performed therein. However, the prayer of dedication does not, of itself, have the power to make the space sacred. Indeed, the general sense is that profane activities performed in the sacred space defile it. Thus, again, it is the activity that determines the holiness or profanity of a place, not the choice to dedicate or not dedicate the space for sacred ceremonies.

28. The temple "endowment" is among the highest of LDS liturgical rites, and is perceived as salvific by those who faithfully engage in it. It consists of a series of covenants entered into in ritual fashion, with promises of salvation offered for faithfulness to those same covenants.

29. See Hedges, Smith and Anderson, *Joseph Smith Papers, Journals Volume 2*, 53–54.

30. See Anderson, *Development of LDS Temple Worship*, 16–17, see also xxvi.

31. Locations where singular sacred events once occurred may, with time, lose their sacral sense. However, in the minds of practitioners, even the desacralized *can* provoke a sense of the sacred.

> There are ... privileged places, qualitatively different from all others—a man's birthplace, or the scenes of his first love, or certain places in the first foreign city he visited in youth. Even for the most frankly nonreligious man, all these places still retain an exceptional, a unique quality; they are the "holy places" of his private universe, as if it were in such spots that he had received the revelation of a reality *other* than that in which he participates through his ordinary daily life.[32]

As Eliade suggests, we each have spaces in our minds and hearts that are—in some sense—hallowed because of an experience (sacred or secular) which we had there. Clearly, it is not the space, but the experience that makes such locations sacred, and which fills our hearts and heads with sentimentality regarding them. And just as secular space is, in a sense, hallowed by the meaningful experiences we have there, the religious spaces we visit are also sanctified as we ritualize them—physically, socially, psychologically, or spiritually. When dealing with the realm of the religious, as we create rites of transformation, the precincts in which those rites are performed take on sacredness for the practitioner.

While a majority of the world's religions have sacred space, of course, there are exceptions. One scholar noted: "One key to understanding the difference between Christians happy with having sacred places and those unhappy with the idea lies in the sacraments and the emphasis placed upon sacraments and upon an authorised priesthood trained to administer them."[33] If ritual helps to form sacred space, then traditions with little ritual have little need for holy habitations. As a singular example, low-church Protestants—such as Baptists or Evangelicals—traditionally do not have much in the way of rites or rituals.[34] Sacraments are customarily

---

32. Eliade, *Sacred and the Profane*, 24.

33. Davies, "Christianity," 52.

34. This is in no way intended as a criticism; simply an observation frequently made in academic and liturgical circles. For example, the Willow Creek Community Church near Chicago refrains from the use of any Christian symbolism. See Hoover, "The Cross at Willow Creek," 139–53. Davies similarly noted, "some Christians are extremely happy to say that their meeting places are sacred while others strongly deny it. ... There are contemporary groups of Christians, especially those who are said to belong to House Church Movements, who specifically use for worship buildings originally built for different purposes. One contemporary group meets in a disused cinema, and specifically tries not to put religious signs or symbols into the building. For them the idea of a sacred place does not make much sense, [as] they see the group of believers as the real focus of God's activity through the Holy Spirit and not the place as such." Davies, "Christianity," 51–52.

not seen as salvific by those who identify with these traditions. Consequently, sacred space is also traditionally absent. The sanctuary does not provoke a sense of awe because provocative rites of transformation are absent and, thus, the space is utilitarian rather than sacred and ritually transformative.[35]

Endowing Ritual with Meaning

While ritual can create sacred space, ritual alone is not enough to do so. It should be understood that what makes ritual empowering—and what allows it to turn the profane into the holy—isn't simply engagement

---

35. It has been suggested that the stories of the Bible and the music that celebrates those events and locales have become the "sacred space" of many low-church Protestants. Thus, Douglas Davies wrote:

> Although the Protestant Reformation retained the sacraments of baptism and the eucharist, . . . its stress lay on preaching and the Bible. Excessive emphasis on the lives of the saints, miracles, pilgrimages and sacred places gave way to a rediscovery of the stories of the Bible and the significance of the Bible for understanding God, the Christian religion and personal dimensions of faith.
>
> The death of Jesus lay at the heart of Protestant religion. . . . He was, in other words, part and parcel of the sacred places of the Bible.
>
> The Incarnation . . . brought an added quality of the sacred to the established location of the holy land. His passion and suffering in the garden of Gethsemane, and his crucifixion on the hill of Calvary added even more to their sacredness, and preaching developed the vision of God's acts in time and place and sought to catch up modern believers in those events. The sacred places of Protestantism were based on the locations of Christ's life, taken up into the imagination of believers through these sermons, Bible stories and, as time went on, especially in hymns. These are sacred places of a spiritual geography. . . .
>
> So even in Churches where there would have been no pictures or stained glass windows giving an artistic portrayal of biblical scenes, those scenes would be created in the mind's eye of believers as they sang and as they heard sermons describing the death of Jesus. Their own experience of forgiveness would often be intimately linked with those images and, in many respects, that experience would help give a sense of the sacred to the picture. . . .
>
> The experiences of many Protestants would have taken place in religious buildings. Those buildings may have been devoid of Christian art and bare of ornament but . . . they were filled with imagery through hymns. The power of music to fill a building and add yet another dimension to words must never be ignored when considering sacred places in Christianity. This is especially important for those situations where believers argue that their building is not sacred in any special way.

Davies, "Christianity," 48–49, 51. See also Brereton, "Sacred Space," 12:528; King, "Religion," 12:289; Walton, "Theological Perspectives," 25, 34.

in the rite. Rather, the act of endowing the ceremony with meaning is where the transformative power enters in.[36] (The same could be said of sacred space: "a sacred space comes into being when it is *interpreted* as a sacred place."[37]) Until a given ritual has connotation and significance for the worshiper, it is but words and movement, but it has not power to enchant, to transport—to change the participant from fallen human to communicant with the divine.[38] As evidence of this, one need only look at how the "irreligious" still behave religiously—though often unaware of the fact; and how those "religious" behaviors have no religious impact upon the non-religious because they are not endowed with religious meaning.[39] As an illustration, consider the common practice of circumcision. This minor surgical rite, of dubious medical value, is currently performed on 81 percent of males.[40] For the practicing Jew, it serves as a "mark" of the renewal of the agreement between God and Israel; a symbol of the covenant carved into the flesh. However, for the non-religious, it has no spiritual impact—no transformative meaning or effect.[41] It is merely a common surgical procedure performed on newborns. There are certainly other culturally commonplace superstitions and taboos, and we frequently see the practical retention of numerous "camouflaged

36. By "transformative power," I mean the power to psychologically, emotionally or even spiritually transform the participant. What I *do not* mean, however, is that spiritual transformation is nothing more than a psychological or emotional response to a religious act. I acknowledge that many religious traditions—including my own—hold that the power of ritual is to be found in God's authorization of the rite and in the Spirit associated with it. The only point I wish to make here is that even an authorized ordinance will have limited power in the life of the participant if he or she does not find meaning in the rite—if he or she does not endow the ritual with meaning.

37. Brereton, "Sacred Space," 12:526, emphasis added. Brereton also pointed out that "places are sacred because they perform a religious function, not because they have peculiar physical or aesthetic qualities." Ibid.

38. One scholar of ritual pointed out, "Intonation separates words from mundane speech, emphasizing their ritual function. The voice, which in the spoken form retains the implication that they are the beliefs of the speaker of the text, are becoming transformed into an impersonal voice, which may be thought of as 'the voice of the Church' or 'the voice of the ritual.' . . . To intone signals a move." Hartwell, "Sacred Space and the Singing Voice," 105.

39. "Some social anthropologists distinguish between 'ritual'—stylized repetitious behavior that is explicitly religious—and 'ceremony,' which is merely social even in explicit meaning." Zuesse, "Ritual," 12:405.

40. http://www.cbsnews.com/news/circumcision-rates-declining-health-risks-rising-study-says/

41. See Neusner, *Enchantments of Judaism*, 43–44.

myths" and "degenerated rituals" that originate out of religious rites of the past, each of which are socially important, but hardly religiously so.[42] Thus, though at their core they have religious underpinnings, because participants are unaware of (or reject) those foundations, the rites have no religious impact upon the participant.

The prolific Jewish scholar, Jacob Neusner, pointed out the need to endow ritual with meaning, if the ritual is to have the power to transform and enchant[43] the participant and, thereby, turn the mundane into the sacred. For Neusner, through the working of our imaginations and the power of our intentions, we transform mere words into an entire world of regeneration and rebirth.[44] It is through such intention and imagination that our ordinary day-to-day experiences can be transformed into metaphors for the sacred.[45] Neusner states:

42. See Chidester "Church of Baseball," 213–30; Eliade, *Sacred and the Profane*, 204–5. For example, a Jewish acquaintance of mine was recently wearing a cross. When I enquired about it, she indicated that it wasn't religious; it's was just jewelry to accessorize her outfit. She was displaying an innately religious object, but with purely secular intent. As another example, one source notes, "the secular world often creates its own sacred places, such as national shrines, war graves, and sporting venues. . . . At Graceland, in Memphis, Tennessee, . . . the constant stream of visitors to the former home of rock and roll star Elvis Presley exemplifies 'nonreligious' pilgrimage. . . . For many Elvis fans, the journey to Graceland is a journey toward a sacred center, even though many deny the status of Elvis as a religious figure. In particular, it is the way that the pilgrimage fulfills a need in pilgrims for a type of religious practice that institutional religions fail to. . . . The critical point is that these pilgrims are seeking out locations at which they perceived sources of culture or personal identity, in much the same way as explicitly religious pilgrims do" (Hecht and Biondo, *Religion and Culture*, 183, 184). In a similar vein, "there is no doubt that sport and religion in the twenty-first century are closer than they have ever been previously. . . . Baseball, as an institution, constitutes a 'church' for many Americans. . . . The match season creates a sense of sacred time (it has been noted that the baseball season begins in spring and signals the renewal of the seasons), the rules of baseball are standards that are largely unchanging and create stability in people's lives, baseball grounds are sacred places (many pitchers ritually jump over the boundaries of the field out of respect), and the large fanbase [sic] gives baseball tens of millions of believers, who are united in 'an extended family'" (Ibid., 323–24). In the aforementioned example, the secular is engaged in, but with religious underpinnings. The participant is unlikely to see the parallels with religion, but the connections are clear.

43. For Neusner, "enchantment" means "showing the remarkable in the ordinary, changing the routine into the extraordinary. . . . What happens in a moment of enchantment is change, not in what we are but in what we perceive." Neusner, *Enchantments of Judaism*, 31. See also Pike, "Desert Goddesses and Apocalyptic Art," 154–70.

44. Neusner, *Enchantments of Judaism*, xv.

45. Neusner, *Enchantments of Judaism*, 6.

> Rightly spoken with proper intention, coming from the heart, words bring forth worlds, through enchantment turning the everyday into something remarkable—the enchantment of heart and soul and mind, which comes to expression in deed turned into gesture. A commonplace deed may be to light a candle. A gesture is to kindle a flame to inaugurate the Sabbath. A deed is to eat a cracker. A gesture is to raise a piece of unleavened bread—a cracker of a certain kind—and to announce that it is the bread that our ancestors ate when they hastily left Egypt—and then to eat the cracker.[46]

The same act has religious meaning—or no meaning—contingent upon our intent; upon our desire to experience the sacred in the mundane.[47] Our words and works are able to do their work of "enchantment"—of transformation—when we endow them with significance that changes us into something different from what we were before we spoke them or performed them. When they are endowed with meaning, they have a transformative power beyond what we might otherwise imagine.[48] Neusner adds:

> Through enchantment, transformation of the ordinary so takes place that new worlds of meaning, new realms of being, come about. Words speak to—therefore, for—the mind. But through enchantment, words bring to life this other world of meaning altogether; the world of vision and form, of sound and feeling and gesture, of movement and stillness, [which] speaks to—and, therefore, for—the imagination, which, in God and humanity alike, flourishes in the soul and in heart and in spirit.[49]

---

46. Neusner, *Enchantments of Judaism*, 7.

47. Just as endowing ritual behaviors with meaning gives transformative power to the practitioner, endowing ordinary objects with sacred meaning has the ability to transform them into reminders of the holy. See for example, O'Malley, "Understanding Sacraments," 185–90.

48. Neusner, *Enchantments of Judaism*, 14. As a simple example, one might look at the ordinance or rite of marriage. Two people come together through a ritual, which transforms their status, legally, psychologically, socially, and sexually. By simple words and possible token acts, their status is changed. In reality, nothing is different about them; but they are now formally different persons. They came to the rite single, legally unattached, and perhaps celibate. They leave the ritual partnered, legally bound, committed, intimately engaged, etc. Mere words and behaviors change the entire status of a person, legally, but also socially, psychologically, emotionally, sexually, and spiritually.

49. Neusner, *Enchantments of Judaism*, 18.

Like Neusner, Douglas Davies also pointed to the reality that "things are *potentially* sacred, but ... they require a suitably sacred mind to appear in their true character."[50] Where ritual can turn the mundane locale into a sacred precinct, intentionality in ritual turns mere movement and words into the holy and provocative. Through ritual, "We are creators of worlds. For good or ill, we live by our power to create, beginning with the strength of intellect and imagination to create ourselves: something out of nothing—before, in death, we return to nothing, and wait."[51]

We spoke above of entering sacred space to perform "the work of the gods."[52] This principle of divine "work" is at the heart of sacred space and its purpose. Our English word "liturgy" comes from a Greek word that means to "labor."[53] Similarly, the Hebrew word for "divine service"—such as that performed in the Jewish temple cult of antiquity—is *abodah*, which also means to "work."[54] The part of ritual that is "work" is not the attending, nor the participation, but the discovery of meaning that ultimately enchants. Spiritual transformation is work—*hard work!* But one's ability to turn simple space into sacred space—one's ability to turn the everyday word, act, or object into the other-worldly—requires work and intent; and it is through such work and intent that sacred space and empowering rites find their life. While many religions do well in providing rituals for their parishioners, most do not do well in helping their adherents to find meaning in those rites. The onus, of course, must be upon the initiate. However, many struggle to know how to understand ritual, let alone how to use it to have a transformative experience.

The Loss of Ritual in the Post-Modern World

Scholars of ritual and sacred space generally sense that there has been "a modern loss of the sacred, or [an] alienation from the sacred, or [loss of] nostalgia for the sacred. ... Primitives had [a sense of the sacred]; some peasant folk ... retained it; but moderns [have] entirely lost it."[55]

50. Davies, "Introduction," 3, emphasis added.
51. Neusner, *Enchantments of Judaism*, 216.
52. Eliade, *Sacred and the Profane*, 28, 29.
53. See Thayer, *Thayer's Greek-English Lexicon*, 375, s.v. #3009. See also Neusner, *Enchantments of Judaism*, 17.
54. See Brown, Driver, and Briggs, *The Brown-Driver-Briggs Hebrew and English Lexicon*, 715, s.v. #5656. See also Neusner, *Enchantments of Judaism*, 17.
55. Chidester and Linenthal, "Introduction," 8–9. They added, "This historical and

Generally speaking, people today do not communicate as well through symbols and ritual as they once did. Indeed, symbolism and ritual have largely become lost languages. For the most part, Western societies are no longer bilingual; we can speak the language of the secular, but the sacred has fallen from our collective vocabulary. Perhaps a number of things have contributed to this; shifts in the content of our education,[56] evolution in culture,[57] a more scientific world-view,[58] globalization,[59] post-

---

essentially political situation of exile from the sacred entail[s] two theoretical implications . . . : the most sacred places were remote, and the most authentic religious experiences in relation to sacred space was homesickness. 'The house is an organic unity . . . whose essence is some definite power, just as much as is the temple or church.' The modern house, however, [is] not sacred. Its unity [has] been dispersed, its position displaced, its boundaries dissolved, its sovereign ownership alienated. As a result of modernization, . . . 'it is difficult for us, semi-americanized as we already are, to form any idea of its unitary power.' In the politics of exile, the sacred was positioned in relation to human beings who found themselves to be out of position. The historical 'pivotings of the sacred' in the modern world had made all 'semi-americanized' human beings political exiles from the sacred." Ibid., 9.

56. American observers, following the Prussian war efforts in pre–World War I, noted the efficiency of their scientific education that led, in their estimation, to victory in the war. As a result, education began to place less emphasis on liberal arts, and greater emphasis on vocational and scientific training. While faith and science can certainly co-exist and compliment one another, a purely scientific approach to education may neglect the student's yearning for the sacred. Without an exposure to the liberal arts, a student may not feel the need (or have the tools) to seek answers for the great questions of life, and a sense of wonder, or *eros*, is most likely to be lost. Absent the enthusiasm or curiosity for the unexplainable, a student may not be inclined to seek after the sacred.

57. Following the cultural revolution of the 1960s, less people have been inclined to participate in traditional religious practices, as it became culturally acceptable—and even culturally encouraged—to not participate. See Levin, *Fractured Republic*, 157–62.

58. René Descartes revolutionary philosophy of the self ("I think, therefore I am") became an important touchstone for the scientific method, as it assumes that only the observable is knowable. As a result, the adoption of the Cartesian mindset throughout culture has led to the belief by many that science is the *only way* of "knowing." However, for others, sacred experiences open us to "wonder" and "enchantment" as alternative and powerful ways of "knowing."

59. In a recent podcast, Rusty Reno spoke about how citizens throughout the world have become less focused on liberal and conservative principles, and more focused on globalism and nationalism. As the world becomes increasingly homogenized through globalization, there are concerns that everyone must accept everyone else's worldview or culture as equally legitimate. While tolerance and kindness are certainly commendable, the removal of distinction may invalidate individual views of the sacred, as pressure increases to accept everyone else's view as truth, leading to relativism in society and religion. See Reno, "Conservative's New Terms," April 17, 2017.

modernism,[60] the de-sacralizing of the body,[61] etc. The "updating" of the Mass (for the Catholics) and the temple Endowment (for the Mormons), and the rejection of once accepted rituals (as in the case of Community of Christ), has, for some, served to dilute the power of those rituals to enchant the participant. As sacred rituals lose their symbolism they lose some of their power. And as rites lose their power in the lives of adherents, there is an increased likelihood that sacred space will lose its place and impact in the life of modern people. We have experienced a "desacralization of the cosmos" and, consequently, lost many of the things that have traditionally had the most transformative effects upon society.[62] As ritual in the post-modern world is streamlined, modernized, and simplified, the sacred is placed at risk.

60. Post-modernism deconstructs the foundations of traditional culture. Writers like Foucault, Derrida, and Rorty seek to show that everything we "know" is merely a construct of the human mind. Thus, the sacred that resides outside of humanity is disregarded and dismissed as merely a human construct.

61. In Christian tradition, the body is commonly seen as a temple of the Holy Spirit (1 Cor 3:16). In antiquity, defilement of that temple was thought to bring eternal destruction upon the defiler (1 Cor 3:17). A lifestyle void of moral purity—or one that comprised engagement in behaviors deemed immoral by recognized societally standards—was seen as a primary source of defilement, cutting one off from the blessings of the Creator. One source suggested, "If embodied practices can consecrate, they can also desecrate a sacred place. Throughout the history of religions, the production of sacred space has depended upon control over purity." Chidester and Linenthal, "Introduction," 10. That being said, the more purity is perceived as relative in contemporary society, the more sacred space and sacred rites are at risk; and the more treatment of the body is seen as not determinant upon one's ability to interact with the divine, let alone upon one's salvation.

62. See Eliade, *Sacred and the Profane*, 51. "Man inhabits the body in the same way that he inhabits a house or the cosmos that he has himself created. . . . Inhabited territory, temple, house, body are all . . . cosmoses. . . . In one way or another, the cosmos that one inhabits . . . communicates above with a different plane that is transcendent to it. Just as modern man's habitation has lost its cosmological values, so too his body is without religious or spiritual significance. In a summary formula we might say that for the nonreligious men of the modern age, the cosmos has become opaque, inert, mute; it transmits no message, it holds no cipher. . . . As for the Christianity of the industrial societies and especially the Christianity of intellectuals, it has long since lost the cosmic values that it still possessed in the Middle Ages. . . . The religious sense of urban populations is gravely impoverished. The cosmic liturgy, the mystery of nature's participation in the Christological drama, have become inaccessible to Christians living in a modern city. Their religious experience is no longer open to the cosmos. In the last analysis, it is a strictly private experience. . . . But in these man-God-history relationships there is no place for the cosmos. . . . Even for the genuine Christian, the world is no longer felt as the work of God." Ibid., 176–77, 178–79.

Are there consequences for the loss of ritual and the consequent forfeiture of sacred space? Certainly, one is a general irreverence in contemporary culture—a loss of the sense that certain things are sacred, and must be treated with propriety, reverence and respect. Resulting from this is a general disrespect for religion and the beliefs of practitioners of religion. It has been suggested that this loss of respect for the religious has, as a consequence, brought a loss of respect for the family. In times past, there was a general sense that the family unit was sacred. Home and Temple were essential once.[63] This perception stemmed from religious belief, which has largely been lost; and, as a consequence of the breakdown of the home, we see a stark increase in divorce rates, and a lack of fidelity to spouse and children.

Another potential consequence of the loss of ritual and sacred space may be the loss of corporate identity. Joel P. Brereton explained: "To call a place sacred asserts that a place, its structure, and its symbols express fundamental cultural values and principles. By giving these visible form, the sacred place makes tangible the corporate identity of a people and their world."[64] If creating sacred space facilitates corporate identity (i.e., religion-specific community and distinctiveness), the loss of such space must surely bring a fracturing of societal values, norms, and unity.

Finally, an additional consequence of the loss of ritual and sacred space may be that secular humanism continues to rise as people become their own god and, therefore, make and play by their own rules.[65] Eliade summarized the consequences in this way:

---

63. McDannell, "Creating the Christian Home," 214. McDannell pointed out, "Homes are places where real people interact with one another in the hopes of promoting specific religious and cultural values. Domestic religion is experienced differently by men, women, and children. The 'unitary power' of the home is as much an ideological position as a phenomenological model. As residents in a post-Freudian world, we know that the 'unquestioned reality' of domestic sacred space . . . is filled with both spoken and unspoken conflict. Perhaps it is our own disenchantment with family life that leads us to question the easy association of house and temple." Ibid., 214.

64. Brereton, "Sacred Space," 12:534.

65. The Capuchin friar Father Keith Clark noted: "When we break off making space and making symbols, we tend to feel as if we are taking our lives into our own hands. We set out to be the producer/director of a film in which we star" (Clark, *Make Space, Make Symbols*, 96). In other words, for some, sacred space is controlling or limiting. The rejection of such space—and its associated symbols—implies liberation; liberation from God, authority, rules, etc. Sacred space assigns one place, duty and meaning. The rejection of such is really a change in identity, from subordinate to independent.

> The nonreligious man refuses transcendence.... Modern nonreligious man ... regards himself solely as the subject and agent of history, and he refuses all appeal to transcendence. In other words, he accepts no model for humanity outside the human condition as it can be seen in the various historical situations. Man *makes himself*, and he only makes himself completely in proportion as he desacralizes himself and the world. The sacred is the prime obstacle to his freedom. He will become himself only when he is totally demysticized. He will not be truly free until he has killed the last god.[66]

By their nature, ritual and sacred space seek to provoke unity. Secular humanism, on the other hand, offers individuality—as it authorizes humans to determine for themselves what *should be* perceived as ethical, and what *should be* socially acceptable practice. The latter is not, of itself, evil. However, a society that—as Eliade suggests—raises itself to the level of god, is sure to fall into moral decay and narcissism, as sexuality, eating, and entertainment (three of the "most rudimentary of bodily experiences"[67]) become their only *needed* rituals—and, in a real way, the focus of their existence.

While secularism offers "freedom" from societally sponsored rules and restraints, religious ritual perceives itself as offering "freedom" from chaos and eventual self-destruction. As humans "demysticize" and "desacralize" their day-to-day experience, they create ambivalence in the world and, more particularly, in their lives and psyche. Ritual and sacred space seek to reverse that growing trend. Indeed, the act of "ritualization provides a means of coping with ambivalence."[68] Ritualization of space and actions is humanity's way of finding meaning in the contradictions of human existence. It allows one to deal with the seeming spiritual polarities that he or she experiences almost daily. It provides a means of understanding the conflicting forces that impinge upon our individual and

---

66. Eliade, *Sacred and the Profane*, 203. Eliade uses "transcendence" in a decidedly religious way; but human beings may also seek the transcendental in an entirely secular way. For example, ComicCon (i.e., comic book conventions) are held worldwide, gathering fans from throughout the region who have an almost religious-like devotion to certain comic book characters, narratives, and franchises. In some cases, this obsession elevates the characters to a god-like status with a devotion exhibited by the attendee that is tantamount to religious observance. Some who attend these conventions feel a strong sense of community that is perceivably transcendental in a secular way.

67. Zuesse, "Ritual," 12:411.

68. Bokenkotter, *Dynamic Catholicism*, 172.

collective existence: things, such as life and death, meaning and absurdity, good and evil, or sacred and profane. These seeming contradictions must somehow be unified—harmonized—if we, as humans, are ever to achieve wholeness and inner peace; if we are ever to perceive the mortal experience as anything other than chaos and chance. The ritualization of space, action, and word provides a means of holding the opposing realities of the mortal experience together. It offers peace and place in an otherwise meaningless world.[69]

---

69. See ibid., 172.

Bibliography

Anderson, Devery S. *The Development of LDS Temple Worship—1846-2000: A Documentary History*. Salt Lake City: Signature, 2011.

Bokenkotter, Thomas. *Dynamic Catholicism: A Historical Catechism*. New York: Doubleday, 1992.

Bremborg, Anna Davidsson. "Creating Sacred Space by Walking in Silence: Pilgrimage in the Late Modern Lutheran Context." *Social Compass* 60, no. 4 (December 2-13) 557.

Brereton, Joel P. "Sacred Space." In *Encyclopedia of Religion*, edited by Mircea Eliade, 12:526-35. London: Macmillan, 1986.

Brown, Francis, et al. *The Brown-Driver-Briggs Hebrew and English Lexicon*. Peabody, MA: Hendrickson, 1999.

Chidester, David. "The Church of Baseball, the Fetish of Coca-Cola, and the Potlatch of Rock n' Roll." In *Religion and Popular Culture in America*, edited by Bruce David Forbes and Jeffrey H. Mahan, 213-32. Rev. ed. Berkeley: University of California Press, 2005.

Chidester, David, and Edward T. Linenthal. "Introduction." In *American Sacred Space*, edited by David Chidester and Edward T. Linenthal, 1-42. Bloomington, IN: Indiana University Press, 1995.

Clark, Keith. *Make Space, Make Symbols*. Notre Dame, IN: Ave Maria, 1979.

Craughwell, Thomas J. *Saints Preserved: An Encyclopedia of Relics*. New York: Image, 2011.

Davies, Douglas. "Christianity." In *Themes in Religious Studies: Sacred Place*, edited by Jean Holm with John Bowker, 33-61. New York: Pinter, 1994.

———. "Introduction: Raising the Issues." In *Themes in Religious Studies: Sacred Place*, edited by Jean Holm with John Bowker, 1-7. New York: Pinter, 1994.

Dues, Greg. *Catholic Customs and Traditions*. Rev. and exp. ed. New London, CT: Twenty-Third, 1992.

Eliade, Mircea. *The Sacred and the Profane: The Nature of Religion—the Significance of Religious Myth, Symbolism, and Ritual within Life and Culture*. New York: Harcourt, Brace & World, 1959.

Gesler, Wilbert M. *Healing Places*. Lanham, MD: Rowman & Littlefield, 2003.

Glassé, Cyril. *The Concise Encyclopedia of Islam*. San Francisco: HarperSanFrancisco, 1989.

Hartwell, Robin. "Sacred Space and the Singing Voice." In *Sacred Space: Interdisciplinary Perspectives within Contemporary Contexts*, edited by Steve Brie, Jenny Daggers, and David Torevell, 103-13. Cambridge: Scholars, 2009.

Hecht, Richard D., and Vincent F. Biondo III, eds. *Religion and Culture: Contemporary Practices and Perspectives*. Minneapolis: Fortress, 2012.

Hedges, Andrew H., Alex D. Smith, and Richard Lloyd Anderson, eds. *The Joseph Smith Papers, Journals Volume 2: December 1841-April 1843*. Salt Lake City: Church Historian's, 2011.

Hoover, Stewart M. "The Cross at Willow Creek: Seeker Religion and the Contemporary Marketplace." In *Religion and Popular Culture in America*, edited by Bruce David Forbes and Jeffrey H. Mahan, 139-53. Rev. ed. Berkeley: University of California Press, 2005.

Hecht, Richard D., and Vincent F. Biondo III, eds. *Religion and Culture: Contemporary Practices and Perspectives*. Minneapolis: Fortress, 2012.

Hopko, Thomas. *The Orthodox Faith Volume 2: Worship*. Yonkers, NY: St. Vladimir's Seminary, 1972.

Hubert, Jane. "Sacred Beliefs and Beliefs of Sacredness." In *Sacred Sites, Sacred Places*, edited by David L. Carmichael et al., 9–19. New York: Routledge, 1994.

King, Winston L. "Religion." In *Encyclopedia of Religion*, edited by Mircea Eliade, 12:282–93. London: Macmillan, 1986.

Kunin, Seth. "Judaism." In *Themes in Religious Studies: Sacred Place*, edited by Jean Holm with John Bowker, 115–48. New York: Pinter, 1994.

Levin, Yuval. *The Fractured Republic: Renewing America's Social Contract in the Age of Individualism*. New York: Basic, 2016.

Matthews, Robert J. "Adam-Ondi-Ahman." *BYU Studies* 13 (1972) 27–35.

McBrien, Richard P., ed. *The Harper Collins Encyclopedia of Catholicism*. San Francisco: HarperSanFrancisco, 1995.

McConkie, Bruce R. *The Millennial Messiah*. Salt Lake City: Deseret, 1982.

McDannell, Colleen. "Creating the Christian Home: Home Schooling in Contemporary America." In *American Sacred Space*, edited by David Chidester and Edward T. Linenthal, 187–219. Bloomington, IN: Indiana University Press, 1995.

Morisy, Ann. "Seven Cairns in the Creation of Sacred Space in the City." In *Sacred Space: House of God, Gate of Heaven*, edited by Philip North and John North, 117–33. New York: Continuum, 2007.

Neusner, Jacob. *The Enchantments of Judaism: Rites of Transformation from Birth through Death*. Atlanta: Scholars, 1991.

Nibley, Hugh. "The Meaning of the Temple." In *Temple and Cosmos: Beyond This Ignorant Present*, 1–41. Provo, UT: Foundation for Ancient Research and Mormon Studies, 1992.

———. "What Is a Temple?" In *Mormonism and Early Christianity*, 355–90. Provo, UT: Foundation for Ancient Research and Mormon Studies, 1987.

Nickell, Joe. *Looking for a Miracle*. New York: Prometheus, 1993.

North, Philip, and John North. "Introduction." In *Sacred Space: House of God, Gate of Heaven*, edited by Philip North and John North, 1–7. New York: Continuum, 2007.

O'Malley, William J. "Understanding Sacraments." *America* 166 (March 7, 1992) 185–90.

Pike, Sarah M. "Desert Goddesses and Apocalyptic Art: Making Sacred Space at the Burning Man Festival." In *God in the Details: American Religion in Popular Culture*, edited by Eric Michael Mazur and Kate McCarthy, 154–73. 2nd ed. New York: Taylor & Francis, 2011.

Reno, Rusty. "Conservative's New Terms." *First Things: Religion & Public Life*, podcast, episode 27, April 17, 2017, https://soundcloud.com/firstthings.

Ross, Ellen. "Diversities of Divine Presence: Women's Geography in the Christian Tradition." In *Sacred Paces and Profane Spaces*, edited by Jamie Scott and Paul Simpson-Housley, 93–114. New York: Greenwood, 1991.

Tavinor, Michael. "Sacred Space and the Built Environment." In *Sacred Space: House of God, Gate of Heaven*, edited by Philip North and John North, 21–41. New York: Continuum, 2007.

Thayer, Joseph H. *Thayer's Greek-English Lexicon of the New Testament*. Peabody, MA: Hendrickson, 1999.

Tvedtnes, John A. "Priestly Clothing in Bible Times." In *Temples of the Ancient World*, edited by Donald W. Parry, 649–704. Provo, UT: Foundation for Ancient Research and Mormon Studies, 1994.

United States Catholic Catechism for Adults. Washington, DC: United States Conference of Catholic Bishops, 2006.

Walton, Heather. "Theological Perspectives on Christian Pilgrimage." In *Christian Pilgrimage, Landscape and Heritage*, edited by Avril Maddrell and others, 22–42. New York: Routledge, 2015.

Webb, Diana. "Pilgrimage." In *Encyclopedia of Christianity*, edited by John Bowden, 939–44. New York: Oxford, 2005.

Weir, David. "Liminality, Sacred Space and the Diwan." In *Sacred Space: Interdisciplinary Perspectives within Contemporary Contexts*, edited by Steve Brie, Jenny Daggers, and David Torevell, 39–54. Cambridge: Scholars, 2009.

Zuesse, Evan M. "Ritual." In *Encyclopedia of Religion*, edited by Mircea Eliade, 12:405–22. London: Macmillan, 1986.

Sacred Thread

7

Symbolism of Ancient Clothing
Conviction in Covering Oneself

Rory Scanlon

In the beginning of the Book of Genesis, Adam and Eve had coats of skins made for them by the Lord God to clothe them because they were naked.[1] The Bible story chronicles this couple's first recognition that their own God-given skin was inadequate. We can naturally reason that this couple had, by this point, come to realize that some of the elements in their new world created physical problems. Cool nights made them cold and uncomfortable. The smallest insects could irritate or pierce their fragile skin. Now, on top of these complications, the cunning serpent had awakened Adam and Eve to a much more troubling fact. They now knew that they were "naked" and that this was inappropriate in the human social order. According to the Bible narrative, this was their first realization of this concept.

In his book *Clothes*, James Laver discusses three main reasons why we, as human beings, wear clothing. The first purpose given is that "we wear them . . . to protect ourselves against cold and damp."[2] We have already acknowledged that Adam and Eve may have come to this conclusion on their own, though the Bible story does not elaborate. We, in our

1. Gen 3:10–11, 21; KJV.
2. Laver, *Clothes*, 23.

contemporary world, understand this fact as one of the principle reasons we put on or take off clothing items today.

James Laver's second principle reads: "we wear them ... to denote our social status."[3] This second purpose for clothing touches directly on what Adam and Eve had learned from the serpent. There is a social order in the communities within which we exist as human beings, and there are social norms to which we must adhere to be accepted into these communities. Our first earthly couple came to realize that covering their natural selves was part of that social acceptance. This realization brought Adam and Eve to a new level of self-awareness. Genesis records that they tried to cover themselves initially with fig leaves,[4] but their merciful God stepped in to show them another resource to create a more permanent clothing supply through the use of animal skins.

The earliest archeological findings prove that man did, indeed, use leather as an early resource[5] not only for covering himself from the elements, but early man also used straps of leather for binding important artifacts to his body so they would be readily available for his use. A leather strap could help also in holding larger animal pelts to the body, thus permitting the wearer to move more effectively. This allowed for needed agility to hunt, gather vegetation and other daily physical human tasks.

However, James Laver's third principle becomes even more crucial in our understanding of the evolution of body coverings. Humans are visual creatures and our earliest ancestors came to recognize clothing as more than a simple wrapper for their naked bodies. The descendants of Adam and Eve would discover clothing pieces could become a form of physical adornment. Laver puts it this way: "we wear them ... to make ourselves as attractive as possible within the lines laid down by the current mode."[6]

Humankind would come to understand that body coverings could become a form of outward communication as real as the spoken word. Clothing can communicate physical dominance, one's own sexuality and even the physical essence of religious adherence.[7] Some of the earliest artifacts archaeologists have uncovered demonstrate man's realization that

---

3. Ibid.
4. Gen 3:7.
5. Forbes, *Studies*, 172.
6. Laver, *Clothes*, 23.
7. Barber, *Women's Work*, 148.

what he wears could be much more than a covering from the weather. This includes the discovery of hand-shaped beads made from pieces of bone and ivory found along the great Paleolithic ice sheet in southern France and Spain.[8] This Gravettian culture existed around 20,000 BC. Specimens of hand-carved beads were found in excavation mounds from this civilization, discovered in "neat rows"[9] suggesting they had originally been strung on strands or sewn to leather pieces that had decomposed. These beads denoted a form of status: man's ability to conquer beasts of the forest. But according to ethnographic professor Victoria Rivers, early man may also have worn them in belief that by wearing these bone fragments the hunting skills of these animals could be "transferred to [the] wearers."[10] Here, perhaps, is our first evidence of man's attempt to adorn himself, to make an impression of personal importance to others in his community.

From James Laver's three principles, we can understand that clothing became, early in human history, a means of protecting ourselves, a way of becoming acceptable within our social community, and a visual statement of our personal belief about ourselves, about our community and about our God.

While early man made use of the animals with whom he lived, he also learned how to use other natural resources, such as plant fibers. We may have naturally assumed that man's acquaintance with animal skins would lead the descendants of Adam and Eve into making the first textiles from the fibers of animal hair, such as that of the wooly sheep. However, historic wool samples show that early sheep hair was more brittle than contemporary sheep, since they were not yet domesticated. Consequently, while their whole pelts were commonly worn as garments, spinning the wool itself as a fiber into usable yarn was not man's first choice.[11]

Humans realized early that vines and strips of bark could be woven into mats and baskets.[12] In one of the tusk ivory engravings recovered from the Gravettian culture of Southern France, we have an engraving of a female wearing a rustic skirt made from cording. The artist who created

---

8. Ibid., 43.
9. Ibid.
10. Rivers, *Shining Cloth*, 68.
11. Barber, *Women's Work*, 189.
12. Forbes, *Studies*, 172.

this engraving even captured the actual "twists in each string."[13] The image also suggests the frayed ends of these strings hanging out at the bottom of the skirt as individual fibers. This ancient engraving confirms that man learned at an early stage to twist fibers together into a continuous piece of string.[14] While this engraving shows that twining was a known art to early man, we do not find actual evidence of such real string manufacturing until around 15,000 BC in the caves of Lascaux, France.[15] Here archaeologists have discovered actual plant fibers twisted to form a heavy cord. This small artifact combined three two-ply strings, "twisting their component strands in the other direction from that in which they had originally been spun."[16] This important find was our first example of man-made cording. With its discovery came our realization that plant fibers had been used for the manufacturing of string and cording much earlier than otherwise believed. Because of these facts, most archaeologists today believe that the oldest fiber known to man for spinning and weaving would have been the flax that grew naturally in much of the Mesopotamian region. This flax would, therefore, make "linen" the earliest man-made textile.[17]

Spinning and weaving are perhaps the oldest arts of mankind. After the domestication of sheep, wool fibers became popular for string and thread manufacturing. This is supported by the Old Testament as stated in Proverbs that "'the lambs are for thy clothing' and the women spin the wool so that man '[warms himself] with the fleece of [his] sheep.'"[18] We also know that this art began as a home art, and was therefore most commonly the work of women.[19] However, in Palestine, once the art of making fabric became a significant business trade, historically this work became the labor of men.[20] Most likely the principle reason for this was because once spinning and weaving left the privacy of the home, women were socially excluded.[21]

13. Barber, *Women's Work*, 44.
14. Barber, *Women's Work*, 45; Forbes, *Studies*, 149.
15. Barber, *Women's Work*, 53; Schoeser, *World Textiles*, 12.
16. Barber, *Women's Work*, 52.
17. Harris, *5,000 Years*, 54; Forbes, *Studies*, 27, 149.
18. Forbes, *Studies*, 9; Prov 27:26, 31:13; Job 31:20.
19. Drooker and Webster, *Beyond Cloth*, 2; Harris, *5,000 Years*, 57.
20. Forbes, *Studies*, 229.
21. Ibid., 160–61.

In the manufacture of early cloth, the major countries naturally leaned to a dominate fiber because of the abundance of certain natural resources. Additionally, some social beliefs also influenced these choices. Linen, for example, was embraced by the early Egyptians who actually forbade the use of wool in their temples, most likely because it was seen as a living product since it was made from the "hair" of an animal.[22] Flax quickly became the major source for the fabric of this country. While not completely native to the arid climate of Egypt, flax was most likely introduced "from Western Asia in very early times."[23]

Mesopotamia, on the other hand, used wool abundantly, at least for over garments. Historically, this culture had a much closer relationship with sheep in general. Bible writings are abundant in their parables based on the art of raising sheep and the strong use of the lamb as a symbol of Christ.[24] The Mesopotamian culture did, however, use linen for garments closest to the body and God Himself required the use of linen in the costumes of the temple priests.[25]

Thus, linen and wool were most likely our first fibers used for man-made textiles. Much later in the history of the world, India will become known for its use of cotton and China for its introduction of silk.

Unfortunately, our ancient study of fibers, fabrics and their effect on fashion must be based on little evidence.[26] There are not enough tangible artifacts from the earliest civilizations, due to the fact that fabric decomposes so easily in the vast majority of the world's climates. Some of the earliest fabrics discovered were small fragments wrapped around other hand-made artifacts. Early archaeologists frequently discarded these fabric scraps as they removed them to study the artifacts beneath, not realizing the value of these textile samples themselves. Fortunately, modern archaeologists are much wiser in their current practices. We are gathering more and more fabric samples to assist in this important study.

We naturally have a better understanding of the evolution of fabric and fashion from more recent Bible periods because we have many more fabric artifacts to prove that evolution. Even so, a study of ancient costume is always as much a process of guesswork as it is scholarly research. We

22. Ibid., 5.
23. Ibid., 27.
24. Isa 53:7.
25. Ezek 44:18.
26. Forbes, *Studies*, 172.

must remember that "research" suggests from its own prefix that it must be constantly worked out. We never know what future discoveries might eventually reveal. As geologist Robert M. Schoch put it, "It should always be remembered that an absence of evidence is not evidence of absence."[27] In our continued study of ancient textiles, perhaps the words of Elizabeth Wayland Barber in her book *Women's Work: The First 20,000 Years* sums it up best. She asks the reader,

> What did ancient people try to accomplish when they deliberately made cloth bear meaning? . . . For one thing, it can be used to mark or announce information. It can also be used as a mnemonic device to record events and other data. Third, it can be used to invoke "magic"—to protect, to secure fertility and riches, to divine the future, perhaps even to curse. Today clothing is also used as an indicator of fashion, but the subtleties of that expression, which change so very rapidly, are largely beyond our ability to reconstruct in the ancient world.[28]

We trust that future discoveries in this important area of textile research will offer us more understanding of the "magic" of these past civilizations. What we do know now is that ever since man began to cover his nakedness, he not only conquered the cold but also began to find acceptance into his social community. And maybe even more importantly, he learned to express himself more fully as an individual. We can only hope that our future encounters with past cultures will continue to open our eyes to the way our ancestors viewed and embraced Laver's three principles on why we wear clothing.

---

27. Schoch, *Voices*, 54.
28. Barber, *Women's Work*, 149.

Bibliography

Barber, Elizabeth Wayland. *Women's Work: The First 2000 Years*. New York: Norton, 1994.
Drooker, Penelope Ballard, and Laurie D. Webster. *Beyond Cloth and Cordage: Archaeological Textile Research in the Americas*. Salt Lake City: University of Utah Press, 2000.
Forbes, R. J. *Studies in Ancient Technology*. Vol. 4. Leiden: Brill, 1956.
Harris, Jennifer, ed. *5,000 Years of Textiles*. Washington, DC: Smithsonian, 2010.
Laver, James. *Clothes*. London: Burke, 1952.
Rivers, Victoria Z. *The Shining Cloth: Dress and Adornment that Glitter*. New York: Thames & Hudson, 1999.
Schoch, Robert M. *Voices of the Rocks*. New York: Harmony, 1999.
Schoeser, Mary. *World Textiles: A Concise History*. New York: Thames & Hudson, 2003.

8

Arrayed in Dazzling White
The Goddess Ta'it and Clothing in Ancient Egyptian Rituals of the Old Kingdom

JOHN S. THOMPSON

Carved on the stone walls inside fifth- and sixth-dynasty royal pyramids (c. 2350–2100 BCE) are the ancient Egyptian Pyramid Texts, some of the earliest extant religious texts in history. These texts remained in use among the ancient Egyptians for roughly two and half millennia and are the canonical foundation of the ancient Egyptian Coffin Texts and Book of the Dead corpora of later eras. Their importance to the religious culture of ancient Egypt throughout its existence cannot be underestimated.

Contemporary to and even preceding the advent of the Pyramid Texts are the texts and images found in the aboveground chapels of the non-royal tombs surrounding the pyramids, with earliest *in situ* examples dating as far back as c. 2600 BCE. Recent research demonstrates that combined sequences of priests in the central "offering table" scene of these non-royal tomb chapels matches the general sequence and descriptions of the Offering List rites in the Pyramid Texts, suggesting that many of the ideas and concepts codified in the Pyramid Texts already existed and were in use even among the non-royal elite.[1] This sequence of rites found in both the royal and non-royal sources is roughly as follows:

1. Thompson, "Iconography of the Memphite Priesthood."

1. Libation
2. Censing
3. Natron Washing (Opening of the Mouth)
4. Meal
5. Anointing
6. Clothing
7. Censing
8. Natron Washing
9. Meal
10. Clothing
11. Bringing the Foot
12. Reversion of Offerings
13. Execration
14. Natron Washing
15. Libation
16. Censing
17. Sealing

In temple and religious tradition generally, censing often serves as a liminal or transitional rite. That seems to be the case here as well. Not only does censing appear in the opening and closing moments of the sequence as a whole (nos. 2 and 16 above), but a more central censing rite (no. 7) seems to mark a moment of division between the previous set of rites that are, for the most part, repeated again after the censing—more specifically, a libation, censing, natron washing, meal, and clothing rite appear both before and after the central censing rite.

Details within the sources suggest that these repetitions may be progressive in nature. For example, the textual and artistic details concerning the meals in both the royal pyramids and non-royal elite tombs indicate that the first meal is small and simple compared to the second meal which is an elaborate feast.[2] The Pyramid Texts related to the closing censing rite repeats the words from the opening censing rite but includes some additional phrases: "You of *great* purity . . . let your scent be on Unis and

2. Ibid., comparing the small feast discussed at 292–99 with the grand feast discussed at 314–21.

purify Unis. . . . May you become *high and big* toward Unis."³ The words for "great," "high," and "big" do not appear in the texts of the first censing, suggesting the second was understood to be of a higher magnitude.

This study focuses primarily on the first of the two clothing rites in the sequence, providing additional detail and context to this ritual that the goddess Ta'it provides. Comparing and contrasting their details in order to further illustrate the progressive nature of the sequence and to better understand those ideas the clothing rites are meant to convey.

The Goddess Ta'it and the Initial Clothing Rite in the Offering List Sequence

The artistic reliefs of those priests carved to represent the initial clothing rite in the non-royal elite tomb chapels are typically shown offering long thin rectangular-shaped objects, grasped at one end and hanging down from each of their outstretched hands (see figure 19).⁴ Some of these depictions have the text label *wnꜣw(j)* indicating that the rectangular objects are "two rolls/strips of cloth."

Figure 19: Figure from the tomb of Netjer-Weser (drawing by author)

3. Egyptian Pyramid Texts 200; cf. Egyptian Pyramid Texts 25; see Allen, *Ancient Egyptian Pyramid Texts*, 28, Unas spell 137b; cf. 19, Unas Spell 20.

4. Figure based on Murray, *Saqqara Mastabas*, 1:XXIII, from the tomb of Netjer-Weser.

The corollary clothing ritual in the Pyramid Text offering list sequence also mentions the offering of two rolls/strips of linen but provides some additional detail in what may have been the liturgy spoken when this offering was made: "May you awake in peace. Awake, Ta'it, in peace! Awake, you of Ta'it town, in peace. . . . You whom the made-up women receive, you who adorn the great one in the sedan chair."[5]

That these strips of linen, personified and addressed as the Egyptian goddess Ta'it (a goddess associated with linen and weaving),[6] are said to "adorn" or "decorate" a "great one" and are received by "made-up" women implies that the two rolls/strips represent something one wears. In fact, the parallel text at this point of the sequence in Pepy I's pyramid contains a variant reading that links the offering of these two strips/rolls of linen to the idea of being clothed: "Ho, Pepi! Receive your dazzling garment (sšp), receive your bleached garment (ḥ'tj) on you, and get dressed (wnḫ.k) in Horus's eye [the offering] from Ta'it-town . . . ."[7]

The Egyptian word sšp translated here as "dazzling garment" derives from its verbal meaning "to illuminate" or "brighten."[8] In this context, the word appears in a nominal form written with two determinatives, one representing linen and the other a sun with rays shining down, suggesting bright, shiny cloth. Indeed, the next phrase is a parallel and indicates that the garments being received in this initial clothing rite are ḥ'tj which James Allen translates as "bleached garments."[9] It is not certain how ancient Egyptians bleached their linens. They could have simply laid them out in the sun or used a substance such as natron to help with that process, though natron would break down the fibers preventing frequent use, but the significant point is that the garments are made to be a bright white.[10]

The meaning that this quality of brightness with regard to the linen may have had for the ancient Egyptians is not explicitly stated in the earlier sources, though the idea of joining with and becoming radiant like the sun god Re in his solar journey is one of the central features of

---

5. Egyptian Pyramid Texts 81; see Allen, *Ancient Egyptian Pyramid Texts*, 22, Unas spell 54.

6. el-Saady, "Reflections on the Goddess Tayet," 213–17.

7. Egyptian Pyramid Texts 414; see Allen, *Ancient Egyptian Pyramid Texts*, 112, Pepi I spell 108; cf. 85, Teti spell 220.

8. Hannig, *Ägyptisches Wörterbuch*, 1235.

9. Allen, *Ancient Egyptian Pyramid Texts*, 85, Teti spell 220.

10. See Nicholson and Shaw, *Ancient Egyptian Materials and Technology*, 280.

the Egyptian religion from the Old Kingdom Pyramid Texts to the latest periods. The Pyramid Texts in Teti's complex includes this phrase: "Your mother Ta'it will clothe (✥bs) you and carry you to the sky in her name of kite [a division of birds],"[11] suggesting that one of the purposes for the clothing of Ta'it is to prepare the recipient for an ascension into the sky, like the sun.

Another passage in the Pyramid Texts provides additional insight into the meaning the clothing of Ta'it may have held for the ancient Egyptians. A prayer to this garment as goddess describes one of her functions as a protection and binding for the body: "Greetings, Ta'it, . . . Care for the King's head, so it does not pass away; gather together the King's bones, so that they will not pass away, and put the love of the King into the bowel of every god who shall see him."[12]

In the late-period temple at Dendera, the clothing of the cult statues in the temples are called "the great adornments of Ta'it."[13] The king is even called "the express image" of Ta'it when he presents deities with their ritual clothing.[14] Ta'it is hailed as "mother of the Gods, mistress of the Goddesses, who arrays the images [the cult statues] in her handiwork, gives sweetness to their flesh, clothes their bodies and gives health to their frames."[15] Other passages refer to Ta'it as "she who purifies the Goddesses, who did spin of old and was the first to weave."[16] A text from the temple of Khnum at Esna states that "the beautiful clothes" which are "to beautify the body" of Khnum have been woven by Tayet herself.[17] So, at least in this later time period, Ta'it and her clothing in temple settings was also associated with the concept of beautifying the body, receiving health, and being pure. The ancient Egyptian Book of the Dead declares of the owner: "Thou puttest on the pure garment; thou layest aside the thick garment," possibly indicative of moving from something coarse to something more pure and refined.[18]

---

11. Egyptian Pyramid Texts 417; see Allen, *Ancient Egyptian Pyramid Texts*, 85, Teti spell 223.

12. Egyptian Pyramid Texts 415; see ibid., 85, Teti spell 221.

13. Cauville, *Dendera I–IV*, IV:106, 3–4.

14. Ibid., III:119, 11; IV:56, 15–16.

15. Ibid., IV:101, 12–13.

16. Ibid., IV:125, 5–6.

17. Sauneron and Hallof, *Esna*, 5:190, 7–8.

18. Book of the Dead 172.

The Goddess Ta'it and the Clothing Rite in the Ancient Egyptian Funeral

The appearance of Ta'it in the initial clothing ritual of the offering list sequence in the Old Kingdom's royal Pyramid Texts and non-royal chapels has some parallel to her appearance in initial clothing rites of the ancient Egyptian funeral. While the ritual program of the funeral should be treated separate from those outlined in the royal pyramids and non-royal chapels, having their own unique purposes,[19] comparing and contrasting their many similarities can still be instructive.

The relationship of Ta'it to the funeral is generally demonstrated from a passage in the Middle Kingdom story of Sinuhe: "A night is made for you with ointments and wrappings from the hand of Ta'it. A funeral procession is made for you on the day of burial...."[20] The night of ointments and wrappings indicated here likely refer to the oil and linen mummy bandages used to anoint and wrap the body of the deceased. Consequently, burial linens are also associated with Ta'it.

The Old Kingdom elite tomb of Vizier Ptah Hotep depicts a funeral procession which appears to contain a reference, at the beginning, to a "weaving house." The caption for this part of the scene is *sḏ't ḏ't m pr r jmnt [nf]rt ḫr nṯr* '' "proceeding from the weaving house to the beautiful west and before the great god." The determinative below the word *pr* "house" is a woman with a weaving apparatus according to Hermann Junker.[21] John Wilson admits that the significance of the weaving house here "escapes" him, and speculates that it was probably a reference to the deceased person's manor or estate,[22] but in light of Ta'it's relation to weaving and the ritual clothing of the funeral perhaps this needs to be reevaluated.

The early stages of the ancient Egyptian funeral procession includes a stop at an *jbw* "purification tent." According to the Coffin Texts, it is inside the purification tent where the body is washed and clothed/wrapped and that a curtain hangs therein: "Hail Osiris N! You go down. You clean yourself with Re in the Lotus Pool.... You put on clothes in the

---

19. On this see Thompson, 209–26.
20. Lichtheim, *Ancient Egyptian Literature*, 229.
21. Junker, *Gîza*, 3:210–11. The figure is that of a woman with a weaving apparatus on her lap; Lepsius, *Denkmäler aus Aegypten und Aethiopien*, 2:20, a; 103; Cairo 1447. Borchardt, *Denkmäler des Alten Reiches*, 1:131.
22. 209, fn. 29, cf. 203, fn. 12.

purification tent and live [again?] behind its curtain."²³ Possibly referencing this curtain, a Coffin Text passage elsewhere mentions a "curtain that Ptah has embroidered and Ta'it has woven herself."²⁴

The funeral procession depicted in the Old Kingdom elite tomb of Qar at Giza includes a scene, early in the sequence, of a purification tent (see Figure 2).²⁵ James Hoffemeier states that this tent "shows the intricate detail of woven material."²⁶ The weave across the top suggests the structure was woven from reeds being that the mythological place of purification was called "the field of reeds." The weave pattern down the center of the image could perhaps be the curtain that hangs in this house, partitioning it into the two "ways" (the hieroglyphic texts on the left and right uprights of the building). The text in each compartment of the *jbw* in Qar's tomb reads (on the left) "The requirements of the lector priest (two chests)" and (on the right) "The requirements of the purification tent. A meal."²⁷

Caption: Figure from the tomb of Qar (drawing by author)

23. Buck and Gardiner, *Egyptian Coffin Texts*, 1:187d–88a.
24. Ibid., 1:254c.
25. Simpson, *Mastabas of Qar and Idu*, 5.
26. Hoffmeier, "Possible Origins of the Tent of Purification."
27. Figure based on Simpson, fig. 24, from the tomb of Qar.

These two "ways" may represent the funeral procession's journey leading to the purification tent and the journey leading from it. Depictions of the funeral procession on tomb chapel walls show that it approaches an *jbw* by water on boats but then leaves the *jbw* on land as it heads west across the desert towards the *wʿbt* ("pure place") and finally to the tomb for burial—the three major stops of the funeral procession. Rather than two "ways," the depiction of the purification tent in the Old Kingdom tomb of Mereruka has two hieroglyphics for "doors" on each end of the tent and a "sky" hieroglyphic across the top that Brovarski reads as "the doors of heaven."[28]

Taken together, everything above can suggest that the purification tent may be the "weaving house" of Ta'it and represents the door or gate by which one enters heaven. This gate requires a purification that includes a washing, anointing, and clothing of the body by Ta'it, as well as a ritual meal. A curtain of Ta'it also seems to hang in this place, though its purpose is not specified except that one comes "alive" behind it.

The washing, anointing, clothing, and meal in the initial stages of the funeral procession are the same rituals required in the initial sequence of the offering list. These two ritual programs should not be conflated since their contexts and purposes serve different purposes in the religion of the ancient Egyptians, but the general meaning of preparatory purification prior to ascending to a higher order is likely a purpose of both sets of rituals.

Clothing with Insignia

The second clothing rite in the offering list sequence of the Pyramid Texts and non-royal tomb chapels, after the central censing, is more ornate than the first. Whereas the first focuses on plain, though bright, simple linen, the Pyramid Texts indicates that the second clothing rite bestows insignia items. Although this study will leave the details of this ritual for a future day, it is important to provide a quick overview in order to provide context for the initial clothing rite already addressed.

The second clothing rite of the Pyramid Texts opens with the label: "presenting him with all his insignia (*sʿḥ*) in each of his places," repeated four times.[29] The recipient is told to "get dressed in your body" and come

---

28. Brovarski, "Doors of Heaven," 107–8.
29. The term translated "insignia" derives from the verbal form meaning "ennoble,

to the gods, "clad in leopard skin, ... kilt, ... [and] reed sandals." He also receives a "water-lily-bud scepter at the fore of the living" and a "staff at the fore of the akhs [glorified and effective dead]."[30] The purpose for all these seems to be outlined in the phrase "you have gone that you may govern Horus's mounds, you have gone that you may govern Seth's mounds, you have gone that you may govern Osiris's mounds." In other words, the insignia represents that the recipient of these items has obtained power to govern among the gods. Again, this stands in contrast to the more simple *wnḫwj* ritual of "two strips of cloth" or "bleached garments" given earlier.

The Old Kingdom elite tomb of Hezi contains a brief sequence of the offering list rite that may contain a representation of this second clothing rite. A lector priest, making an offering gesture with the label *wdn ḫt jn ḫrj-ḥbt* "offering things by the lector," faces the deceased who sits behind his offering table. Behind the lector stands a figure who simply holds a scepter or baton in his hand. The label above him states *šdt s'ḫ 'š' wrt* "reciting a great many glorifications."[31]

Conclusions

In another study, I explored how the sequence and nature of the Offering List rites in the Egyptian Pyramid Texts and elite tomb chapels are strikingly similar to the layout of ritual performances along the architectural path of the biblical temple tradition.[32] The libation, censing, washing with simple meal, anointing, and clothing in the initial set of rituals of the ancient Egyptian Offering List provide a point of comparison to the libation, censing, washing, anointing, simple linen clothing, and simple meal of the priests in connection with the altar and laver of the courtyard and in preparation for entering the "holy place" of the biblical temple. The progression of the Egyptian funeral service can now be seen following a similar pattern wherein a washing, anointing, clothing, and simple meal are performed in the purification tent as a preparation for the procession to the *wꜥbt* or "pure place."

---

honor, reward." See Hannig, *Ägyptisches Wörterbuch*, 1078.

30. Egyptian Pyramid Texts 224; Allen, *Ancient Egyptian Pyramid Texts*, 71, Teti spell 141.

31. Kanawati and Abder-Raziq, *Teti Cemetery at Saqqara. Vol. 5, The Tomb of Hesi*, 50, pl. 64.

32. See Thompson, "Context of Old Testament Temple Worship," 156–83.

However, the ancient Egyptians did not believe that the mere performance of the rituals alone prepared them for their powerful state in the afterlife. The writing on their tombs walls assert that they also did those things which created ma'at or "order," such as giving food to the hungry, clothing the naked, honoring their parents, etc. For example: "I carried out maat which is what the god loves; I propitiated the god in respect of all that which he loves; I made invocation offerings for the akhs; I was respectful of my father and kind to my mother. I buried him who had no son; I ferried him over who had no boat; I rescued the wretched man from the (more) powerful one; I gave the share of the father to his son."[33]

Likewise, the clothing rites may not have been viewed solely as a symbol of status, rank, or progression. The goddess Ta'it was closely associated with the god of grain, Neper, and they both appear in a text on the stela of Mentuhotep: "I gave bread to the hungry and clothes to the one who was naked. I was a son of Neper, the husband of Ta'it."[34] The two lines are in parallel. Giving bread to the hungry is parallel with Neper, the god of grain. Giving clothes to the naked is parallel with Ta'it, the goddess of weaving and linen. Consequently, the ancient Egyptians may have understood that the offering and reception of the linens of Ta'it were not just part of a preparatory purification for one's ascension, but they were also a cultural reminder of certain character qualities one was to possess—namely being generous and thoughtful towards the poor and needy. Just as they were being clothed by a goddess, so should they clothe others.

Further, Mentuhotep's expression suggests that the ancient Egyptian's viewed the act of feeding and clothing the poor as a means by which a deep relationship is created between the giver and the gods—a relationship that the text describes as familial, using terms for sibling and spouse. They may have employed such terms, in part, due to humanity's shared understanding of the deep emotional attachment and love that exist in such familial relationships. The implied meaning then is that when you are in the service of your fellowman, you are not only creating a stronger relationship to others in your community, you are creating a deep bond with the gods as well.

---

33. Hawass, "Inscribed Lintel," 219–24. See also Strudwick, *Texts from the Pyramid Age*, 294–95.

34. Stele des Mentuhotep (London UC [University College collection] 14333); see Brunner, *Altägyptische Weisheit*, 370–73, 510–11.

Recall again this aforementioned Pyramid Text: "Greetings, Ta'it, ... Care for the King's head, so it does not pass away; gather together the King's bones, so that they will not pass away, and put the love of the King into the bowel of every god who shall see him."[35] The last phrase is interesting for it juxtaposes the purpose of the clothing to not only gather and protect the king's body but to draw the king and the gods together within a bond of love.

So, at least in the contexts explore herein, the ritual clothing associated with Ta'it is representative of the preparation one is to make prior to ascending to a higher order. It appears to be symbolic of the recipient's readiness-state of purity and beauty for making their ascent. It is also a reminder of one's civic duty to not forget the poor and needy, but to clothe the naked as they themselves are clothed by the gods. Ta'it's clothing also represents divine blessings such as the binding and protection of the body that it not "pass away." Lastly, her cloth is said to facilitate the love that can exist between the recipient and the gods, perhaps due to recipient's purity and good works to the poor that the cloth can represent. This love is characterized as deep and unique as familial love.

In light of Ta'it's ritual clothing representing love, perhaps it would be fitting to end this brief study with a familiar Pauline admonition, and perhaps even distant echo: "Therefore, as God's chosen people, holy and dearly loved, clothe yourselves with compassion, kindness, humility, gentleness and patience. Bear with each other and forgive one another if any of you has a grievance against someone. Forgive as the Lord forgave you. And over all these virtues put on love, which binds them all together in perfect unity" (Col 3:12–14).

---

35. Egyptian Pyramid Texts 415; see Allen, *Ancient Egyptian Pyramid Texts*, 85, Teti spell 221.

Bibliography

Allen, James P. *The Ancient Egyptian Pyramid Texts*. Writings from the Ancient World, no. 23. Atlanta: Society of Biblical Literature, 2005.

Borchardt, Ludwig. *Denkmäler des Alten Reiches (ausser den Statuen) im Museum von Kairo, nr. 1295-1808*. Catalogue général des antiquités égyptiennes du Musée du Caire. 2 vols. Berlin: Reichsdruckerei, 1937.

Brovarski, Edward. "The Doors of Heaven." *Orientalia* 46 (1977) 107-15.

Brunner, Hellmut. *Altägyptische Weisheit: Lehren für das Leben*. Bibliothek der alten Welt Reihe der alte Orient. Zürich: Artemis, 1988.

Buck, Adriaan de, and Alan H. Gardiner. *The Egyptian Coffin Texts*. 7 vols. Chicago: University of Chicago Press, 1935.

Cauville, Sylvie. *Dendera I–IV: Traduction*. Louvain, Belgium: Peeters, 1997.

el-Saady, Hassan. "Reflections on the Goddess Tayet." *Journal of Egyptian Archaeology* 80 (1994) 213-17.

Hannig, Rainer. *Ägyptisches Wörterbuch. I, Altes Reich und Erste Zwischenzeit. Kulturgeschichte der antiken Welt*. Mainz am Rhein: Philipp von Zabern, 2003.

Hawass, Zahi. "An Inscribed Lintel in the Tomb of the Vizier Mehu at Saqqara." *Lingua Aegyptica* 10 (2002) 219-24.

Hoffmeier, James K. "The Possible Origins of the Tent of Purification in the Egyptian Funerary Cult." *Studien zur altägyptischen Kultur* 9 (1981) 167-77.

Junker, Hermann. *Gîza*. Denkschriften der Akademie der Wissenschaften in Wien. Philosophisch-historische Klasse. 12 vols. Wien, Leipzig: Hölder-Pichler-Tempsky, 1929-55.

Kanawati, Naguib, and Mahmoud Abder-Raziq. *The Teti Cemetery at Saqqara. Vol. 5, The Tomb of Hesi*. Warminster, UK: Aris and Philips, 1999.

Lepsius, Richard. *Denkmäler aus Aegypten und Aethiopien*. 12 vols. Berlin: Nicolaische Buchhandlung, 1849-59.

Lichtheim, Miriam. *Ancient Egyptian Literature*, Vol. 1. Berkeley: University of California Press, 1973.

Murray, Margaret Alice. *Saqqara Mastabas* [in English]. 2 vols. London: British School of Archaeology in Egypt and B. Quaritch, 1905-37.

Nicholson, Paul T., and Ian Shaw. *Ancient Egyptian Materials and Technology*. Cambridge: Cambridge University Press, 2000.

Sauneron, Serge, and Jochen Hallof. *Esna*. 8 vols. Le Caire: l'Institut français d'archeologie orientale, 1959.

Simpson, William Kelly. *The Mastabas of Qar and Idu (G7101 and 7102)*. Giza Mastabas. Boston: Museum of Fine Arts, 1976.

Strudwick, Nigel C. *Texts from the Pyramid Age*. Writings from the Ancient World. Atlanta: Society of Biblical Literature, 2005.

Thompson, John S. "The Context of Old Testament Temple Worship: Early Ancient Egyptian Rites." In *Ascending the Mountain of the Lord: Temple, Praise, and Worship in the Old Testament*, edited by Jeffrey R. Chadwick, David R. Seely, and Matthew J. Grey, 156-83. Provo, UT: Brigham Young University Religious Studies Center. Salt Lake City, Deseret, 2013.

———. "The Iconography of the Memphite Priesthood in Egypt's Elite Tombs of the Old Kingdom." PhD diss., University of Pennsylvania, 2014.

Wilson, John A. "Funeral Services of the Egyptian Old Kingdom." *Journal of Near Eastern Studies* 3, no. 4 (1944) 201-18.

9

A Few of the Ways by which the High Priest's Sacred Clothing Sets Him Apart

Selena Billington

This paper presents a small portion of a PhD dissertation that I completed in 2014, which concerned the social function of cloth and clothing in Israel's tabernacle.[1] That dissertation was an anthropological study, which used three forms of data: (1) the Hebrew Bible, (2) extra-biblical literature, and (3) archeological evidence. Part of the thesis of that dissertation is that Aaron's consecration attire clearly identifies the high priest as on a par with ancient Near East (ANE) kings and pharaohs, and conveys the status of the high priest as the one person of most elite status in the society reflected in the tabernacle narratives.

For this paper, the biblical data come from Exod 28 (and Exod 39)[2]—part of the tabernacle narratives. In the tabernacle narratives, the Lord instructs the Israelites to build a tabernacle and to make special garments in which to consecrate Aaron (who is the prototype high priest) and his sons (who are prototype priests). Appropriately for this volume of conference papers, with its theme of "Sacred Space, Sacred Thread," Aaron's special garments are specifically described in the biblical text as being sacred; they are *qodesh*.[3] Various English translations render the Hebrew

---

1. Billington, "Glorious Adornment." The dissertation has not yet been released for distribution, pending publication as a book.

2. Exodus 39 repeats (and slightly modifies) much of Exod 28.

3. The complete phrase is sometimes *bigde qodesh* (Exod 28:2, 4) and sometimes

term *qodesh* as "sacred" or "holy," and render the word for clothing in this context as "garments" or "vestments." Therefore, in translations of Exod 28:2 and Exod 35:19, for example, Aaron's special garments are variously rendered as "sacred garments,"[4] "sacred vestments,"[5] "holy garments,"[6] or "holy vestments."[7]

Exodus 28:2–3 begins the introduction and overview of the description of Aaron's sacred vestments in Exod 28 with the pronouncement, "You shall make sacred vestments for the glorious adornment of your brother Aaron. And you shall speak to all who have ability, whom I have endowed with skill, that they make Aaron's vestments to consecrate him for my priesthood."[8] After that introduction, the overview continues with a list of vestments to be made: a breastpiece, an ephod (and also a specially woven band associated with the ephod), a robe, a tunic of some particular weave structure, a special headdress, and a sash.[9] We are then told that there are three materials to be used: (1) gold; (2) dyed stuff (translated in the NRSV as "blue, purple, and crimson yarns"); and (3) a particular type of linen.[10]

Following this introduction in Exod 28:2–5, the biblical text in the rest of chapter 28 goes on to give detailed descriptions of each of Aaron's liturgical garments, including information about every aspect of their manufacture: (1) the fiber content; (2) the special mode of spinning; (3) the luxury dyes used; (4) the different weave structures involved for different garments; and (5) specific details about the design elements such as the multiple hems, hem pendants, and neck opening of Aaron's robe, for example.

---

bigde haqodesh (Exod 31:10; 35:19; 39:1, 41; 40:13). Elsewhere the phrases *bigde qodesh* and *bigde haqodesh* are used to refer to the all-linen garments worn by the Aaronide (high) priest when entering the holy of holies on the day of atonement (Lev 16:4, 32).

4. E.g., Exod 28:2: New International Version (NIV).

5. E.g., Exod 28:2: New Revised Standard Version (NRSV), New Jerusalem Bible (NJB). Or "sacral vestments": New Jewish Publication Society (NJPS)

6. E.g., Exod 28:2: New American Standard Bible (NASB), New King James Version (NKJV), Jewish Publication Society (JPS).

7. E.g., Exod 35:19: NRSV.

8. Unless otherwise noted, all translations in this paper are from the NRSV.

9. "These are the vestments that they shall make: a breastpiece, an ephod, a robe, a checkered tunic, a turban, and a sash" (Exod 4a).

10. "When they make these sacred vestments for your brother Aaron and his sons to serve me as priests, they shall use gold, blue, purple, and crimson yarns, and fine linen." (Exod 4b–5).

For this paper, I focus on just two of the details that the text provides about Aaron's consecration attire, both of which depend on the fact that Aaron's sacred vestments are made using the dyed stuff. The first is that Aaron's robe is "entirely of blue," or is of "pure blue."[11] My conclusion will be that the cloth used for Aaron's robe is an example of the sumptuousness of the high priestly sacred clothing, and is part of the evidence presented by the biblical authors that the high priest is on a par with contemporary kings. The second detail on which I focus is that Aaron's ephod, the specially woven band associated with it, and his breastpiece, are all woven from a combination of the dyed stuff and fine linen. My conclusion about this will be that this combination of materials used in the high priestly sacred clothing serves to distinguish the high priest from all other Israelites.

Both of the details about Aaron's consecration attire upon which this paper focuses depend on the fact that Aaron's sacred vestments are made using the dyed stuff. Therefore, before discussing those two details, an overview of the three dyes used for the dyed stuff is appropriate here.

The Three Dyes

The phrase "*tekhelet, 'argaman,* and *tola'at shani,*" which is rendered in the NRSV as "blue, purple, and crimson yarns," occurs over twenty-five times in the tabernacle narratives.[12] The three individual terms in that phrase are used biblically to designate colors and materials dyed in those colors, and in the secondary literature the terms are used also to refer to the dyes themselves. With respect to their colors, I suggest visualizing the first (*tekhelet*) as a purplish-blue, the second (*'argaman*) as a reddish-purple, and the third (*tola'at shani*) as a purplish-red, although it might have instead been an orangish-red, depending on the exact scale insect that was used to produce the dye.[13]

---

11. The Hebrew phrase (*kelil tekhelet*) can be interpreted either as "pure/perfect blue" or as "entirely of blue." The phrase occurs only three times in the biblical text: describing the robe of the ephod in Exod 28:31 and 39:22, and in Num 4:6, in which such a cloth is used to wrap the ark from the "most holy" space in preparation for traveling.

12. "[and] [in] *tekhelet* and *'argaman* and *tola'at shani/hashani*": Exod 25:4; 26:1, 31, 36; 27:16; 28:5, 6, 8, 15, 33; 35:6, 23, 25, 35; 36:8, 35, 37; 38:18, 23; 39:1, 2, 3, 5, 8, 24, 29.

13. Considerable research and literature has been devoted to the actual colors of the three dye terms, as reviewed in my dissertation. Concerning the color of the third

All three dyes are animal-based. Hundreds of plants have been used to create dyes, but very few animal species. According to Dominique Cardon, the recognized authority on natural dyeing, there are only about twenty-five animal species altogether that have been used for dye production: about fifteen species of molluscs (all of which produce purples such as *tekhelet* and *'argaman*) and about ten species of scale insects (all of which produce reds such as *tola'at shani*). Animal-based dyes create brighter colors than plant-based dyes, are color-fast, and labor-intensive. Thus, as noted by many, and articulated succinctly by Cardon, "[a]nimal dyes represent extreme examples of the role of coloured textiles as status symbols."[14]

The purplish-blue *tekhelet* and the reddish-purple *'argaman* together were known as the "sea purples."[15] The sources of the "sea purples" of the ancient Mediterranean world were two species of murex (or sea snail)[16] and one species of rockshell.[17] All three are marine molluscs of

---

dye, there are two possibilities for the identity of the scale insect from which *tola'at shani/hashani* is derived. One possibility is the endangered species *Kermes vermilio*, which lives only on the kermes oak, which in turn is found around the Mediterranean, and which produces an orangish-red dye (scarlet). The other possibility is the endangered species *Porphyrophora hamelii*, which feeds on the roots of two different host grasses, in two different geographic sites only, both in modern-day Armenia, and which produces a purplish-red dye (crimson). Dyed stuff from both species was a prestige-status indicator in the ANE. *Tola'at shani/hashani* is erroneously associated in older literature with *Coccus ilicis*; that species is related to *Kermes vermilio*, but contains *no* red colorants.

14. Cardon, *Natural Dyes*, 551.

15. The information in this paragraph is a distillation of a considerable corpus of literature reviewed in my dissertation. One especially helpful source for "sea purples" is Bradley, *Colour and Meaning*. Two especially helpful sources for the species of dye-bearing molluscs are Cardon, *Natural Dyes*; and Rosenberg, "Characterisation of Historical Organic Dyestuffs." There are numerous sources of information about recent experiments dyeing with *tekhelet*; especially helpful among these are Elsner, "Solution of the Enigmas" and the many contributions of I. Irving Ziderman (e.g., Ziderman "Purple Dyeing in the Mediterranean World"). For a recent dialogue between a proponent of *tekhelet* as blue-purple (Zvi Koren) and a proponent of *tekhelet* as an indigo-like blue (Baruch Sterman), see Biblical Archaeology Society Staff, "Scholar's Study: The Great *Tekhelet* Debate," Bible History Daily, http://www.biblicalarchaeology.org/daily/archaeology-today/biblical-archaeology-topics/scholars-study-the-great-tekhelet-debate/. The starting point in that dialogue is Sterman and Sterman, "Great *Tekhelet* Debate."

16. *Murex trunculus* (also known as *Hexaplex trunculus* or as *Phyllontus trunculus*) and *Murex brandaris* (also known as *Bolinus brandaris*).

17. *Stramonita haemastoma* (also known as *Purpura haemastoma* or as *Thais*

the same family,[18] and all three yield a red-violet colorant, leading to the reddish-purple *argaman*. In addition, one of the three—the sea snail *Murex trunculus*—is unique in yielding, in addition to the red-violet colorant, the same blue colorant that is found in indigo plants. One way of manufacturing dye from this sea snail yields a very dark violet-blue—the combination of red-violet and indigo blue. However, if the last stage in the manufacturing process is done is direct sunlight, the violet-red colorants oxidize, leaving only the indigo colorants, so that the resulting color (*tekhelet*) is a purplish-blue, similar to indigo.[19]

There is considerable archaeological and extra-biblical evidence for all three of these dyes—or the materials dyed with them—being among the most precious objects in the ANE. For example, dyed stuff from the Levantine shores were so consistently taken as booty or demanded as tribute by conquerors that by the fourteenth century BCE, the word for the reddish-purple *argaman* had also come to mean "tribute" in both the Ugaritic and Hittite languages.[20] And, of course, more than half a millennium after the book of Exodus was written, the reddish-purple was *the* indicator of high status both for men and women in Roman antiquity (ultimately becoming the imperial purple reserved for the emperor).

Aaron's Robe—Entirely of Blue

Within Exod 28, more complete information is given about each of the garments listed in Exod 28:4a. In particular, the description of the robe provided in Exod 28:31–34 is as follows: "You shall make the robe of the ephod all of blue. It shall have an opening for the head in the middle of it, with a woven binding around the opening, like the opening in a coat of mail, so that it may not be torn. On its lower hem you shall make pomegranates of blue, purple, and crimson yarns, all around the lower

---

haemastoma).

18. Cardon, *Natural Dyes*, 566. "Today, all marine molluscs used as sources of purple in all parts of the world—including the historical purple-producing species of the Mediterranean area—are classified as part of the Muricidae family." Cardon, *Natural Dyes*, 565.

19. During the rabbinic period at least, biblical blue (*tekhelet*) was the purplish-blue, rather than the very dark violet-blue, because there is commentary in the Talmud on the similarity of appearance between *tekhelet* and indigo. (Greenspan, "Search for Biblical Blue," 36).

20. Reinhold, *History of Purple*, 10–11.

hem, with bells of gold between them all around—a golden bell and a pomegranate alternating all around the lower hem of the robe."

The pomegranates of "blue, purple, and crimson yarns" are of *tekhelet*, *'argaman*, and *tola'at shani*, and Aaron's robe of the ephod—"all of blue"—is made entirely of *tekhelet*.

Three points are made in the passage. First, the robe is all of blue (or is pure blue).[21] Second, it has a special woven edge for the neck opening. Third, it has special hems, with decoration.[22] The Priestly writers of the tabernacle narratives consistently list things in decreasing order of importance (as in the list of Aaron's garments in Exod 28:4a, in which the breastpiece and ephod are listed first).[23] In this case, presumably the characteristics of Aaron's robe are listed in the order of importance to the Priestly writers for the purpose of showing Aaron's elite status. In this respect, the fact that the robe is entirely of *tekhelet* is its most important property.

Similarly, of the three dyes *tekhelet*, *'argaman*, and *tola'at shani*, it is evident that *tekhelet* was valued most highly by the Priestly writers, because it is *always* listed first whenever presented in conjunction with any other dyed stuff.[24] Further evidence of the primacy of *tekhelet* is from Num 4:5–15, a P (Priestly writers) account that lists in decreasing order of importance the furnishings of the tabernacle and the cloths that are used for wrapping them for transport. In that account, neither of the two cloths used for wrapping the set of least important items is *tekhelet* (Num 4:13–14). For wrapping each of the more important items, one of the two or three cloths is *tekhelet* (Num 4:5–12). Significantly, for the most important item furnishing the tabernacle (the ark of the covenant from the holy of holies), one of the three cloths is *kelil tekhelet*—"pure/perfect *tekhelet*" or "entirely of *tekhelet*" (Num 4:5–6).[25]

21. See Note 11.

22. The term in 28:33–34 rendered as "hem" in the NRSV is plural; lit. "hems."

23. The biblical texts dealing with the cloth and clothing of the tabernacle are Exod 25–31, 35–40 (the "tabernacle narratives"), and Num 4. These are some of the components of a corpus of texts which concern Israelite religious practices. The texts of this corpus, known in the literature as the Priestly writing (P), display a unity of style and language, and have been assumed, since the time of Julius Wellhausen in the late eighteenth century CE, to have been written by the same author or authors, to whom I refer as "the Priestly writers" in this paper.

24. See Brenner, *Colour Terms*, 146; and Haran, *Temples and Temple-Service*, 160.

25. It may be that a distinction is being made between the cloths of *tekhelet* that were used to wrap various sets of items and the possibly unique cloth "entirely of

At this point, I would like to summarize the three points made so far. First, cloths dyed with the animal-based dyes *tekhelet*, *'argaman*, or *tola'at shani* were the most precious textiles known in the ANE, and were extreme examples of symbols of high status. Second, the most important characteristic of Aaron's robe of the ephod, as far as the Priestly writers were concerned, was that it was made entirely of stuff dyed with *tekhelet*. Third, stuff dyed with *tekhelet* was considered by the Priestly writers to be more valuable than stuff dyed with *'argaman*, or *tola'at shani*; cloth made from stuff dyed with *tekhelet* was the single most precious textile known to them.

The fourth point I would like to make is that the design of Aaron's robe required a lot of cloth. My analysis of the description of the robe in Exod 28:32–34, presented in full in my dissertation and forthcoming book, indicates that the robe uses at least as much as three times the cloth as would be needed for a simple tunic style of garment.[26] Furthermore, the text emphasizes that this cloth is to be *entirely* of *tekhelet*. This is an ostentatiously superfluous use of the most sumptuous possible cloth known to the biblical writers. The wearer of such a garment would have been immediately identifiable by anyone in the ANE as a person of extreme elite status. The cloth used for Aaron's robe is an example of the sumptuousness of the high priestly sacred clothing, and is part of the evidence presented by the Priestly writers of the tabernacle narratives that the high priest is on a par with contemporary kings.

Dyed Stuff and Fine Linen

In the list of the components of Aaron's consecration attire in Exod 28:4a, the breastpiece and ephod are first and second, respectively. Within Exod 28, detailed descriptions are given first for the ephod, second for a specially woven band associated with the ephod, and third for the breastpiece. Clearly for the Priestly writers, the breastpiece, ephod and the

---

tekhelet" (*kelil tekhelet*) which was used as the third layer of cloth wrapping the ark (Num 4:6), in the same way that a distinction clearly is made in the description of materials for the tabernacle between gold and "pure gold." If so, apparently *kelil tekhelet* was valued even more highly than the otherwise most highly prized *tekhelet*. Another possibility is that the phrase *kelil tekhelet* is intended to emphasize that, even though the cloth wrapping the ark was necessarily a large piece of cloth, it nevertheless was entirely of *tekhelet*.

26. Billington, "Glorious Adornment," 220–31.

ephod's band were Aaron's most important garments. The second detail about Aaron's sacred vestments that is a focus of this paper is that these three liturgically important garments are all woven from a combination of the dyed stuff and twisted fine linen (Exod 28:6, 8, 15).[27]

The new information that needs to be introduced at this point is that the stuff dyed with *tekhelet*, *'argaman*, and *tola'at shani* must be wool. There are several lines of evidence for this. First, the only two fibers in common use in the ANE at this time were linen and wool, so the dyed materials must have been either linen or wool. The biblical text itself, with its clear distinction between the fine linen and the dyed stuff, strongly suggests that the dyed stuff was *not* linen. Therefore it *was* wool. Second, although linen bleaches nicely, it "is notoriously difficult to dye well.... The problem is caused by the fibers' hardness, which keeps the dye from penetrating well into the fiber where it won't wash or rub off."[28] Linen *could* be dyed, albeit with difficulty. On the other hand, white wool can be dyed easily. Third, there is archaeological evidence from the ANE for the dyeing of wool with some of the animal-based dyes discussed above: specifically, the sea-purples *tekhelet* and *'argaman* derived from molluscs, as well as an orangish-red derived from the scale insect *Kermes vermilio*.[29] Fourth, there are extra-biblical texts in which the terms *tekhelet* and *'argaman* are unambiguously synonymous with dyed wool. Thus, the authoritative *Assyrian Dictionary of the Oriental Institute of the University of Chicago* provides two meanings for the cognate of *'argaman*: "red purple wool" and "tribute."[30] Similarly, the cognate of *tekhelet* is defined as "a precious blue-purple wool," with a following sub-heading: "as raw material (often beside other dyed wools)"[31]

Obviously, the insight that the dyed materials are wool is not original with me; in fact, biblical commentators who explicitly mention the fiber

---

27. The word for "fine linen" is one of seven terms in the Hebrew Bible for linen, linen garments, or flax. One of the other terms is used also in the tabernacle narratives, in the description of the priestly undergarments (Exod 28:42).

28. Barber, *Prehistoric Textiles*, 15.

29. Wool textiles dyed with *Kermes vermilio* have been excavated at 'En Rahel (Shamir, "Coloured Textiles") and at Palmyra (Böhmer and Karadag, "New Dye Research").

30. The Assyrian cognate of *'argaman* is *argamannu*. See entry in Reiner, *The Assyrian Dictionary*.

31. The Assyrian cognate of *tekhelet* is *takiltu*. See entry in Reiner, *The Assyrian Dictionary*.

content of the dyed materials universally call them wool.³² However, in my experience, it can be a surprise to people that Aaron's garments are to be woven of dyed wools and linen, given the well-known biblical prohibitions in Lev 19:19 against putting on "a garment made of two different materials" and in Deut 22:11 against wearing "clothes made of wool and linen woven together." However, there is no inherent conflict between the Lord's commandment, on the one hand, that Aaron in particular, as prototype high priest, is to wear garments of wool and linen woven together, and the Lord's commandment, on the other hand, that Israelites in general are never to wear garments of wool and linen woven together. The two commandments together constitute an example of a sumptuary law—a law which either *forbids* or *prescribes* the wearing of specific styles by specific classes of persons.³³ In this case, Israelites in general are *forbidden* to wear garments like the sacred ones *prescribed* for the high priest in particular. This is all related, of course, to the fact that Aaron's garments are sacred—holy—and that only Aaron or his successors as high priest may wear these "sacred threads."

There are numerous examples of sumptuary laws in history.³⁴ One famous example is the reservation of Imperial purple (*'argaman*) for garments of the emperor of Rome. The effect of the biblical sumptuary law pertaining to the wearing of garments of wool and linen woven together is that the high priest is distinguished from all other Israelites.

Conclusion

I have presented two examples from the many details, provided in the tabernacle narratives of the book of Exodus, about the sacred vestments

---

32. E.g., Propp, *Exodus 19–40*; Meyers, *Exodus*; Milgrom, *Leviticus 1–16*.

33. Lurie, *Language of Clothes*, 115. Lurie's exact quote defines sumptuary laws as those which "prescribe or forbid the wearing of specific styles by specific classes of persons." Lurie describes sumptuary laws as originally entailing restrictions on the color and shape of garments that could be worn. More generally, a sumptuary law is "a law . . . to prevent extravagance in private life by limiting expenditure for clothing, food, and furniture" (Webster's Third New International Dictionary).

34. A commonly quoted example of sumptuary laws are those of the Massachusetts Colony (1651), which prohibited any person whose net worth was less than £200 from wearing, for instance, gold and silver buttons, and which more generally prohibited persons from wearing clothing which "exceeds their ranks" ("Colonial Laws of Massachusetts, 1651," Constitution Society, http://www.constitution.org/primarysources/sumptuary.html).

that constitute Aaron's consecration attire. The first is that Aaron's robe is "entirely of blue," or is of "pure blue." I conclude that the cloth used for Aaron's robe is an example of the sumptuousness of the high priestly sacred clothing, and is part of the evidence presented by the biblical authors that the high priest is on a par with contemporary kings. The second is that Aaron's ephod, the specially woven band associated with it, and his breastpiece, are all woven from a combination of dyed wool and fine linen. I conclude that this combination of materials used in the high priestly sacred clothing serves to distinguish the high priest from all other Israelites.

I chose to focus on these two particular aspects of Aaron's sacred vestments/holy garments for my presentation at the "Sacred Space, Sacred Thread" conference, in the hope of triggering an interesting conversation—perhaps involving a comparison between the way that the Israelite high priest's sacred threads set him apart from his coreligionists, on the one hand, and the way or ways that liturgical garb functions in contemporary worship environments, on the other hand.

I thank the Widtsoe Foundation for sponsoring the "Sacred Space, Sacred Thread" conference, and thank Jacob Rennaker and Jack Welch for organizing it. I am grateful to have been invited to participate.

Bibliography

Barber, E. J. W. *Prehistoric Textiles: The Development of Cloth in the Neolithic and Bronze Ages, with Special Reference to the Aegean.* Princeton: Princeton University Press, 1991.

Billington, Selena. "Glorious Adornment: The Social Function of Cloth and Clothing in Israel's Tabernacle." PhD diss., Iliff School of Theology and the University of Denver, 2014.

———. "Prestige Elements of Clothing in the Ancient Near East, according to the Hebrew Bible." Paper presented at the annual meeting of the American Schools of Oriental Research. Chicago, IL, 17 November 2012.

Böhmer, Harald, and Recep Karadag. "New Dye Research on Palmyra Textiles." In *Dyes in History and Archaeology*, edited by Jo Kirby, 88–93 London: Archetype, 2003.

Bradley, Mark. *Colour and Meaning in Ancient Rome.* Cambridge: Cambridge University Press, 2009.

Brenner, Athalya. *Colour Terms in the Old Testament.* Journal for the Study of the Old Testament Supplement Series 21. Sheffield, UK: JSOT, 1982.

Cardon, Dominique. *Natural Dyes: Sources, Tradition, Technology and Science.* London: Archetype, 2007.

Elsner, Otto. "Solution of the Enigmas of Dyeing Tyrian Purple and the Biblical tekhelet." In *Dyes in History and Archaeology*, 11–16. York, UK: Textile Research Associates, 1992.

Greenspan, Ari. "The Search for Biblical Blue." *Bible Review* 19, no. 1 (2003) 32–39, 52.

Haran, Menahem. *Temples and Temple-Service in Ancient Israel: An Inquiry into Biblical Cult Phenomena and the Historical Setting of the Priestly School.* 1978. Reprint, Winona Lake, IN: Eisenbrauns, 1985.

Lurie, Alison. *The Language of Clothes.* New York: Random House, 1981.

Meyers, Carol. *Exodus.* The New Cambridge Bible Commentary. Cambridge: Cambridge University Press, 2005.

Milgrom, Jacob. *Leviticus 1–16: A New Translation with Introduction and Commentary.* Edited by William Foxwell Albright and David Noel Freedman. The Anchor Bible. New York: Doubleday, 1991.

Propp, William H. C. *Exodus 19–40: A New Translation with Introduction and Commentary.* The Anchor Bible. New York: Doubleday, 2006.

Reiner, Erica, et al., eds. *The Assyrian Dictionary of the Oriental Institute of the University of Chicago.* 21 vols. Chicago: Oriental Institute, 1956–2010.

Reinhold, Meyer. *History of Purple as a Status Symbol in Antiquity.* Collection Latomus 116. Bruxelles: Latomus, 1970.

Rosenberg, Erwin. "Characterisation of Historical Organic Dyestuffs by Liquid Chromatography-Mass Spectrometry." *Analytical and Bioanalytical Chemistry* 391 (2008) 33–57.

Shamir, Orit. "Coloured Textiles found along the Spice Route joining Petra and Gaza—Examples from the First to Eighth Centuries AD." In *Colour in the Ancient Mediterranean World*, edited by Liza Cleland, Karen Stears, and Glenys Davies, 49–52. British Archaeological Reports International Series 1267. Oxford: John and Erica Hedges, 2004.

Sterman, Baruch, and Judy Taubes Sterman. "The Great *Tekhelet* Debate—Blue or Purple?" *Biblical Archaeology Review* 39, no. 5 (September/October 2013) 28, 73.

Ziderman, I. Irving. "Purple Dyeing in the Mediterranean World: Characterisation of Biblical *Tekhelet*." In *Colour in the Ancient Mediterranean World*, edited by Liza Cleland, Karen Stears, and Glenys Davies, 40–45. British Archaeological Reports International Series 1267. Oxford: John and Erica Hedges, 2004.

10

Dressed to Impress

Adam as a Priestly Figure in Eden

Jacob Rennaker

The puzzle I hope to solve today is this: How was it possible for perhaps the most well-known man without clothes in the Hebrew Bible to be compared with perhaps the most well-known man wearing the most sacred of clothes in Jewish thought? During Judaism's Second Temple period, several authors drew connections between the temple and the creation stories recorded in Genesis, even going so far as to describe the Israelite high priest and his clothing in terms of Adam. I will examine several texts written during this period of time in order to tease out what interpreters saw as Adam's priestly role in Eden, and will explore how these authors may have discerned such ideas from the very first chapters of Genesis.

The temple in Jerusalem stood as the focal point of Israelite religion when it was destroyed by the Babylonians in the late sixth century BCE. Having been forcefully estranged from this beating heart of their religious life, Jewish exiles in Babylon possessed a heightened sensitivity to the temple and its related imagery.[1] Such sensitivity is evident in the bibli-

---

1. Concerning both temple and Eden imagery, Michael Fishbane writes, "It was not until the woe and dislocation of the exile, and with it the destruction of the land and Temple, that the symbolism of Eden emerges with singular emphasis. In the mouths of the post-exilic prophets, this imagery serves as the organizing prism for striking

cal writings of Ezekiel, a prophetic figure who bridged the gap between those who had lived in the shadow of the Jerusalem temple their entire lives, and those who knew nothing but the ruins of this sacred structure upon their return. In describing his vision of the temple,[2] Ezekiel uses language evocative of Eden, humanity's very first (and perhaps most important) home. For instance, this is evident in the regular appearance of cherubim—a very specific type of heavenly being—in Ezekiel's narrative. While the six gates of the temple's courtyards were all decorated with palm trees (Ezek 40:16, 22, 26, 31, 34, 37), indicating a garden-like setting, the walls and doors of the sanctuary proper were decorated with both palm trees and cherubim, the walls and doors of the sanctuary proper were decorated with both palm trees *and* cherubim (Ezek 41:20, 23, 25a). This, of course, is suggestive of Adam's eastward expulsion from Eden—Genesis states that cherubim were placed "at the east of the Garden of Eden" to prevent a westward return to the garden.

This correlation between Eden and the temple may explain the particular term that God uses consistently to address Ezekiel in his temple visions—the phrase *ben-'ādām,* can be translated as both "mortal" and as "son of Adam." The image of Ezekiel as a priestly "son of Adam" becomes even more significant when we take into account the fact that only the high priest was authorized to enter the temple's Holy of Holies (Lev 16), where both the doors to this most sacred room and the Ark of the Covenant within this sacred space were guarded by cherubim, as was the Garden of Eden.[3]

Earlier in the book of Ezekiel, the author made this connection between Adam and the Israelite priesthood more explicit. Chapter 28 describes Eden as being at the top of a mountain, and uses language evocative of the Israelite tabernacle and temple to describe it. The text also refers to an inhabitant of this sacred space as wearing precious stones (Ezek 28:13) similar to those worn by Aaron as he officiated in the tabernacle

---

visions of spatial renewal." Fishbane, *Biblical Interpretation in Ancient Israel,* 369–70. And, regarding the perception of temple imagery during this period, Carla Sulzbach noted that "The assorted strands of references to sacred places that were still clearly discernible in the earlier strata of the Hebrew Bible were mined by the various Second Temple period texts and these were then fused into one grand, intricately contrived temple image." Sulzbach, "Of Temples on Earth, in Heaven, and in-Between," 173.

2. See Ezek 40–48.

3. See Sweeney, "Ezekiel: Zadokite Priest and Visionary Prophet of the Exile," 141–42.

and shown here (Exod 28:15–20).⁴ In the verses that follow, God explains that because of this individual's "sin" (חטא), "I cast [him out] as a profane thing from the mountain of God," or Eden (Ezek 28:16). Thus, it appears as though the individual banished from Eden was wearing priestly attire before being expelled, which also seems to imply that this individual was performing priestly duties within the garden.⁵ This, then, seems to be an early connection between Adam and ornate priestly clothing, which was presumably manufactured by God.

After the Jerusalem temple was rebuilt by the Jewish people in the early sixth century CE, several authors made similar, yet more expansive conceptual connections between Eden and creation as they wrote about this restored temple in Jerusalem. These texts suggest a creative and complex understanding of what the temple, its rituals, and its worshippers symbolized. For instance, several authors suggested that the temple was symbolic of Eden, and that the high priest was a representative of Adam. As we will see, from this perspective, the Israelite high priest effectively reversed humanity's expulsion from the presence of God.

One example of such thinking was written by the author of *Liber Antiquitatum Biblicarum*, which states that the tabernacle and temple ritual somehow restored what was lost through Adam and Eve's disobedience in Eden. According to this account, God showed Moses "the measurements of the sanctuary, and the number of the offerings, and the signs by which they shall begin to examine the heavens. And [God] said: These are the things which were forbidden to the race of men after they had sinned."⁶ This likely reference to Adam and Eve's actions in Eden suggest

---

4. While the Masoretic (Hebrew) Text of Ezekiel only mentions this figure wearing nine of the twelve stones mentioned on Aaron's priestly breastplate, the Greek text mentions all twelve stones. For a detailed comparison and analysis of the Hebrew and Greek texts of Ezek 28:11–19, see Stordalen, *Echoes of Eden*, 332–56.

5. Fletcher-Louis agrees with this reading: "The office of high priest was thought to recapitulate the identity of the pre-lapsarian Adam. This goes back at least as far as Ezek 28:12ff. where the prince of Tyre wears precious stones which are simultaneously those worn by the *Urmensch* in the garden of Eden and those of the Aaronic ephod according to Exodus 28." See Fletcher-Louis, "Worship of Divine Humanity as God's Image," 394, 408.

6. *Liber Antiquitatum Biblicarum* XIX.10–11. In his commentary on this passage, C. T. R. Hayward states that this reference to Adam and Eve suggest these first parents were "responsible for losing privileges which human beings should properly have retained. Among these are the ways to Paradise: these and other gifts are, it would seem, partly restored to Israel with the building of the tabernacle and the conduct of its Service. The due celebration of the annual festivals, in particular, give Israel some part

these first parents lost privileges that humans should have retained in other circumstances. The construction of the tabernacle and its various rituals, in part, seem to have restored certain of these privileges that were lost. Here, then, God gives Israel a significant role in affairs that affect humanity as a whole.[7] Thus, the creation of the tabernacle and temple could be seen as functional replacements for Eden's primal sacred space.

The book of *Jubilees* also makes conceptual ties between Eden, Adam, and the temple. In this text, Adam and Eve are created outside of the garden; God brings Adam and Eve into the garden at different times—Adam enters the garden after forty days, then Eve enters the garden after eighty days (Jubilees 3:9–13).[8] The author makes clear that these procedures reflect the priestly laws governing entrance to the temple in Leviticus 12:2–8, and suggests that the Garden of Eden had a similar level of sanctity as did the temple. This particular idea is made explicit in Jubilees 8:19, where the narrator describes Noah as knowing "that the Garden of Eden is the holy of holies, and the dwelling of the Lord."[9] The significance of this statement can be summarized in the following: If "Adam and Eve were brought into the Holy of Holies prior to their disobedience [then] their expulsion from Eden [was a] removal from the place where God's Presence ... [was] most immediate for Israel. The high priest's entry [into] the Holy of Holies on [the holy day of] Yom Kippur [would symbolically] correspond to the first man's return to Eden,"[10] albeit temporarily.[11]

Interpretations of Adam's apparel suggest an additional priestly connection. In the Wisdom of Ben Sira (in Hebrew), we find a list of

---

in the divinely appointed order of things which themselves directly affect the whole human race" (Hayward, *Jewish Temple*, 167).

7. Hayward, *Jewish Temple*, 167.
8. See also Hayward, *Jewish Temple*, 89.
9. Translation of Hayward, *Jewish Temple*, 89.
10. Hayward, *Jewish Temple*, 89.

11. In understanding Eden as a sort of primeval temple, Adam's role is equated with the priestly roles later performed by Levites. This is seen clearly in the description of Adam's actions in Jubilees immediately following his expulsion from Eden: "And [God] made for them coats of skin, and clothed them, and sent them forth from the Garden of Eden. And on that day which Adam went forth from the Garden, he offered as a sweet savor an offering, frankincense, galbanum, and stacte, and spices in the morning with the rising of the sun from the day when he covered his shame" (Jubilees 3:26–27). Adam's offering here appears to be fulfilling the priestly requirements for daily offerings in the tabernacle (and later, the temple) given in Exod 30:1–8.

several biblical figures whose grave sites were visited by their faithful descendants. The author then writes that "above every living thing is *the beauty* of Adam" (49:16; emphasis added). The very next verse begins, "Greatest of his brothers and *the beauty* of his people was Simeon the son of [Y]ohanan the priest; In whose generation the house was visited and in whose days the Temple was strengthened" (50:1; emphasis added). While a passing reference to Adam just before a sustained description of the high priest Simeon may seem like a non sequitur, this juxtaposition was not haphazard: "The description of Sim[e]on as the 'beauty,' [or] *tip'eret*, of his people establishes more than a formal link with the preceding chapter (49:16), where the 'beauty,' [or] *tip'eret*, of Adam is named."[12] Here, the author "implies that Adam's [clothing] is analogous to Sim[e]on's high priestly robes: if so, he may suggest here . . . that the high priest's [clothing] are the garments of the first man,"[13] which God made before expelling him from Eden.

In any case, the Wisdom of Ben Sira establishes at the very least a conceptual connection between the perception of Adam and the perception of the Jewish high priest Simeon as he functioned within the Jerusalem temple. This comparison suggests that the author saw the high priest as a latter-day representative of Adam, and that the regular rituals performed in the temple were, in fact, offered on behalf of the whole world.[14] From this perspective, then, the aforementioned privileges originally granted to Adam in Eden were recapitulated in Simeon, the high priest,[15] who offered sacrifices on behalf of humanity within the latter-day equivalent of Eden.

A similarly relation between Eden, Adam, and the temple appears in several Qumran texts. In the Community Rule, we read: "For God has chosen them [the community] for an everlasting covenant, and all the glory of Adam is theirs" (1QS 4:22–23). The curious phrase "all the glory of Adam" appears in one of the *Hodayot*: "And you [God] are causing [the community] to inherit all the glory of Adam and an abundance of days" (1QH 4:15). This association between the Qumran community and Adam is further demonstrated throughout the *Hodayot*. For example, one passage reads, "I will recount your glory in the midst of the sons of

---

12. Hayward, *Jewish Temple*, 44.
13. Hayward, *Jewish Temple*, 45.
14. Hayward, *Jewish Temple*, 14.
15. Hayward, *Jewish Temple*, 45.

Adam; and in the abundance of your goodness my soul delights" (1QH 19:6–7).[16] In fact, Fletcher-Louis observes that much of this collection "is a sustained and extended meditation on the anthropology of Genesis 2:7,"[17] which describes the creation of Adam from the dust of the earth.[18] These examples suggest that the Qumran community considered the character of Adam as glorious, and believed that they could somehow participate in that glory.

Given the evidence that both the Wisdom of Ben Sira and Jubilees were preserved at Qumran,[19] it is not surprising that additional texts there may contain imagery that associates high priestly figures with the concept of Adam and a return to the presence of God. While the Qumran community saw themselves as inheritors of "all the glory of Adam," they also saw themselves as priests. These two views are joined in 4Q Florilegium (4Q174 1 i:6–7) "And he has commanded that a sanctuary of Adam[20] be built for him; that there they may send up, like the smoke of incense,

---

16. I have chosen to render בני אדם here as "sons of Adam" instead of "sons of men." The first lines of this hymn, "I thank you, my God, for you have dealt wonderfully with dust (עפר), and in forming (וביצר) clay you have made very mighty" (1QH 19:3), allude to the imagery employed in the creation of man as recorded in Gen 2:6–7. By analogy, the particular phraseology בני אדם translated as "son of Adam" appears to be more appropriate than "son of man" or "human" in late Second Temple texts. Marvin Sweeney argues: "Later texts of the Second Temple period . . . note that the priest in the Temple represents Adam in the Garden of Eden, which may explain the appellation ben-'adam, 'son of Adam' or 'mortal,' that is consistently applied by YHWH to Ezekiel throughout the book. The fact that only the high priest may enter the Holy of Holies, where the Ark of the Covenant is guarded by cherubim much like the Garden of Eden, reinforces this image" (Sweeney, "Ezekiel: Zadokite Priest and Visionary Prophet of the Exile," 141–42).

17. Fletcher-Louis, *All the Glory of Adam*, 108.

18. An excellent example of such a meditation from this collection is the following: "(God) lifts up the poor from the dust to the [eternal height,] and to the clouds he magnifies him in stature, and (he is) with the heavenly beings in the assembly of the community." 4QHodayot[set superscript a] 7 ii, 8–9. Based on the translation in Chazon and others, *Discoveries in the Judaean Desert XXIX*, 100.

19. Hayward, *Jewish Temple*, 39–40, 85.

20. Some have translated מקדש אדם as "sanctuary of human beings" (for example, Elwolde, *Dictionary of Classical Hebrew, Vol. 1*, 125, s.v. אדם). However, if the author wanted to be explicit about the sanctuary being composed of humans, rather than referring to Adam, he or she could have used the more specific אנוש "human," which appears frequently in the Dead Sea Scrolls (see Elwolde, *Dictionary of Classical Hebrew, Vol. 1*, 334–35, s.v. אנוש). At the very least, this statement is ambiguous enough to be alluding to Adam (see Elwolde, *Dictionary of Classical Hebrew, Vol. 1*, 124, 129, s.v. אדם I, IV).

the works of the law.²¹" Michael Wise and Carla Sulzbach agree that the translation of מקדש אדם as "sanctuary / Temple of Adam" is preferable to the much more generic "sanctuary / Temple of humanity" in view of the Edenic overtones they see in this text.²² It is possible that the Qumran community saw themselves as a conceptual sanctuary consisting of priestly individuals who had each received the "glory of Adam," thus becoming a "Temple of Adam." It is also possible to combine this idea with the importance of a physical location to perform priestly duties at Qumran. Sulzbach suggests that, "in light of other historical precedents, it may be assumed that *Miqdash Adam* [sanctuary / Temple of Adam] refers to a certain place, the designated *maqom*, where worship and divine service takes place (for the moment, until better times). Perhaps even the synchronized angelic-human [priestly] service as described in the [*Songs of Sabbath Sacrifice*] could thus have taken place in the *Miqdash Adam*."²³

If the *Songs of Sabbath Sacrifice* in particular were used in a liturgical setting, then its second Song may support the view that the community saw themselves individually as representatives of Adam. Referring to those in the heavens, the Instructor asks: "[What] is the offering of our tongues of dust (לשון עפרנו) (compared) with the knowledge of the g[ods?] (4Q400 2 6–7)." This is a possible allusion to Gen 3:19, where God says to Adam, "For you are dust, and unto dust you will return." This passage from the second Song is the only instance where humanity comes close to being viewed negatively in the *Songs*; elsewhere, the emphasis is always on glorious figures (often portrayed using priestly language). It should be remembered that by reading *Ben Sira* and *Jubilees* together, the high priest entering the Holy of Holies most likely represented Adam returning to Eden, and therefore signified a return to the presence of God.²⁴ If the Qumran community embraced this imagery in *Ben Sira* and *Jubilees*, then perhaps the community also understood these *Songs of Sabbath Sacrifice* as somehow functioning to reverse the sentence pronounced upon Adam in Gen 3:19; instead of returning to the dust, community members would ritually receive the glory originally intended for Adam. Such a liturgical experience would have held a special significance for

---

21. For this last clause, I follow the translation of Geza Vermes in *The Complete Dead Sea Scrolls in English*, 525.

22. See Wise, "4QFlorilegium and the Temple of Adam," 131; Sulzbach, "Of Temples on Earth, in Heaven, and in-Between," 177.

23. Sulzbach, "Of Temples on Earth, in Heaven, and in-Between," 178.

24. See above.

those at Qumran, who were unable to participate in the various priestly rituals at the temple in Jerusalem.[25] In fact, by laying claim to the "glory of Adam," it is possible to see the Qumran community as appealing to a tradition even older than the Jerusalem temple in order to justify their community's performance of priestly functions.[26]

Taken together, these several Second Temple texts display a complex understanding of how the temple and its priests were conceptually related to Eden and Adam—that the temple itself was in some way a recreation of Eden and that the rituals performed by the temple's priests made restitution not only for Adam and Eve's disobedience, but the that temple rituals also made positive offerings on behalf the entire human race. In what follows, I will demonstrate why this interpretation was plausible (and perhaps natural) by focusing on the language and imagery used in the Eden narrative and will outline how the idea of a priestly Adam was a real interpretive possibility in Gen 2–3.

The first verbal cues that alert us to Adam's priestly possibilities occur in Gen 2:15. Here, God takes the man and places him[27] in the Garden of Eden "to till it and keep it." These verbs are elsewhere translated as "serve" (עבד) and "keep [or] guard" (שמר), and are most often used together to describe the priestly actions of "serving" God and "keeping [or] guarding" God's word.[28] With this connection in mind, some have

---

25. Carol Newsom writes: "What was specifically needed at Qumran ... were not merely arguments couched in visionary form to demonstrate the authenticity of the claims of the group but rather some form of experiential validation of their claims. I would suggest that the cycle of songs in the Sabbath Shirot was developed precisely to meet this need for experiential validation. ... To the extent that the worshipper experienced himself as present in the heavenly temple through the recitation of the Sabbath Shirot, his status as a faithful and legitimate priest would have been convincingly confirmed in spite of the persistent contradiction of his claims in the world" (Newsom, *Songs of the Sabbath Sacrifice*, 71–72).

26. The author of the Hebrews makes a similar rhetorical move by claiming Jesus as a priestly heir of the pre-Levitical Melchizedek (e.g. Heb 7).

27. Solomon was described as having installed sacred furniture in the temple using a similar form of the same verb: 2) ויּנח Chr 4:8). In other temple-related contexts, this verb and verbal form are used to describe the placement of divine images in their temples. See 2 Kgs 17:29 and Zech 5:5–11.

28. See Num. 3:7–8; 8:25–26; 18:5–6; 1 Chr 23:32; Ezek 44:14. See also Cassuto, *Commentary on Genesis, Part I*, 122–23, Wenham, "Sanctuary Symbolism in the Garden of Eden Story," 21; and Parry, "Garden of Eden: Prototype Sanctuary," 144. For a more technical discussion, see Beale, *Temple and the Church's Mission*, 67 n. 89.

suggested that "if Eden is seen ... as an ideal sanctuary, then perhaps Adam should be described as an [ideal Israelite priest]."[29]

Other elements within Genesis 2–3 point to an understanding of Eden's inhabitants as functioning within temple-related sacred space. The prohibition against eating from the tree of the knowledge of good and evil stated that if this was violated, Adam would "surely die" (Gen 2:17).[30] This is significant because, according to early Jewish interpreters, "the [tabernacle] was [seen as] the centre of life, because ... God was present [there. And] to be excluded from the camp of Israel ... was to enter the realm of death."[31] From this perspective, then, God's statement that Adam and Eve would "surely die" if they ate a particular fruit was less about the length of their lives, as it was about their ability to remain ritually pure within a particular sacred space.

This concept of maintaining ritual purity within such space points us back to Adam's responsibilities in the Garden of Eden: to "serve" and "keep [or] guard" it. For Israelite priests, one notable aspect of "guarding" meant protecting the tabernacle and temple from ritually impure individuals or creatures entering its precincts.[32] It may have been possible to see the entrance of the serpent, an unclean animal (see Lev 11), as a failure on Adam's part to guard the temple-like Garden of Eden. The cherubim's stated purpose of "guarding" the sacred space of Eden could then be interpreted as God's replacement of Adam as caretaker of Eden's sacredness.[33] As the cherubim's duties are described using the same verb that outlines Adam's responsibility to "guard" (שמר) the garden in the

---

29. Wenham, "Sanctuary Symbolism in the Garden of Eden Story," 21.

30. See also Gen 3:3–4.

31. Wenham, "Sanctuary Symbolism in the Garden of Eden Story," 24. Wenham finds evidence for this view in the language of Leviticus. See Wenham, *Book of Leviticus*, 177, 201; and Wenham, "Why Does Sexual Intercourse Defile?" 432–34.

32. For example, Num 3:6–7, 32, 38; 18:1–7; Neh 11:19; Ezek 40:45; 44:14; 1 Chr 9:17–27; 2 Chr 23:19.

33. Beale notes that this priestly responsibility to guard sacred space "appears to be relevant for Adam, especially in view of the unclean creature lurking on the perimeter of the Garden who then enters." He goes on to explain: "When Adam failed to guard the temple by sinning and letting in a foul serpent to defile the sanctuary, he lost his priestly role, and the cherubim took over the responsibility of 'guarding' the Garden temple: God 'stationed the cherubim ... *to guard* the way to the tree of life' (so Gen 3:24; see also Ezek 28:14, 16). The guarding function of the cherubim probably did not involve gardening but keeping out the sinful and unclean, which suggests that Adam's original role stated in Genesis 2:15 likely entailed much more than cultivating the soil, but also 'guarding' the sacred space" (Beale, *Temple and the Church's Mission*, 69–70).

previous chapter, it may be inferred that Adam's duty there was priestly in nature.

Two final elements suggest a priestly context for understanding the roles of Adam and Eve within the garden; these appear in the description of their actions—as well as the actions of God—after Adam and Eve ate the fruit (Gen 3:6). Upon hearing the voice of God in the garden, they hid themselves "from the presence of the LORD God." It has been suggested elsewhere that, "in general, any [ritual] activity [using the phrase] 'before the Lord' can be considered an indication of . . . a temple at the site, since this expression stems from the basic conception of the temple as a divine dwelling-place and actually belongs to the temple's technical terminology."[34] If this is the case, then Adam and Eve's previous actions within the garden could have been viewed as paralleling the actions of priests in the Israelite tabernacle and temple. This suggestion is strengthened by the actions of God that follow Adam and Eve's indictment: God "clothes" them (וילבשם) with "garments" (כתנות) of skin. The same verb meaning "to clothe" (לבש) appears several times in passages that describe Moses clothing the priests of the tabernacle with "garments" (כתנות) (again, the same word used in Genesis), suggesting that God's clothing of Adam and Eve could be seen by its audience as having had priestly overtones.[35]

The inclusion of Eve in these temple-oriented passages certainly complicates the idea of an all-male priesthood in ancient Israel. Nevertheless, from the aforementioned Second Temple writings, it is clear that there was a common perception of Adam in the Genesis narratives as a sort of priestly figure; an idea so potent that it was seen by some as radiating into the present from primeval times, and by others as an interpretive lens through which to illuminate the stories of humanity's beginnings. While some ancient interpreters saw Adam as being dressed in sacred clothing (presumably manufactured by God) while walking about Eden, many others at the very least saw similarities between the role and function of Adam in Eden and that of the High Priest in the temple. This idea

---

34. Haran, *Temples and Temple Service in Ancient Israel*, 26.

35. For example, Exod 28:41; 29:8; 40:14; Lev 8:13. See also Wenham, "Sanctuary Symbolism in the Garden of Eden Story," 21–22; and Parry, "Garden of Eden: Prototype Sanctuary," 145. For a discussion of early Jewish and Christian traditions that make a similar association between Adam's garment and priestly clothing, see Tvedtnes, "Priestly Clothing in Bible Times," 649–62; and Anderson, *Genesis of Perfection*, 122–24.

of one person making offerings to God on behalf of humanity as a whole endowed both the space of the Jewish temple and the threads worn by the High Priest with sacred significance.

Bibliography

Anderson, Gary. *The Genesis of Perfection: Adam and Eve in Jewish and Christian Imagination.* Louisville, KY: Westminster John Knox, 2001.
Beale, G. K. *The Temple and the Church's Mission: A Biblical Theology of the Dwelling Place of God.* Leicester, UK: Apollos, 2004.
Cassuto, Umberto. *A Commentary on the Book of Genesis Part I: From Adam to Noah: Genesis I–VI.* Translated by Israel Abrahams. 1944. Reprint, Jerusalem: Magnes, 1961.
Chazon, Esther, et al., eds. *Discoveries in the Judaean Desert XXIX: Qumran Cave 4 XX, Poetical and Liturgical Texts, Part 2.* Oxford: Clarendon, 1999.
Elwolde, John, ed. *The Dictionary of Classical Hebrew, Vol. 1.* Sheffield, UK: Sheffield Academic Press, 1993.
Fishbane, Michael. *Biblical Interpretation in Ancient Israel.* Oxford: Clarendon, 1985.
Fletcher-Louis, Crispin. *All the Glory of Adam: Liturgical Anthropology in the Dead Sea Scrolls.* Boston: Brill, 2002.
———. "The Worship of Divine Humanity as God's Image and the Worship of Jesus." In *The Jewish Roots of Christological Monotheism: Papers from the St. Andrews Conference on the Historical Origins of the Worship of Jesus,* edited by Carey C. Newman, James R. Davila, and Gladys S. Lewis, 112–28. Leiden: Brill, 1999.
Haran, Menahem. *Temples and Temple Service in Ancient Israel.* Oxford: Clarendon, 1978.
Hayward, C. T. R. *The Jewish Temple: A Non-Biblical Sourcebook.* London: Routledge, 1996.
Newsom, Carol. *Songs of the Sabbath Sacrifice: A Critical Edition.* Atlanta: Scholars, 1985.
Parry, Donald W. "Garden of Eden: Prototype Sanctuary." In *Temples of the Ancient World: Ritual and Symbolism,* edited by Donald W. Parry, 126–51. Salt Lake City: Deseret, 1994.
Stordalen, Terje. *Echoes of Eden: Genesis 2–3 and Symbolism of the Eden Garden in Biblical Hebrew Literature.* Leuven: Peeters, 2000.
Sulzbach, Carla. "Of Temples on Earth, in Heaven, and in-Between." In *The Changing Face of Judaism, Christianity, and Other Greco-Roman Religions in Antiquity: Presented to James H. Charlesworth on the Occasion of his 65th Birthday,* edited by Ian H. Henderson and Gerbern S. Oegema, 166–85. Gütersloh: Gütersloher Verlagshaus, 2006.
Sweeney, Marvin. "Ezekiel: Zadokite Priest and Visionary Prophet of the Exile." In *Form and Intertextuality in Prophetic and Apocalyptic Literature,* 125–43. Tübingen: Mohr Siebeck, 2005.
Tvedtnes, John A. "Priestly Clothing in Bible Times." In *Temples of the Ancient World: Ritual and Symbolism,* edited by Donald Parry, 649–62. Salt Lake City: Deseret, 1994.
Vermes, Geza. *The Complete Dead Sea Scrolls in English.* New York: Penguin, 2004.
Wenham, Gordon. *The Book of Leviticus.* Grand Rapids: Eerdmans, 1979.
———. "Sanctuary Symbolism in the Garden of Eden Story." In *Proceedings of the Ninth World Congress of Jewish Studies, Division A: The Period of the Bible,* 19–25. Jerusalem: World Union of Jewish Studies, 1986.

---. "Why Does Sexual Intercourse Defile?" *Zeitschrift für die Alttestamentliche Wissenschaft* 95, no. 3 (1983) 432–34.

Wise, Michael. "4QFlorilegium and the Temple of Adam." *Revue de Qumran* 15 (1991) 103–32.

11

The Making and Meaning of the Colored Fabrics of the Temple

Margaret Barker

There was a huge curtain that separated the holy of holies from the main part of the temple. It was known as the veil of the temple, and it was a magnificent piece of woven fabric. The second-century CE geographer Pausanias described it as "a woolen curtain, adorned with Assyrian weaving and Phoenician purple, which was dedicated by Antiochus."[1] Because the temple veil was a tangible symbol of sacred Hebrew culture, it became the target of various parties interested in controlling the Hebrews. More than once it was taken as loot by invading armies. In 70 CE, after the Roman conquest of Jerusalem, Titus took that curtain to Rome and kept it in his palace, together with the scrolls of the Law.[2] Yet while foreign conquerors proudly displayed this ornate curtain, it was regarded with secrecy and a level of controversy by the Hebrews themselves. From early writers of the Bible, we know that there was a beautiful curtain in the desert tabernacle, "a veil of blue and purple and scarlet stuff and fine twined linen; in skilled work it shall be made, with cherubim" (Exod 26:31).[3] However, the veil symbolized something that the supporters of King Josiah's temple purges in 623 BCE did not like, and what they did not

---

1. Pausanias, *Description of Greece*, 4.
2. Josephus, *Jewish War* 7:162.
3. This is my own translation.

like, they did not mention. Even though Solomon's temple in Jerusalem was a larger version of the tabernacle, the supporters of the seventh-century BCE temple purges omitted the veil, the great golden throne, and the cherubim when they wrote about the holy of holies in the book of Kings.[4] The Chronicler, a later writer, did mention these items in the book of Chronicles, the Greek title of which—*paraleipomenōn*—literally means "The Things That Have Been Left Out." In it, the Chronicler writes, "He made a veil of blue and purple and crimson fabrics, and fine linen, and worked cherubim on it" (2 Chr 3:14).

The veil of the temple and the cherub throne represented something in the original temple that King Josiah tried to remove through purges, but he could not remove this symbol from the memory of his people. This is why we shall explore today not only how the great curtain was made, but what it meant.

First, the Curtain Symbolized the Fabric of Creation

In the book of Proverbs, there is a wonderful poem about weaving the creation, although you would probably not find the word "weave" in an English translation. The poem is about Wisdom, the heavenly Mother who was beside the Creator as he made heaven and earth (Prov 8:22–31). She was there, says the poem, *before* the Creator began to work, and she was weaving.

There is now a problem: how did Wisdom relate to the Creator? Many of the Hebrew words are not easy to translate, and so scholars have suggested changing some letters to give a better sense of the poem's message. The Old Greek translation of Proverbs says that Mother Wisdom was established as a firm foundation for the creation, and some English versions concur with this reading. But this involves changing one Hebrew letter in and also adding a letter to a difficult-to-translate word. The word actually means "I was weaving," *nāsakhtî*, and so the text says that before the earth was created, Wisdom was weaving. At the end of the poem, Wisdom says she was beside the Creator— and then there is another problematic word, *harmozousa*. The Old Greek translation of the word is "the woman who holds things firm" or "the woman who joins together:"

---

4. The RSV (UK) version of the Bible is used except where I indicate my own translation.

Wisdom was beside the Creator, weaving and holding all things together. The creation was woven by Wisdom.

This is very different from other creation stories in the ancient Near East, which depict the gods in violent conflict who overcame hostile forces or one hero god who killed the chaos monster. There is just a hint of Mother Wisdom weaving in the Genesis creation story, in fact, in the very first word. "In the beginning" is not the only way to read those Hebrew letters. Origen, the great Christian scholar who died in 253 CE, transliterated the word in his Hexapla as *"by means of the net, barēsēth*, God created heaven and earth." The creation was held in place by a great net, and Proverbs 8 shows that the weaver of the net was Mother Wisdom. This picture of creation is drawn from a woman's life: taking the fleece of sheep or the stalks of flax, preparing them, spinning them, dyeing them with colors taken from plants and small creatures, and then setting up her loom to weave a cloth. We find images drawn from this process all through the Bible and in other Hebrew and early Christian texts outside the Bible. They carry important teachings about the creation and the bonds between heaven and earth.

The tabernacle built by Moses and the temple built by Solomon both represented the entire creation—heaven and earth. The holy of holies was heaven, and the hall of the temple was the earth. The curtains that formed the tabernacle and the curtain that separated heaven and earth represented the matter of creation. They were made from four colors: white linen formed the vertical warp of the cloth, and the weft was red, blue, and purple wool. At least, we assume it was wool—the Hebrew text does not say what the colored threads were, but later writers said they were wool.

The multi-colored nature of the cloth is strange, because in Hebrew law it was forbidden to mix different fibers in one cloth. The rule was "You shall not wear a mixed [cloth], wool and linen together" (Deut 22:11; Lev 19:19). Perhaps cloth made this way was especially holy, and it was forbidden in ordinary uses precisely because it was only for temple use. The colored dyes for the wool were also forbidden because they were made from unclean creatures. The purple and the blue dyes came from sea snails, and the red dye came from a worm that lived in oak trees. Snails and worms were unclean for the Jews, and yet the dye for the temple fabrics was made from them. All these dyes were also very expensive to make, and so the temple curtains were very valuable.

There is much about temple fabrics that we do not understand. Nobody knows, for example, how the colors were woven together. Some people think that colored threads were woven closely together so that the cloth looked purple. We do know that each color represented one of the four elements: earth, air, fire, and water. The blue represented the air; the red represented the fire; and the purple represented the water because, they said, the purple dye came from a sea creature (a sea snail). The white linen had a double meaning: it represented the earth, because linen was made from flax which grew in the earth, but it was also used for the garments of angels in heaven. The vertical linen thread linked earth and heaven.

There is nothing in the Hebrew Bible about this color symbolism. In fact, there is nothing in the Hebrew Bible about the meaning of the temple and its furnishings—only the high priests had that knowledge. Weaving the various fabrics was described in great detail, but there is nothing to say why they had to be made in that way. The only two people who wrote about the color symbolism were Philo, a Jew in Egypt who lived at the same time as Jesus, and Josephus, a Jew in Palestine who lived about thirty years later. Both came from a high-priestly family, and both provided the same symbolisms for the colors in the temple curtain. Presumably they knew the secret teachings of the high priests, but they broke the rules and revealed the meaning of the colors.[5]

There are technical words in Hebrew that describe weaving, but nobody knows for certain what they mean. There is a short piece about making the veil in the *Mishnah*, which is an account of Jewish rules and customs in the time of Jesus. The curtain at this time was ten meters wide and was woven by eighty-two young women. This was far too big to be woven in one piece; the rest of the text seems to say that the curtain was woven in seventy-two long strips, and each strip had twenty-four linen warp threads.[6] Each strip was about fourteen centimeters wide [one handbreadth], and so they must have been sewn together to form the ten-meter-wide temple curtain.[7] This is the curtain that tore when Jesus died; there was an earthquake and the curtain tore from top to bottom (Matt 27:51), down one of these seams between two of these seventy-two strips.

Temple mystics saw the meaning of the veil in their visions. Rabbi Nehunyah, for example, lived near Jerusalem at the end of the first century

---

5. Philo, *Questions on Exodus*, 85; Josephus, *War*, 5:213.

6. Or this may mean that each linen warp thread was 24-ply, to give strength. b. B. Yoma 71b.

7. m. Shekalim 8:5.

CE, and in his visions, he stood before the throne of God in heaven, in the holy of holies. He saw the back of the great curtain and said that he saw the whole creation. An approximate translation of a difficult text containing Nehunyah's visions shows what he saw upon the curtain—the mysteries, the secrets, the bonds, and the wonders that took place in the weaving of the fabric that perfects the creation. He saw the interweaving upon it and the beauty of heaven and earth. He saw all distant parts of the earth and the inhabited world; he saw the distant parts of the firmament on high, and the bindings, the stitches, and the seams.[8] These elements of his visions stemmed from the strips of fabric, sewn together. His pupil Rabbi Ishmael saw the secret weaving of the creation with all its mysteries. In his vision, he saw the curtain where all history was drawn, and a great angel showed him the details.[9] Another Jewish mystic saw something very similar. He wrote: "Your hovering throne which fastens the peg[10] of the weaving of the fabric that makes perfect the Creation and its interweaving. . . . Standing upon it are many years and generations without end."[11] Again, this is an approximate translation.

How old was this belief about the curtain? All the evidence I have given so far is rather late in terms of the Jerusalem temple. The rabbis I have quoted all lived after the Jerusalem temple was destroyed by the Romans in 70 CE, but there is good reason to think that the temple curtain had always represented the creation and history. The book of Isaiah shows his well, and the earliest parts of the book were written long before the Mother Wisdom and her weaving were banished from the temple.

The prophet Isaiah had many disciples over many generations, but the master of the school lived before 700 BCE—about eight hundred years before the rabbis who saw creation as a woven cloth. Like them, Isaiah had a vision of standing by the throne in heaven. He saw the Lord's robe filling the hall of the temple, and he heard the heavenly seraphs proclaiming that the glory of the Lord filled the whole earth (Isa 6:1–3). Since the hall of the temple represented the earth, Isaiah saw the Lord's robe as his glory filling the earth. In other words, the glorious cloth of his robe was the creation.

---

8. Schäfer, *Synopse*, 201.
9. Charlesworth, *Old Testament Pseudepigrapha*, 296–99.
10. Some texts have "cord," a similar word.
11. Schäfer, *Synopse*, 98.

A disciple who lived about 150 years later reported that he had a similar experience, but what he saw was history on the curtain. The Lord, he said, had stretched out the heavens like a curtain. The prophet had stood beyond that curtain, at the beginning of all history. He had seen how princes and mighty men were carried away, and so he could proclaim with confidence the future of his own people (Isa 40:21–24).

The Psalms were the hymns of the temple, and they too describe creation as the Creator's robe of glory. Psalm 104 says that the Lord is clothed with light like a garment; he has stretched out the heavens like a tent curtain, and he has clothed the earth with the sea as its garment (Ps 104:1, 2, 6). The Lord made all these things with Wisdom (Ps 104:24), but there is no way of knowing from the Hebrew text whether this was wisdom (meaning knowledge) or Wisdom (meaning the Mother Wisdom). What is certain, though, is that the creation is described in the Hebrew Bible as a piece of woven cloth, and that Mother Wisdom was the weaver.

Second, Weaving Knowledge

The early Christians knew and wrote about the high priestly traditions of the temple. The book of Hebrews claimed that Jesus was the Great High Priest (Heb 4:14), and Ignatius, bishop of Antioch at the end of the first century CE, said that "to Jesus alone as our high priest were the secret things of God committed."[12] The imagery these Christian writers used suggests that they knew not only traditions of the high priests but also the meaning of temple weaving. Below, I present some lines from early Christian books—lines that are not found in the New Testament—that add to our understanding of what the temple curtain may have symbolized.

First, from the *Gospel of Philip*, the process of dyeing is the image for the transformation from an earthly to a heavenly state:[13] "God is a dyer. Just as good dyes, said to be genuine dyes, dissolve into what is dyed in them, so also those whom God dyes become immortal through his colors, for his dyes are immortal. And God baptizes those to be baptized in water" (*Gos. Phil.* 61). The fabric and the dye become one, but the fabric is a new color.

Then there is a parable about the work of Jesus restoring all material things to their heavenly state; he goes to the place where the temple fabrics

---

12. Ignatius, *Letter to the Philadelphians*, 91–97.
13. Meyer, *Nag Hammadi Scriptures*.

were made, and the reference seems to be to the seventy-two strips that formed the veil and represented the material world: "The master went into the dye works of Levi; he took seventy-two cloths and threw them into a vat. He drew them out and they were all white. He said: the Son of Man has come as a dyer" (*Gos. Phil.* 63).

The second excerpt comes from the *Teaching of Silvanus*, a work attributed to the friend of St. Paul and St. Peter who was a leader of the church in Jerusalem. He is mentioned several times in the New Testament, sometimes as Silas (e.g., Acts 15:22; 2 Cor 1:19; 1 Pet 5:12). The *Teaching of Silvanus* is a mainstream Christian text that was used by the first monks in Egypt, and it was written in the style of Wisdom teaching. Here are the extracts:

- My son, put on the holy teaching like a robe.
- Wisdom summons you in her goodness, saying, "Come to me, all of you, O foolish ones, that you may receive a gift, the understanding which is good and excellent. I am giving you a *high priestly garment that is woven from all wisdom.*"
- Clothe yourself with wisdom like a robe, put knowledge upon you like a crown, and be seated upon a throne of perception.
- My son, return to your divine nature.
- Return, my son, to your first Father, God, and Wisdom your Mother, from whom you came into being.

The imagery here is the glorious garment of the high priest. In Solomon's temple, the king was the high priest, and here we have Wisdom his Mother giving him a garment woven from all wisdom and inviting him to sit on the throne of perception. This was a memory of what actually happened when the king was crowned. It is not possible to reconstruct all the details of the ritual because the texts are so old, and it seems that some were deliberately damaged.

Psalm 110 is a good example of early Christians' understanding of the symbolisms associated with the curtain. The first Christians understood the psalm as a prophecy of Jesus, and it is quoted many times in the New Testament. The psalm describes how a man was transformed into the royal high priest Melchizedek. He was anointed, he was given a glorious garment, he was seated on the throne, and he was "born" as a divine being. These are the images that Silvanus used to describe Mother

Wisdom and her child: anointing gave the gift of understanding; the glorious garment was the robe of wisdom; the throne was the throne of perception; and the heavenly birth was a return to his divine nature. The words of Silvanus are an exact parallel to Psalm 110 but were written many centuries after the psalm, showing how the early Christians understood it.

The verse that describes the temple ritual, however, is almost unreadable in the Hebrew, but it does make sense if the vowels are changed and the words are read differently. The text itself is not changed. Verse three can be read as:

> Your Mother graciously offers to you
> the glorious garments on the day of your birth.
> From the Compassionate One I have begotten you
> with the dew as the Morning Star.[14]

Here we find the Mother Wisdom offering her son—newly anointed with the dew (or anointing oil) and newly born as a divine being—a glorious garment when he is seated on the throne.

Psalm 2 is similar to Psalm 110; it describes how the king was born when he was "put" on Zion, the holy mountain. But the word "put" is in fact the word "weave," and so the line is literally "I have woven his king on Zion his holy mountain" (Ps 2:6). Presumably this means that someone had given a woven garment to the Lord's king. The Hebrew is usually changed to give "I have set *my* king on Zion, *my* holy hill," but in fact the speaker is someone else who has set the Lord's king on Zion. "I have woven his king on Zion his holy mountain" (Ps 2:6).

When Jesus was born, St. Luke says that his Mother "wrapped him round"—gave him his garment—and then put him in a manger. Although St. Luke wrote in Greek, this story was first told in Hebrew, where the word for manger sounds almost the same as the old name for Jerusalem: manger was *"ēbûs,"* and Jerusalem was *"yᵉbûs."* The people who first told this story described Jesus as the son of the Mother Wisdom, wrapped in her garment and set in Jerusalem.

---

14. This is my translation.

Third, the Garment of Wisdom

The temple curtain, you remember, was woven to represent the creation. In his vision, Isaiah saw the Lord's train filling the hall of the temple, showing that his glory filled the earth. The high priest's garment, the ephod, was made from the same fabric as the veil, and it too represented the creation. Not long before the time of Jesus, a book written in Egypt called the Wisdom of Solomon said, "On Aaron's long robe was the whole creation" (Wis 18:24). There was, however, one difference between the fabric of the veil and the fabric of the high priest's ephod. The high priest's garment was interwoven with gold thread (Exod 28:5-6; 39:2-3). The Hebrew text only says that hammered gold was cut into threads to work into the fabric, but experts think the gold was probably rolled around a linen thread to give it strength. We shall look later at the meaning of these gold threads, and we will first look at the various Hebrew words used for weaving.

Sometimes it helps to look at the Old Greek translation, to see what words they chose for the technical terms. The curtain for the door of the tabernacle was made of *roqēm* fabric (Exod 26:36). This Hebrew word seems to mean "woven from several colors" or perhaps "embroidered with several colors." The Old Greek says it was made from many colors, but we do not know how. The same Greek word was also used in the New Testament in a very interesting context; it referred to hidden Wisdom that was revealed by Jesus. St. Paul wrote to the church at Ephesus that he was called to preach the unsearchable riches of Christ, "the plan of the mystery hidden by God who created all things, that through the Church the *many-colored* wisdom of God might now be made known to the principalities and powers in the heavenly places" (Eph 3:9-10, my translation).

The veil across the holy of holies and the high priest's ephod garment, however, was made from a different type of cloth called ḥōšēbh work. While the Old Greek says it was "woven cloth" (*huphanton*), which is not much help, the Hebrew word ḥōšēbh implies knowledge or skill, and so many translations say that the cloth for the veil and the ephod was "skilled work." It was certainly skilled work, but the word may imply more than that. It may mean that the work itself, or the *creation* of the fabric, symbolized the weaving together of knowledge and skill—or wisdom—and so the cloth represented the creation itself and was a weaving of Wisdom. The high priest's ephod was, as Silvanus said, a garment woven from all wisdom that signified the high priest's return to his divine nature as a child of Mother Wisdom.

The ḥōšēbh veil across the holy of holies was also woven "with cherubim" (Exod 26:31). Whenever the curtain is described, it is "ḥōšēbh work, cherubim;" there is no "with" in the Hebrew text. Cherubim are usually thought to be creatures like winged sphinxes, and there were two of them that formed the throne in the holy of holies of Solomon's temple. In Moses's tabernacle there were two smaller cherubim over the ark of the covenant (Exod 25:18-20). The interior walls of the temple were decorated with carved cherubim and palm trees (1 Kgs 6:23-29). The cherubim of the ḥōšēbh curtain are often imagined as golden sphinxes woven into the cloth, but nobody really knows what "ḥōšēbh work, cherubim" means.

Silvanus, you will recall, said that Wisdom seated her child on the throne of perception, so the cherubim that formed the throne must have represented an aspect of wisdom. Philo—and remember his family were high priests who had the secret knowledge—said that "cherub" meant "full knowledge and much understanding."[15] In another place, he said the word meant "full knowledge" and "a wealth of understanding poured out."[16] Now, there is no Hebrew word that obviously links "cherub" to knowledge, even though there have been ingenious suggestions. Philo must have known that the cherubim represented an aspect of wisdom, and so he thought of the cherubim throne in the same way as Silvanus: a throne of perception or knowledge.

The really interesting word that Philo used is "poured out," or kechumenē ("understanding poured out") because in Hebrew, "poured out" is the same word as "woven." Had Philo heard talk in Hebrew about cherubs and misunderstood the meaning of the Hebrew word? The cherub represented not "a wealth of understanding poured out," but *a wealth of understanding woven together.*

The prophet Ezekiel, who saw the Mother Wisdom and her chariot throne leaving the temple—he called her the Living One—wrote about a cherub, dressed in jeweled robes, who was the heavenly high priest (Ezek 28:12-19). Many of the words in this text are difficult to translate, but is seems that the cherub was anointed, clothed, and then set on the holy mountain, and he was full of wisdom and perfect in beauty (Ezek 28:14).

---

15. *Epignōsis kai epistēmē pollē*. Philo, *Life of Moses*, 2:97.

16. *Epignōsis pollē*, and *epistēmē plousia kai kechumenē*. Philo, *Questions on Exodus*, 62.

This is exactly what happened to the royal high priest, according to Psalm 2 and Psalm 110, when he was anointed and clothed with wisdom.

*****

What did the royal high priest wear? In the holy of holies, he wore white linen, the dress of an angel among the angels, but when he returned to the world, he passed through the great curtain of the temple that represented all physical matter and put on a garment made of the same fabric as the veil. Aaron the high priest, you recall, wore a robe that represented the whole creation (Wis 18:24).

Thus, the Christians understood the robe as a symbol of incarnation; the one who came from heaven was clothed in matter—that is, in a human body. The curtain tore when Jesus died; the writer of the Book of Hebrews described it *without any explanation*: "[We] enter the holy of holies] . . . by the new and living way which [Jesus] opened for us through the curtain, that is, through his flesh" (Heb 10:19–20). The first Christians also said that Mary had been a temple weaver. She was spinning wool to make a new curtain for the temple when Gabriel spoke to her, and so she was weaving the new veil of the temple as she was pregnant with her child.[17] The Hebrew idiom for the growth of an unborn child was "weaving," as we can see from the psalmist who wrote: "You wove me in my mother's womb" (Ps 139:13b, translating literally). Mary was weaving a new veil and a new creation, just as Mother Wisdom had been weaving in the beginning (Prov 8:23).

The Golden Garment

And now we come to the golden threads that were woven through the high priest's ephod. They represented heavenly wisdom woven though the fabric of creation, and the task of the high priest who wore the ephod was to weave the wisdom of heaven through the fabric of creation. He was Wisdom's messenger, her angel. The ephod was bound onto his shoulders (Exod 28:7, 12), and later texts show that it was a symbolic yoke, a sign that he was the Servant. Isaiah knew that the promised royal child would be called "Wonderful Counselor, Mighty God, Everlasting Father, Prince of Peace," and that the government would be *"upon his shoulder"* (Isa 9:6). In other words, he would wear the colored ephod of the royal high

---

17. See *The Infancy Gospel of James*, 10–11.

priest, interwoven with golden wisdom. The Old Greek translated his four names as just one title: "The Angel of Great Counsel."

Four hundred years after the royal high priests had left the temple, people still remembered the imagery of the golden robe and that it represented Wisdom's imparted knowledge. Jesus Ben Sira, who lived about 200 BCE, was a wisdom teacher in Jerusalem. He advised his students to seek Wisdom and wear her like a glorious robe:

> You will wear her like a glorious robe,
> and put her on like a crown of gladness. (Sir 6:31).

The Hebrew text of Ben Sira is a complicated piece of wordplay in the traditional style of Wisdom teaching, and the Hebrew text here is slightly different from the Greek that is used for English translations. You will not find this symbolism in an English Bible of Ben Sira 6:18–31. The Hebrew text shows that Ben Sira compared the golden robe to Wisdom's bonds—perhaps the bonds of her covenant and the fibers that, as described in Proverbs 8, allow Wisdom to hold all things together. Ben Sira told his student to hold out his shoulder and wear wisdom, that she would give birth to him in garments of gold and crown him with glory.[18] Wisdom's net would hold him secure. The ephod was also compared to the yoke of Wisdom's teaching. For Jewish teachers, the yoke represented a system of teaching; wearing a yoke meant that a pupil accepted that master's teaching. Jesus said that his yoke was easy (Matt 11:29–30) in comparison with the rules of the Law of Moses. For Ben Sira, the high priest's ephod symbolized the yoke of Wisdom.

Toward the end of his book, he included a poem about the great high priest Simon, whom he had seen coming out into the temple court, wearing the golden ephod:

> How glorious was he when the people gathered round him,
> As he came out of the house of the curtain.
> He was like the Morning Star among the clouds, like the moon when it is full.
> He was like the sun shining upon the temple of God Most High

---

18. Ben Sira plays with the sound of the word for "bond" and the word for "discipline." He says: "For discipline is like [Wisdom's] name." Here *mûsār*, discipline, is similar to *môsēr*, bond, and both sound like the name of Ashratah. (Sir 6:22). Ben Sira compares Wisdom to the heavy weight of the oracle stones. Ben Sira tells his student: "Hold out your shoulder and wear her ... she will give birth to you in garments of gold" (Sir 6:29). And finally, he declares: "she will dress you in garments of glory and she will crown you with a crown of beauty" (Sir 6:31, my translation).

> Like the rainbow shining in glorious clouds . . .
> When he put on his glorious robe
> And clothed himself with superb perfection
> And went up to the holy altar,
> He made the court of the temple glorious. (Sir 50:5–7, 11, my translation)

The Morning Star was a title for the king, the son of the Mother Wisdom; the shining rainbow was the colored ephod with its golden threads; the clouds around him were the priests in their white linen clothes. The high priest coming out of the temple into the world was the light of dawn from heaven.

About two hundred years after Ben Sira, in the time of Jesus, Philo said that gold represented the pure being of heaven[19] and that the golden ephod itself represented heaven.[20] He showed that all the imagery of the golden ephod was still known in the time of Jesus. Philo knew that the ephod was a garment woven from the same fabric as the temple curtain—red, blue, purple, and white—but it was also interwoven with gold. It represented the knowledge of creation interwoven with the light of heaven. This is a paraphrase of his complicated text: "The high priest is not a man but a divine Logos. . . . He is the child of parents incorruptible and wholly free from stain, his father being God, who is likewise Father of all, and his Mother Wisdom. Through her the universe came into existence. His head has been anointed with oil, which means that his mind has been illuminated with a brilliant light." This is the anointing which symbolized the gift of wisdom. Philo continued: "Thus he is thought worthy to put on the garments. Now the garments . . . that he puts on are the world, for he clothes Himself in earth and air and water and fire. . . . For the Logos is the bond of all existence, and holds and knits together all the parts, preventing them from being dissolved and separated."[21]

The weaving of the ephod represented the four elements of the creation enlightened with gold, the splendor of heaven, and the high priest wore this after he had been anointed and his way of thinking had been illuminated. His person and his teaching held the creation together.

Philo's description of enlightenment through the donning of a priestly fabric matches that of the early Christian Wisdom text by Silvanus

---

19. Philo, *Questions on Exodus*, 73.
20. Philo, *Moses*, 2:122.
21. Philo, *On Flight and Finding*, 108–12.

cited above in which Wisdom, the divine Mother, speaks to her child. "Return, my son, to your first Father, God, and Wisdom your mother, from whom you came into being...."[22]

Then the Mother clothes her child as her high priest: "Wisdom summons you in her goodness, saying, 'Come to me, all of you, O foolish ones, that you may receive a gift, the understanding which is good and excellent. I am giving you a high priestly garment, which is woven from every wisdom.... Do not become desirous of gold or silver, which are profitless, but clothe yourself with wisdom like a robe, put knowledge upon you like a crown, and be seated upon a throne of perception.... From now on, then, my son, return to your divine nature.'"[23] Mother Wisdom and her many-colored weaving have disappeared from the way that we read the Old Testament today, but images drawn from weaving are found in the older texts. The book of Job uses the language of fabric to describe the creation: "[God] stretches out the north ... and hangs the earth upon nothing" (Job 26:7). Job takes the textile imagery further in the phrase "God wraps up the waters in clouds and the clouds do not tear, he covers the moon and spreads a cloud over it" (Job 26:8–9). Isaiah described the foolish plans to make an alliance with Egypt as "Weaving a cloth that is not of my Spirit" (Isa 30:1, my translation). These are all images of a cloth: stretching out, wrapping, covering, tearing, and weaving.

Mother Wisdom had been honored in the first temple in Jerusalem, before King Josiah's temple purges, but he removed her and her weavers from the temple. He organized a great purge in his kingdom in 623 BCE, not unlike the Reformation in Europe. He removed all traces of pagan practices, but he also removed many of the older ways of the temple. He took from the temple everything connected with the Mother Wisdom: the great tree that represented her—the tree of life—and the house(s) of the holy ones in the temple area where the women wove linens for the Mother Wisdom.

Despite Josiah's removal of the temple curtain, there is archaeological evidence that weaving took place in other shrines before Josiah's reign, during the time of Solomon's temple.[24] Loom weights and weaving tools have been found there, as well as the remains of looms and small quantities of flax and other yarns—some linen, some red and blue wool.

22. Ibid., 91.
23. Ibid., 89, 90.
24. In this section, I draw on Ackerman, "Asherah," 19ff.

With the knowledge that a symbolically colored, woven fabric was placed in the early temples, we now know these artifacts may provide concrete proof that the temple's colored veil did exist.

Temple theology is gradually recovering the world of the original temple in Jerusalem. As the evidence accumulates, so it becomes easier to recognize other elements whose significance has until now been missed—words that seemed to make no sense, loom weights and colored yarns in shrines that could not be explained. We are, so to speak, weaving together the threads of a world that was almost lost, and restoring the many-colored Wisdom of the temple. But why? What is the purpose of all this, of assembling a conference such as this to examine the smallest details of the temple and its textiles?

I have focused on one element in the ancient temple: the colored threads and the gold in some of the fabrics. But every item, every detail, every measurement was significant. The measurements of the temple, for example, represented the precise proportions and harmonies of all creation and human society. In Ezekiel's vision of how the temple should be, the guiding angel showed him the temple's exact appearance, plan, and measurements. The prophet had to teach these to his people because the temple was in some way a reflection of their own condition: "Describe to the house of Israel the temple, that they may measure the pattern and be ashamed of their *iniquities*" (Ezek 43:10; emphasis added).

The complex wordplay used by the temple teachers may well have intended three meanings here. While its English translation implies "sins" or "wrongdoings," "iniquities" in Hebrew is the same word as "distortions," or things that are bent out of their natural state or crooked (We still talk about people being crooked, or crooks!). It is also very like the Hebrew word for "dwelling." The dwelling place that the people of Israel had built—that is, the temple—was distorted, and this was a sign of their iniquity. Their lives were wrong, and so was their temple's construction.

If you ask people what was revealed to Moses on Sinai, you will probably be told, "The ten commandments." Very few people realize that some fifteen chapters of the revelation on Sinai are details about how to build the place of worship. The temple was the template for all life and for all ways of understanding creation. Each element was a statement not only about being in the temple, but also about living in the world. The Lord should be at the center; the system was created that way. When Moses was told to build the tabernacle, the Lord said, "Let them make me a holy place that I may dwell in their midst" (Exod 25:8). The Greek translation here is slightly different: "You shall make for me a holy place and I shall be seen among you." *The temple in all its detail was the visible revelation and guide just as much as the Scriptures were.*

The psalmist wrote: "Open my eyes that I may see wondrous things out of thy Law" (Ps 119:18), a prayer to understand the written words. But Mother Wisdom also opened eyes; it was one of her gifts to her children. The Weaver gave spiritual sight, enabling them to see her weaving, all the wonders of form and pattern, and how everything joined together. *Every detail of the temple was a visual, not verbal, revelation of the divine and a guide to living.*

The linen exhibition we have here explores one aspect of this. The process of making linen was a parable about the trials and tribulations of everyday living. The exhibition shows how the rough fibers grown from the earth are prepared and spun, then woven, bleached, and polished by human skills. On another level, the process shows how the basic stuff of human life is transformed: it comes rough from the earth, it is washed and then whitened by the light of divine glory, and it is polished by the trials and sufferings of daily life into a shining garment. Thus, the rough stuff of life becomes the glorious garment of heaven.

We find these parables in every part of the temple. Today and tomorrow we shall explore in detail many aspects of the temple: sacred clothing and fabrics, sacred spaces, temple worship. Each is part of the greater whole, and although we shall, for very practical reasons, deal with several aspects separately, one at a time, we must then weave them all together, stand back and reflect, and try to contemplate the whole.

There are many curiosities about the words used in the Hebrew texts that describe the temple, its fabrics, and other furnishings. Since the temple teachers used wordplay as a way to emphasize their message, it is not inappropriate to speculate a little here about the two words: "angel or messenger" and "craft skill." The Lord communicated through his angel messengers, but it seems that the Lord also communicated through craftworkers. The words "angel" and "craft worker" or "craft skill" are related: "angel or messenger" is a masculine form, *mal'ākh*, and its feminine form is "craft skill," *mᵉlā'khâ*. This word "craft skill" is used for the work of God in creation and its results, and it is used for the work on the tabernacle and its furnishings—"to come to do *the work*" (Exod 36:2; emphasis added). In these examples, the English translation is simply "work," and so the significance is lost: "On the seventh day, God finished his work" (Gen 2:2). In fact, he finished his work as a craftsman.

Of most interest to us today is what the Lord said of Bezalel, the chief craftsman of the tabernacle: "Behold I have filled him with the Spirit of God, with wisdom and discernment, with knowledge and all craft skill" (Exod 31:3). We learn from the skills of the craft-workers just as we do from the words of the scribes, and over the next two days, we shall be learning something of the language of those ancient craft-workers. The ancient texts require patience and skill to translate, and this is also true of the work of the ancient craft workers.

They have been neglected for too long.

Bibliography

Ackerman, Susan. "Asherah, the West Semitic Goddess of Spinning and Weaving?" *Journal of Near Eastern Studies* 67, no. 1 (2008) 1–30.

The Babylonian Talmud, Mo'ed III. Translated by Isidore Epstein. London: Soncino, 1918.

Charlesworth, James H. "3 Enoch." In *Old Testament Pseudepigrapha*, vol. 1. London: Darton, Longman, & Todd, 1983.

Ignatius. "Epistle to the Philadelphians." Translated by Maxwell Staniforth. In *Early Christian Writings: The Apostolic Fathers*. Harmondsworth, UK: Penguin, 1968.

James, Montague R., ed. "The First Gospel of the Infancy of Jesus Christ." *The Apocryphal New Testament: A Collection of Apocryphal Christian Literature in an English Translation*. Oxford: Clarendon, 1980.

Josephus. *Jewish War*. Loeb Classical Library Series. Cambridge: Harvard University Press, 1997.

Meyer, Marvin, ed. *The Nag Hammadi Scriptures*. New York: HarperCollins, 2007.

The Mishnah. Translated by Herbert Danby. Oxford: Oxford University Press, 1989.

Pausanias. *Description of Greece*. Loeb Classical Library Series, vol. 5, book 12. Cambridge: Harvard University Press, 1935.

Philo. *Life of Moses*. Loeb Classical Library Series. Cambridge: Harvard University Press, 1935.

———. *On Flight and Finding*. Loeb Classical Library, Philo vol. 5. Cambridge: Harvard University Press, 1934.

———. *Questions on Exodus*. Loeb Classical Library, Philo Supplement 2. Cambridge: Harvard University Press, 1935.

Schäfer, Peter. *Synopse zur Hekhalot-Literatur*. Tübingen, Germany: Mohr, 1981.

12

The Veil of the Temple in Second Temple Judaism and Early Christianity

Daniel M. Gurtner

The Veil in Israelite Cultic Worship in the Hebrew Bible

The veil of the temple is the innermost barrier separating the holy place from the most holy place in the tabernacle and subsequent temple of the Hebrew Bible. In the earliest texts (Exod 26:31–37) it is said to be violet in color (or light purple) and made with "crimson thread," often thought to signify "royal attire"[1] associated with God's kingly presence within.[2] It was embroidered with images of cherubim (Exod 26:31), which not only "symbolized the presence of Yahweh"[3] but also infers a prohibitive function. Cherubim first appear in the Hebrew Bible (Gen 3:24) where they guarded "the way to the tree of life,"[4] and the veil's function was to

---

1. Much of the present research draws from and expands upon prior work from Gurtner, *Torn Veil*. Brenner, *Colour Terms in the Old Testament*, 146.

2. This is confirmed by the description of Yahweh's presence with Israel as being "enthroned between the cherubim" (1 Sam 4:4; 2 Sam 6:2; 2 Kgs 19:15; 1 Chr 13:6; Pss 80:1; 99:1; Isa 37:16), which when coupled with a reference to God's enthronement "in heaven" (Ps 2:4) may support the notion that the holy of holies was thought to be a replica of heaven. Translations throughout are the author's own unless noted otherwise.

3. DeVries, *1 Kings*, 94.

4. Cf. Hendel, "'Flame and the Whirling Sword,'" 671–74. This seems to set a

separate the holy place from the holy of holies (Exod 26:33).[5] This kind of structural separation (בדל, Exod 26:33) had a cultic function as well. The same language of "separation" is used throughout the priestly code (Lev 11:1–45) for the distinction between "unclean" and "clean" animals (Lev 11:1–47; cf. Lev 10:10; 20:25), as well as in Ezekiel's temple vision for the distinction between the sacred and profane (Ezek 40:1—42:20).[6] Such separation between the holy and unholy, clean and unclean, sacred and profane is appropriate for the cultic contexts in which the veil appears, for within the holy of holies is "where God himself is present."[7] That is, the primary function of the veil was to restrict physical access[8] to the throne of God and thus his very presence,[9] a privilege granted only to consecrated priests on the Day of Atonement (Lev 16:11–28). On this occasion the high priest takes the offering behind the veil as a "sin" or "purification" offering (Lev 16:11) to sprinkle blood on the atonement slate of the ark (Lev 16:14). This rite "laid the foundation for God to forgive the people all sins committed since the previous Day of Atonement."[10]

Veil of the Temple in Second Temple Judaism

When Jerusalem fell to the Babylonians in 587 BCE, the temple was destroyed but soon rebuilt by those returning from exile beginning in 538 BCE. This structure is known as the temple of Zerubbabel, governor of the period, and it was completed in 515 BCE. Lacking the Solomonic temple's rich adornment (cf. Hag 2:1–9), Zerubbabel's temple was apparently damaged several times over the years and was ultimately rebuilt

---

precedent for how they are to be understood in the tabernacle and in subsequent temple depictions on the veil and carved on walls around the Solomonic (1 Kgs 6:29, 32, 35; 7:29, 36; 2 Chr 3:7) and Ezekiel's visionary temples (cf. Ezek 9:3; 10:2–8, 11, 14–20; 11:22; 41:18, 20, 25). This underscores the role of the veil as in some sense guardians of the holy of holies.

    5. Structurally, it also helped to form a holy of holies that was a perfect cube of 10 cubits per side.

    6. Zimmerli, *Ezekiel, Chapters 25–48*, 404.

    7. Zimmerli, *Ezekiel, Chapters 25–48*, 404–5; cf. Allen, *Ezekiel*, 2.235.

    8. This restriction is not merely a physical barrier but also a visual one cf. the "shielding veil" (Exod. 35:12a; cf. 39:20b [MT=34b]; cf. Num 4:5).

    9. Milgrom and Gane, "פרכת," 755–56.

    10. Hartley, "Atonement, Day of," 55. Averbeck ("Sacrifices and Offerings," 710) shows that the basic meaning of כפר, as seen by its Akkadian cognate *kuppuru* ("to wipe clean") means "to purge" particularly with reference to the tabernacle and altar.

by Herod the Great. Herod's work on the temple began between 23 and 19 BCE[11] and was completed, with the exception of detailed additions and adornments, within ten years.[12] Additions were continually added to the structure right up to the outbreak of the Jewish revolt in 66 CE. It was largely patterned after Solomon's temple and likewise had a veil. Yet traditions in Second Temple Judaism pertaining to temple veil are not as prevalent as one might expect and vary from reflections upon the Solomonic temple, to idealizations in a heavenly sanctuary, to physical descriptions of the Herodian veil and legends about what happened to it upon the destruction of the Herodian temple by the Romans in 70 CE.

The Wisdom of Ben Sira (Sir 50:5) mentions a priest coming out of the temple with a phrase which in the Hebrew (מִבֵּית לַפָּרֹכֶת) could be understood "from behind the veil" or, as the Greek takes it, "from the house of the veil" (οἴκου καταπετάσματος). The Greek text seems to use the "house of the veil" as a circumlocution for the temple building (ναός), suggesting not only that the temple is to be identified with respect to its veil, but also an explicit indication that the veil stood for something beyond itself, in this case the temple.[13] In 1 Maccabees the veil is among the objects of worship that Antiochus IV Epiphanes plundered from the Jerusalem shrine in his attempt at "erasing the telltale signs of their Jewish heritage" (1:22; RSV)[14] Later in 1 Maccabees (4:51), it is among the curtains rehung in the reconstituted Jerusalem temple.

The *Letter of Aristeas* purports to give an eyewitness account of an ambassadorial visit to Jerusalem in which the author visits the temple and describes its veil billowing and flowing in the passing breeze which made "a pleasant and unforgettable spectacle" (*Let. Aris.* 86).[15] A strange occurrence of the veil is found in *Joseph and Aseneth*, which purports to narrative events surrounding the biblical Joseph and his marriage to the Egyptian Aseneth (Gen 41:45). Here Aseneth's conversion to Judaism is depicted as the removal of a veil (καταπέτασμα) from before a window (*Jos. Asen.* 10:2). In this respect the author uses a recognizable cultic

---

11. In either the eighteenth (19/20 BCE; Josephus, *Ant.* 15.11.1 §380) or the fifteenth (23/22 BCE; *J.W.* 1.22.1 §401) year of his reign. Sanders (*Judaism: Practice and Belief 63 BCE–66 CE*, 57).

12. Wise, "Temple," 812.

13. See Gurtner, "'House of the Veil' in Sirach 50," 187–200.

14. deSilva, *Introducing the Apocrypha*, 244.

15. Shutt, "Letter of Aristeas," 18.

image for its prohibitive function whereby its removal is an indication of religious conversion.[16]

Lives of the Prophets contains (12:10–13) describes the curtain of the sanctuary (*Dabeir*) torn into small pieces which "will be carried away by angels into the wilderness."[17] *Second Baruch*, written after the destruction of Jerusalem in 70 CE, identifies the veil among the cultic items taken from temple by angels prior to the destruction (*2 Bar.* 6:7–10; 8:2).[18]

Several depictions of the veil are found among the documents from Qumran.[19] The fragmentary accounts in the Temple Scroll (11Q19) say the veil is made of gold (col 7 line 13; Exod 26:31), like other cultic vessels it describes,[20] and may depict an idealized temple to be built in Jerusalem in the future. In the *Songs of the Sabbath Sacrifice* the reader led through the heavenly sanctuary where the veil is seen with a luminous and fiery appearance (4Q405 f15ii–16:3).[21] In its lavish embroidery,[22] this heavenly counterpart to the earthly veil[23] bears animated figures of cherubim, participating in heavenly worship in song to God.[24]

16. Bohak, "*Joseph and Aseneth*" and the Jewish Temple in Heliopolis, 70–71.

17. All this is a portent of the coming of the Lord (*Liv. Prop.* 5:1–2). Though it may well be a Christian interpolation into an earlier Jewish document, it is among the earliest associations of its destruction with that of the temple (Charlesworth, *Old Testament Pseudepigrapha*, 2.393–94). Hare notes that ἅπλωμα is an unusual term for a curtain, but is found in *T. Benj.* 9:4 (Charlesworth, *Old Testament Pseudepigrapha*, 2.393 n. f). "Curtain" here (ἅπλωμα) is recognized as something which is unfolded, or an expanse (LSJ).

18. Charlesworth, *Old Testament Pseudepigrapha*, 1.623. In this setting the protection of the temple is lifted (*2 Bar.* 8:2; cf. *4 Bar.* 4:1; *J.W.* 6.5.3 §300; Tacitus, *Hist.* 5:13). Brown, *Death of the Messiah*, 2:1110.

19. Gurtner, "Biblical Veil in the Dead Sea Scrolls," 57–79.

20. 11Q19 3:8, 9, 12; 11Q19 31:8–9; 32:10; 37:11; 39:3; 41:16–17.

21. The text suggests the veil has two sides (4Q405 f15ii–16:5). DJD XI, 335. It is unclear whether this description is of the veil itself or of its inscriptions, which have "a luminous and fiery appearance." DJD XI, 336. "glorious from their two sides [. . .] curtains of the wondrous inner chambers and they bless [the God of all . . .]. Underlines represent Davila's reconstruction based on 11Q17 v. Davila, *Liturgical Works*, 140.

22. Baumgarten, "Qumran Sabbath Shirot and Rabbinic Merkabah Traditions," 202.

23. Davila, *Liturgical Works*, 140.

24. Davila, *Liturgical Works*, 139. A fragmentary reference to the veil is found in the Damascus Document (4Q266 5 ii 4–5; cf. lines 8, 10, 12) which may simply mean no more than the physical location of the priest with respect to the inner veil and discusses regulations appropriate for it. The final reference to the veil found at Qumran, apart from biblical texts identical to those discussed in chapters 2 and 3, is in the

Philo of Alexandria describes the veil as being made of the same material dyed "dark red and purple and scarlet and bright white" (*Moses* 2.87), though his figurative meaning behind this is debated.[25] More helpful is Josephus, who provides detailed description of the veil in the Herodian temple (*Jewish War* (*J.W.*) 5.5.4 §212; 5.5.5 §219; cf. *J.W.* 5.5.7 §232) which was among the items delivered into Roman hands (cf. *J.W.* 6.8.3 §389) and taken to Rome as plunder (*J.W.* 7.5.7 §162). Josephus is very descriptive and specific. He says the veil was made:

> of Babylonian tapestry, with embroidery of blue and fine linen, of scarlet also and purple, wrought with marvelous skill. Nor was this mixture of materials without its mystic meaning: it typified the universe. For the scarlet seemed emblematic of fire, the fine linen of the earth, the blue of the air, and the purple of the sea; the comparison in two cases being suggested by their colour, and in that of the fine linen and purple by their origin, as the one is produced by the earth and the other by the sea. On this tapestry was portrayed a panorama of the heavens, the signs of the Zodiac excepted. (*J.W.* 5.5.4 §§212–14)

The Babylonian tapestry and the scarlet purple and skill clearly depict royalty[26] and rich in meaning. It is thought to depict the heavenly firmament (Gen 1:6),[27] the separation between heaven and earth.[28] The colors depicted the elements of the universe, and describing it as portraying the "panorama of the heavens"[29] also suggests the firmament imagery, even

---

so–called *Apocryphon of Moses*. The language of 4Q375 1 ii 7 (Apocryphon of Moses Ba) is nearly identical to that of Lev 16:2, and the blood of the offering is likewise sprinkled "before the veil" (לפני פרכת) "And Aa[ron shall sprinkle with some of the blood] 7 before the veil of [the sanctuary and shall approach] the ark of the testimony." Again we encounter the same problem of whether the blood was sprinkled "against" or "before" the veil and the role of the veil in this rite is unclear.

25. Some have argued that these colors represent a "philosophical modification" of the older Hellenistic-Jewish interpretation of the curtain before the holy of holies (Hofius, *Der Vorhang vor dem Thron Gottes*, 24; *QE* 2.91 [to Exod 26:31]; 2.94 [to Exod 26:33b]; *Moses* 2.74ff). In this sense the inner veil is an allegorical projection from the Pentateuch of a cosmic symbol of the four elements (Pelletier, "La tradition synoptique," 161–66).

26. Such Babylonian tapestry likewise served as the coverlet for Cyrus' golden sarcophagus when it was visited by Alexander the Great (Arrian, *Anabasis of Alexander* 6.29.5).

27. Pelletier, "La tradition synoptique," 171.

28. Hofius, *Vorhang*, 23.

29. ὁ πέπλος ἄπασαν τὴν οὐράνιον θεωρίαν.

a visual depiction of the heavens.[30] Josephus' other depictions of the veil will be considered in relation to some early Christian traditions below.

The Veil in Early Christianity

The veil of the temple is scarcely mentioned in the earliest Christian writings found in the New Testament. One is found in all three Synoptic Gospels, where it is said that at Jesus' death "the curtain of the temple is torn in two from top to bottom" (Matt 27:51a; cf. Mark 15:38; Luke 23:45). This suggests at least in part that the prohibitive function of the veil is removed by God himself and caused by the death of Jesus. No other mention of the temple or the significance of this event is described in this context. In the book of Hebrews, the veil tradition discussed at three locations in Hebrews. Here, the believer's hope lies "behind the veil" (6:19) in the holy of holies, where Christ offered himself as a sacrifice (9:3) and has opened for believers a "new and living" way to God through the veil, which, the author says, is Christ's body (10:20). Discussion of the veil in subsequent early Christian literature is almost exclusively focused on these two accounts, with primary attention given to its rending for several reasons.

Writers from early Christianity depict a wide variety of interpretations of the torn veil, such as a declaration of the divinity of Christ[31] or the historical reality of his crucifixion.[32] According to Ephraem the Syrian, the veil was among the innocent sufferers for the sins of humanity.[33] Cyril of Alexandria declares that the rending of the veil marks the advent of the "great day of the Lord" (Joel 2:30–31).[34] Eusebius represents the rending of the veil as the stripping away of the old covenant.[35] Melito of Sardis sees the rending of the veil as a sign of mourning analogues to rending of garments.[36] Origen himself offers a myriad of allegorical interpretations

---

30. Josephus, *Ant.* 2.9.5 §226; 8.5.2 §138; 12.2.9 §66; 12.2.12 §99; 16.5.1 §140; 19.1.12 §81; 19.1.13 §89; *J.W.* 5.5.2 §191.

31. E.g., Origen, *Cels.* 2.33; *Comm. Jo.* 19, 16; §103; John Chrysostom, *Oratio de hypapante* 66.1; *Scand.*, 20.9.1; *Exp. Ps.*, 55.210.44; *Precatio* 64.1065.26.

32. E.g., Eusebius, *Hist. ecc.* 3.8.1–9; *Dem ev.* 19.

33. *Sermo asceticus*, 125.8.

34. *Comm. Minor Proph.*, 1.341.22.

35. *Dem. ev.*, 8.2.119.8.

36. *Pasch.* 98.

largely centered on removing the "veil" of unbelief.[37] This notion of the removal of the temple veil as a depiction of religious conversion we have seen before (*Jos. Asen* 10.2). It is similar to the use of other veil language found in Paul (2 Cor 3:13–16) which, while using language of a face covering (κάλυμμα) rather than a cultic article, is similarly used for its prohibitive function and its removal a connotation of religious conversion.

Christian writers from the second century on have seen the rending of the veil as a symbol of temple destruction. Some see it as a means of vindicating, or fulfilling, Jesus' prediction (Matt 23:38) while others understood it as God's removal of angelic protection of Israel.[38] Others have regarded it as evidence that God himself (or the Holy Spirit) has departed from the temple in judgment against its rejection of Jesus as the Christ.[39] This seems to be the way it was understood by Tertullian (ca. 160–ca. 220)[40] and later by Jerome (ca. 380–409 CE),[41] the latter of whom goes on to say (depending on Josephus) that there was a voice announcing departure spoken at the time of Christ's crucifixion (*Ep.* 46). Others interpret the torn veil as a sign that the temple was handed over to the Gentiles.[42] Yet it is perhaps helpful to note that Jewish authors—notably Josephus and the writer of *2 Baruch*—likewise understand the destruction of the temple as a sign of God's judgment upon Israel, though for very different reasons.

Legends of the Veil

A number of fascinating legends regarding this veil have passed through Jewish, Christian, and other traditions. Josephus (*B.J.* 6.5.3 §§288–309) lists *wonders* that occurred within the temple prior to its destruction. Among them he says the enormous brass eastern gate of the inner court, which could hardly be moved by twenty men, was seen opening by itself at midnight; the priests in the inner court hearing a collective voice at Pentecost, "We are departing from here" (i.e., the sanctuary). Tacitus

37. *Comm. In Matt.* 27:50–54; *Fr. Luke* 151, 251.

38. Tertullian, *Marc.* 4:42; Hilary, *Comm. Matt.* 33:7; *Tract. In Psalm.* 57:10; Melito of Sardis, *Pasch.* 98.

39. Tertullian, *Adv. Jud.* 13.15; *Const. ap.*, 6.5.26; Clement of Alexandria, *Paed.* 3.2.

40. *Adv. Iudaeus* 13.15.

41. *Ep.* 46; cf. *Ep.* 18a; *Comm. Matt* 4. Jerome says that the temple lintels were broken at Jesus' death, and the veil was thereby rent.

42. Pseudo-Macarius, *Hom. spirit*, 50.4.331.

concurs that there were bad omens prior to the fall of the temple, including armies fighting in heaven, opening of the doors to the holy place, the voice of the gods as they depart, and a lighting of the temple (*Hist.* 5.13).[43] Some rabbis (*y. Yoma* 6.43c; *b. Yoma* 39b) say that forty years before the temple was destroyed, the doors that were closed in the evening were found open in the morning, an event which was interpreted by the rabbis as predicting its ultimate destruction.[44] These are among a host of examples from antiquity where deities give extraordinary signs typically at the death of noble figures.[45]

Another tradition recounts an episode involving the Roman general Titus at the time of his utter defeat of the Jews. One text (*b. Giṭ*⊠*t* 56b) claims that upon his victory Titus said, "Where is their God, the rock in whom they trusted [Deut 32.37]?" Then "the wicked Titus who blasphemed and insulted Heaven" committed two atrocities in the temple: First, he "took a harlot by the hand and entered the holy of holies and spread out a scroll of the Law and committed a sin on it." After this, he "took a sword and slashed the curtain. Miraculously blood spurted out, and he thought that he had slain himself."[46] Traditions perhaps related to this account say that following their victory over Jerusalem and plundering its temple, the veil ended up in Rome.[47] R. Eleazar son of R. Jose, who

---

43. Brown, *Death of the Messiah*, 2:1114.

44. Cf. *Sifre* Deut. 328. For more references to the destruction of the temple in Judaism, cf. Evans, "Prediction of the Destruction," 89-147.

45. There was allegedly a lunar eclipse on the night when Herod the Great put Matthaias to death (Josephus, *Ant.* 17.6.4; §167) and a voice from heaven declared the heavenly destiny of a Jewish martyr (cf. *b. Ber.* 61b; *b. 'Abod.* 18a; Brown, *Death of the Messiah*, 2:1113). Similarly, in Greco-Roman thought, there were eclipses at the deaths of Romulus and of Julius Caesar (cf. Virgil, *Georgics* 1.472-90, esp. 466-88).

46. Some understand this as a euphemism for slaying God (Epstein, *Babylonian Talmud*, 259, n. 5). The rabbis then cite Ps 74:4 as a prediction of the mockery displayed by Titus, and then Ps 89:9, praising Yahweh for his forbearance in not striking that "wicked man" dead. The text goes on: "Titus further took the curtain and shaped it like a basket and brought all the vessels of the sanctuary and put them in it, and then put them on board ship to go and triumph with them in his city." Josephus seems to presume the cultic articles were taken intact by the Romans (*B.J.* 6.8.3 §389-91) and displayed in the "Temple of Peace" (*B.J.* 7.5.7 §158-62). Evans, "Predictions of the Destruction," 99.

47. Cf. Légasse ("Les voiles du temple de Jérusalem," 587), who presumes Rome is the origin of the synoptic veil tradition. Cf. also Brandon, "Date of the Markan Gospel," 126-41.

may date to the generation after Bar Kokhba,[48] was said to have seen it in Rome "and there were on it several drops of blood."[49]

Some rabbis understood the blood sprinkled toward the veil on the Day of Atonement (Lev 4:6) would sometimes touch the veil and render it unclean (*b. Yoma* 57a; cf. *m. Yoma* 5.4).[50] This occasioned the need for *cleansing the veil* by a ceremonial immersion either within the temple courts or outside, depending on the degree of uncleanness (*m. Šeqal.* 8.4; cf. *b. Ḥul.* 90b). This required three hundred priests, who descended into the ritual bath to dip the veil (*Exod. Rab.* 50.4 [on Exod 36:35]). After this they would spread it out to dry within the temple complex itself (*m. Mid.* 1.5; *b. Sanh.* 88b) or outside, depending on the degree of uncleanness. Sometimes it would be spread out on the roof of the portico (see *m. Pes.* 1.5; *m. Sukkah* 4.4) "that the people may see how fine is the craftsmanship thereof" (*m. Šeqal.* 85).[51]

The veil said to be the preeminent of the temple hangings (*m. Šeqal.* 5.1, 2; *y. Šeqal.* 5, 49a, 28) both in terms of its *craftsmanship and cost*. It was reportedly "one handbreadth in thickness" (*Exod. Rab.* 50.4 [on Exod 36:35]; *m. Šeqal.* 8.4–5; *Num. Rab.* 4.13 [on Num 4:5]) and "was woven in seventy-two threads" (*Exod. Rab.* 50.4 [on Exod 36:35])[52] with "no knots in the thread" (*Exod. Rab.* 50.4 [on Exod 36:35]). It was said to have been made "by eighty-two young girls"[53] who took their wages from a fund for temple reparations (*y. Šeqal.* 4, 48a, 22).[54] Some Christian accounts suggest the veil was woven by Mary as a child (*Prot. Jas.* 10:2) who, "when a needle accidentally pricked her finger," was "given a foretaste of the pain

---

48. Strack and Stemberger, *Introduction to the Talmud and Midrash*, 22.

49. *b. Me'il* 17b; *b. Yoma* 57a; *Exod. Rab.* 50.4 [on Exod 36:35]

50. "When he sprinkled, the drops were not to reach the curtain, but if they did, they just did" (*b. Yoma* 57a; cf. *m. Yoma* 5.4)

51. Ginzberg (*Legends of the Jews*, 3:159, n. 335) claims, "During the festivals of the pilgrimage the priests used to raise the curtain from the Holy of Holies to show the pilgrims how much their God loved them as they could see in the embrace of the two Cherubim." Yet the texts he cites to support this notion (cf. *b. B. Batra* 99a; *b. Yoma* 54a, b. *Tg. Onk.* Exod 25:20; *Tg. Jer.* Exod 25:20; Josephus, *Ant.* 3.6.4) say nothing of such a tradition.

52. Or "was woven on [a loom having] seventy-two rods, and over each rod were twenty-four threads" (*m. Šeqal.* 8.5).

53. Textual variations read "at a cost of 82 myriad (*denars*)" (cf. *b. Ḥul.* 90b; cf. *m. Shek* 8.5; *b. Tamid* 29a, b).

54. So Rab Huna (d. 297). A conflicting account (*t. Šeqal.* 2.6) says their salary was taken from the "heave-offerings of the [*sheqel-*]chamber."

she would feel at the crucifixion."[55] Presumably the veil eventually work out and two new ones were made each year (*Exod. Rab.* 50.4 [on Exod 36:35]) and two were always available at any given time (*t. Šeqal.* 3.15) one was spread out and used while the other was folded up. The folded one was brought out either on the eve of the Day of Atonement or if the first should somehow become unclean.

Conclusion

The veil has a rich history in the literary contexts of Judaism and Christianity. In Judaism the initial concern is explicitly its preservation of the sanctity of the sanctuary and Israel's God. It is mentioned among the identifiable cultic objects defiled both during the era of the Hasmoneans and the Romans. Even though the temple was long destroyed, rabbis preserved and developed traditions pertaining to its sanctity and care. Also without a temple are the sectarians from Qumran, who project the veil into their conception of angelic worship within the heavenly sanctuary. In Christianity the prohibitive function of the veil is severed precisely because of the sacrificial death of Christ. In Hebrews the veil is Jesus' body through which the Christian passes to the presence of God. Yet it is intriguing that the early Christian sources give no indication that the God of Judaism is in any manner less holy than before, but that in Christ believers are granted a distinct access to the very Presence in a decidedly unprecedented way.

---

55. Clarke, *Gospel of Matthew and Its Readers*, 238. The text further reads, "And the priest said: Choose for me by lot who shall spin the gold, and the white, and the fine linen, and the silk, and the blue, and the scarlet, and the true purple. And the true purple and the scarlet fell to the lot of Mary, and she took them, and went away to her house."

Bibliography

Allen, L. C. *Ezekiel*. 2 vols. Word Biblical Commentary 29. Dallas: Word, 1990.
Averbeck, Richard E. "Sacrifices and Offerings." In *Dictionary of the Old Testament: Pentateuch*, edited by T. Desmond Alexander and David W. Baker, 706–33. Downers Grove, IL: InterVarsity, 2003.
Baumgarten, J. M. "The Qumran Sabbath Shirot and Rabbinic Merkabah Traditions." *Revue de Qumran* 13 (1988) 199–213.
Bohak, Gideon. *"Joseph and Aseneth" and the Jewish Temple in Heliopolis*. Early Judaism and Its Literature 10. Atlanta: Scholars, 1996.
Brandon, S. G. F. "The Date of the Markan Gospel." *New Testament Studies* 7 (1961) 126–41.
Brenner, A. *Colour Terms in the Old Testament*. Journal for the Study of the Old Testament Suppliment 21. Sheffield, UK: JSOT, 1982.
Brown, R. *The Death of the Messiah: A Commentary on the Passion Narratives in the Four Gospels*. 2 vols. New York: Doubleday, 1994.
Charlesworth, J. H., ed. *Old Testament Pseudepigrapha*. 2 vols. New York: DLT, 1983.
Clarke, Howard. *The Gospel of Matthew and Its Readers: A Historical Introduction to the First Gospel*. Bloomington, IN: Indiana University Press, 2003.
Davila, James R. *Liturgical Works*. Eerdmans Commentaries on the Dead Sea Scrolls 6. Grand Rapids: Eerdmans, 2000.
deSilva, David A. *Introducing the Apocrypha: Message, Context, and Significance*. Grand Rapids: Baker, 2002.
DeVries, S. J. *1 Kings*. Word Biblical Commentary 12. Waco, TX: Word, 1985.
Epstein, I., trans. *The Babylonian Talmud*. 18 vols. London: Soncino, 1936.
Evans, Craig A. "Prediction of the Destruction of the Herodian Temple in the Pseudepigrapha, Qumran Scrolls, and Related Texts." *Journal for the Study of the Pseudepigrapha* 10 (1992) 89–147.
Ginzberg, L. *The Legends of the Jews*. 7 vols. Translated by H. Szold and P. Radin. Philadelphia: Jewish Publication Society of America, 1936–47.
Gurtner, Daniel M. "The Biblical Veil in the Dead Sea Scrolls." *Qumran Chronicle* 14, no. 1–2 (2006) 57–79.
———. "The 'House of the Veil' in Sirach 50." *Journal for the Study of the Pseudepigrapha* 14.3 (2005) 187–200.
———. *The Torn Veil: Matthew's Exposition of the Death of Jesus*. Society for New Testament Studies Monograph Series 139. Cambridge: Cambridge University Press, 2007.
Hartley, J. "Atonement, Day of." In *Dictionary of the Old Testament: Pentateuch*, edited by T. Desmond Alexander and David W. Baker, 55–57. Downers Grove, IL: InterVarsity, 2003.
Hendel, R. S. "'The Flame and the Whirling Sword': A Note on Genesis 3:24." *Journal of Biblical Literature* 104 (1985) 671–74.
Hofius, O. *Der Vorhang vor dem Thron Gottes: Eine exegetisch-religionsgeschichtliche Untersuchung zu Hebräer 6,19f. und 10, 19f.* Wissenschaftliche Untersuchungen zum Neuen Testament 14. Tübingen: Mohr Siebeck, 1972.
Légasse, S. "Les voiles du temple de Jérusalem: Essai de parcours historique." *Revue Biblique* 87 (1980) 560–89.

Milgrom, J., and R. Gane. "פרכת." In *Theologisches Wörterbuch zum Alten Testament*, edited by G. Johannes Botterweck, Helmer Ringgren, and Heinz-Josef Fabry, 4:755–56. Stuttgart: Kohlhammer, 1984.

Pelletier, A. "La tradition synoptique du 'Voile déchiré' à la lumière des réalités archéologiques." *Recherches de science religieuse* 46 (1958) 161–80.

Sanders, E. P. *Judaism: Practice and Belief 63 BCE–66 CE*. London: SCM, 1992.

Schlatter, Adolf. *Der Evangelist Matthäus: Seine Sprache, sein Ziel, seine Selbständigkeit*. Stuttgart: Calwer Verlag, 1957.

Shutt, R. J. H. "Letter of Aristeas." In *The Old Testament Pseudepigrapha*, edited by J. H. Charlesworth, 2:7–34. 2 vols. New York: Doubleday, 1983, 1985.

Strack, H. L., and G. Stemberger. *Introduction to the Talmud and Midrash*. Translated by and edited by M. Bockmuehl. Minneapolis: Fortress, 1991.

Wise, M. O. "Temple." In *Dictionary of Jesus and the Gospels*, edited by Joel B. Green, Scot McKnight, and I. Howard Marshall, 811–17. Downers Grove, IL: InterVarsity, 1992.

Zimmerli, W. *A Commentary on the Book of the Prophet Ezekiel, Chapters 25–48*. Translated by J. D. Martin. Philadelphia: Fortress, 1983.

Conversations

13

Muslim, Jewish, and Catholic Perspectives on Sacred Spaces and Sacred Clothing

An Interfaith Panel Discussion

Reuven Firestone, Amir Hussain, and Pim Valkenberg

Sacred Space

Pim Valkenberg, The Catholic University of America

I'll approach this topic from the point of view of a Christian and more specifically, a Roman Catholic. One of the first things to be noted is that there have been discussions about religious buildings, what they should look like, and how they should be oriented. In the Christian tradition, it's an old custom to orient churches towards the east, and that's exactly where the word *orientation* came from. In the Jewish tradition and the Islamic tradition they have similar customs. However, many modern Christian churches no longer follow this practice but originally churches were always oriented towards the east. The reason for that is that Christians used to pray towards the east because they expected Jesus to come back from the east. That is a very old custom that is still preserved in this idea of orientation.

The second thing I would like to mention is that the places of worship where we come together as Christians is a sanctuary, a holy place, or a tabernacle, which, of course, for the Church of Jesus Christ of Latter-day Saints is a famous and well-known word. For Catholics, this is the sacred place where we preserve the body of Christ because we believe that in the Roman Catholic Eucharist the priest consecrates bread and wine to become the body and the blood of Christ. We believe that Christ is not only a memory, but Christ—who died for our sins and for our salvation—is present in the community of Christ so you can say that the term "the body of Christ" has a double meaning: the Catholic community is in a sense the body of Christ, but in a very tangible sense we believe the body of Christ is given to the community in the Eucharist. Our sanctuaries or holy places house the body of Christ in both senses.

Another point to keep in mind concerns the different and similar ways of thinking among religions regarding the borders between the sacred and the profane. What is secular and what is holy? "Sacred" means that this is a place where the usual rules do not apply; you cannot just go there because something special is happening there. I think Christianity derived this principle from the temple worship in Judaism, where you also have a holy space, a kind of a secondary space, and then a secular space. Likewise, in the Christian church buildings, you have the *apse* with the altar (which is the holiest place), and then you have the *nave* or center of the building where the faithful are and then in older Christianity you used to have the *narthex*, the place at the entrance to the church where the catechumens were, the people who were learning to become Christians. We often see this tripartite building structure used to in older Christian churches.

Reuven Firestone, Hebrew Union College

I want to talk about three aspects of space: one is directionality, another is the notion of center, and the third, a notion of actual prayer space—a space in which one engages in prayer. In the Jewish tradition, there is a sense of directionality in prayer, and that directionality is toward Jerusalem. Because the Jewish community tended to shift westward through the centuries, the directionality of prayer is thought of being toward the east as with Christians—but it's not really toward the east. It's really toward Jerusalem. Sometimes Jews forget about that so if you're north of Jerusalem in Syria, for example, you also might point toward the east. But you should really be pointing toward the south in that case. We're not quite as careful as our Muslim colleagues who are much more technically aligned with directionality. Our directionality is a tradition that presumes the ancient sanctity of Jerusalem as the core location of divine holiness. Jerusalem is on the location, according to Jewish tradition, of the *even shetiyah* or the "foundation stone" upon which the earth was established. It is the *axis mundi*, the axis around which, or in relation to which, the entire earth revolves because it is such a sacred place.

All of that having been said, Jews didn't really pay all that much attention to the absolute, sanctified physical location of Jerusalem until the last seventy or eighty years, because Judaism as a religious tradition is—and I will say this is an often unvoiced but accurate statement from the scholarly point of view—all expressions of Judaism today are expressions of a different religion than biblical religion. The two are not the same. Our theology is different, our prayer practices are different, our general orientation is different, our rituals and cultural practices are different. So, for those communities that identify Jews as a very interesting people who still live the biblical life, they are really wrong about that because Jews don't live that particular biblical life.

I'll give you an example of how that works in terms of space and structure. The temple is gone, destroyed. Now, Jewish tradition presumes that the temple will be rebuilt—the Jerusalem Temple will be rebuilt when God decides the time is right to rebuild it. In Israel today, there is a major conflict between communities as to whether or not God has pressed the button that starts the process of redemption. That is, is the State of Israel and its conquest or the absorption of the so-called Holy Land or sacred space (the biblical space) part of God's design and plan? Or is that merely a political development? If it is part of God's design and plan, then everyone in the Jewish community would be obligated to make sure that it remained under Jewish control because it is part of the preliminary activities that will bring the final messianic coming. But if it is not part of God's plan, then engaging in any kind of activity that might suggest that it is part of God's plan would be an act of heresy, because it would be like trying to force God to bring the messiah. In the past, according to Jewish tradition, when such a thing has ever been attempted, it has caused terrible destruction to the Jewish people.

This conflict between these two interpretations is occurring right now in Israel and also in the Jewish Diaspora. The conflict is essentially over the meaning of the State of Israel. Is the establishment of the State of Israel a political act, or is it the beginning of a divine, redemptive act? This question has a very important impact on the notion of sacred space in the Holy Land. But the temple is no longer functional and there is no more functional priesthood. We have people whose names are Cohen or Levi or Kagan—and all kinds of variations of the Hebrew name for priest as it has been translated into various languages—they are still part of the Levitical or priestly tribe in theory, but they have no particular function in Jewish ritual; there are a few very small exceptions, such recital of the Priestly Blessing, but these are minor and insignificant.

And so, the temple service which was central to worship in the biblical period has been transferred from the temple itself to the family table in Jewish practice; this is the way that most Jews around the world practice. The Sabbath table, for example, becomes symbolic of the altar of the great Jerusalem Temple. And Jews basically act out the sacrificial system at home without any actual sacrifice because the temple, where all sacrifices were carried out, no longer exists. The *hallah*, the two braided loaves of bread that are eaten every Sabbath, is symbolic of the showbread that was in the temple. Typically, the head of the family makes a blessing to welcome the Sabbath. After that, all wash their hands with a blessing before eating the hallah. This blessing and washing serves as an act of ritual purification—a symbolic version of what the temple priests did at one time before making the temple sacrifice. Only then do the participants engage in eating of that bread in the ritual, which is part of the Sabbath service. So here we have the transformation of a temple offering into a family offering at home.

Regarding prayer space: there's no consecration of space in Jewish tradition for prayer in post-biblical, Rabbinic tradition. Any place that is a clean place can be a location of prayer. And there is no set synagogue architecture. There are various styles of synagogue architecture, but there is no specific "Jewish" architecture. Just like there's no "Jewish" food. You may think there's "Jewish" food, but there's nothing that's really Jewish food aside from the particular restrictions of what foods may or may not be eaten. *Gefilte* fish, for example, is not really a Jewish food. It's simply one example of a Jewish practice of taking something from the local culture and Judaizing it, making it a *kosher gefilte* fish as opposed to a non-kosher *gefilte* fish. "Gefilte fish," meaning stuffed fish, is a kind of food eaten in some parts of Eastern Europe by everybody—Jews and non-Jews. The same holds true for bagels and other commonly considered "Jewish" food. Bagels are not a uniquely "Jewish" food.

This is also true of architecture. The architecture of synagogues in Poland are particular to Polish styles of architecture. The same is true in Western Europe and in the Muslim world. So yes, synagogues do have a certain architecture, but the distinctiveness of what makes it Jewish is that Jewish sensibilities—Jewish ritual associations and some ritual function—are incorporated into the architecture. But if you were to compare these synagogues with other forms of religious architecture from the same lands, the same area, and the same period of time, you would see that these other buildings have had a profound influence on synagogue architecture. This principle also applies to the temple in Jerusalem. It was patterned upon the old Canaanite pre-monotheist, fully polytheistic, idolatrous temples that were in the vicinity. Then, as synagogue architecture developed in the post-temple age during the first centuries of the common era, one can observe a great deal of similarity between what is "Jewish" in synagogue architecture and other forms of monumental architecture at the time.

Amir Hussain, Loyola Marymount University

When Reuven was talking about sacred space, it made me think of the film version of Umberto Eco's *The Name of the Rose*. There's a great scene in the film where one character at the monastery says, "Master, is this a place abandoned by God?" And the other character turns to him and says, "Have you ever known a place where God would feel at home?" I love that line. Is there a place where God would feel at home? For Muslims, there is a *hadith* or tradition of the Prophet Muhammad that says, "the whole earth is a mosque." There is this idea of the earth being created by God, which is in and of itself a good thing in Jewish and Christian thought as well.

If you look at sacred space for Muslims, the one space that comes up over and over again is the City of Mecca, in what is now Saudi Arabia. I tell my students that Mecca is not important because it is where the Prophet Muhammad was born, even though it is where Muhammad was born. Mecca is not important because it is where Muhammad gets his first revelations, even though it is where Muhammad gets his first revelations.

Rather, Mecca is important because it is where Abraham comes with his son—disputes about whether that son is Ishmael or Isaac notwithstanding—and builds the first place of prayer, the Ka'aba. That is the place, the sacred mosque for Muslims, the Ka'aba in Mecca. And so, when we pray the five daily prayers, we orient ourselves to the Ka'aba.

What makes a mosque a prayer space? A prayer space has a niche (the technical term in Arabic is "*mihrab*") that points in the direction of Mecca. Here in Los Angeles, it's twenty-two degrees northeast. That is where Mecca is located. In other places, it's west, and in other places, it's south, but wherever you are, you pray facing in the direction of Mecca. And so, Mecca becomes the holy place and the Mosque in Mecca becomes the most holy place for Muslims.

One of the companions of the Prophet asked him, "What are the holy places?" And the prophet says first, the Masjid al-Haram, the sacred mosque in Mecca. And then the Masjid al-Aqsa, literally the farthest mosque, which Muslims take to be in Jerusalem. So there is an importance there of Jerusalem for Muslims. And lastly, the mosque of the prophet. Muhammad migrates with his community from Mecca to Medina in 622 CE and the first thing he does is he establishes a place of prayer there. The prophet leaves Mecca more or less not to live there ever again in 622 and so establishes his community in Medina. That's where the first successors of the Prophet have their communities as well, but within the first forty years of Islamic history, roughly thirty-eight of those years have been where Medina was an important city. But even during the time of Ali, the prophet's son-in-law (the fourth Caliph), Ali moves the Islamic capital, if you will, from Medina to Kufa. And then the next dynasty (the Umayyads) moves the capital to Damascus in what is now Syria. The following dynasty (the Abbasids) move it to Baghdad. Here's where I'm going with this—it was only for the first thirty years of Islamic history that Mecca and Medina were centers of any kind of power and authority. They've always been religious centers, but the political center has almost never been in those places and only in the past seventy years or so have those cities reclaimed their former prominence.

I think that sense of sacred prayer space can be any kind of space. If you come to our office space in the Caruso Catholic Center, you'll know which spot is mine because it's the one with the prayer mat folded up sitting on the desk there. When it comes time for the prayer, you take out your prayer mat, you say your prayer, and that's it. You can do them anywhere you want. But for the Friday prayer you have to pray in a congregation, ideally at a mosque. There's no one style of mosques. You have these beautiful mud brick mosques in Mali, and you have sandstone mosques in Delhi. You have mosques with minarets, you have mosques with domes, and you have mosques that don't have those. These are all sacred spaces where you can congregate together for prayer.

Sacred Clothing

Pim Valkenberg, The Catholic University of America

Let's start with identity. I'm a Roman Catholic, but there is no way you can see that I am Roman Catholic. You might be able to see that I'm a somewhat liberal-leaning academic theologian, but you cannot see that I'm a Roman Catholic because I'm a lay person. But when a priest is present, you can see that immediately. So, clothing in Roman Catholic tradition makes a big distinction between those who have a specific religious function and those who do not. Of course, as a lay person, I can be very learned about my religion, but I have no specific religious function, and so I do not wear special clothing. But in the Roman Catholic tradition there is distinctive clothing for the priests and for the monks. They are the two classes, if you will, that distinguish themselves by a specific sort of clothing and if you are very learned, you might be able to distinguish between a Benedictine Monk, a Franciscan or a Dominican Friar, and a Jesuit.

Then, of course, you have the Priests, the Bishops, the Archbishops, the Cardinals, and the Pope. Black is for the common Priest, purple is for the Bishop, red is for the Cardinal, and white is for the Pope. In addition to this, you have the liturgical colors which say something important about the specific phase of the liturgical year. The Priest (and sometimes the Deacon) wears specific liturgical colors, green for the regular time of the year, red for the commemorations of the Saints—specifically the Martyrs, because they witnessed their faith by their blood—and for Pentecost because the color of the Holy Spirit is red. White is worn during the holy days of Easter and Christmas because it is the color of joy, purple during Lent and Advent, which is the color of repentance. All these colors have a specific meaning and give a specific coloring to some of the liturgical moments.

Reuven Firestone, Hebrew Union College

In Judaism, when the functionality of the priesthood ended with the destruction of the Jerusalem Temple, some people say there was a democratizing of authority. Access to particular locations of worship, for example, were no longer restricted to certain classes or tribes, whereas in the temple, different categories of people could get only so close to the Holy of Holies, depending on your tribal affiliation or your gender. But Judaism did retain an old gender distinction in worship services between men and women and that has been something that has been breaking down, especially in the last twenty or thirty years. But in Orthodox Judaism, the gender separation remains.

Regarding sacred clothing, there's no form of clothing that distinguishes, say, a rabbi from a non-rabbi. A rabbi has no special status beyond being recognized as someone who has achieved a certain level of learning. A rabbi is a teacher and doesn't function as a priest. While some more traditional congregations still only allow males to lead worship services, elsewhere anyone can lead as long as they are considered by the congregation to be pious and know what to do. According to Jewish tradition, even events such as marrying and burying don't require a rabbi. In America you need to be licensed in order to perform certain functions such as marriage. It is much easier to become licensed to do so as a rabbi or a cantor, but in Jewish religious practice it is not necessary for a rabbi or cantor to perform a wedding.

As for head coverings, because of a sense of respect and a sense of humility in the Jewish tradition, there is a tradition of covering the head, especially during times of prayer, but it's not required. That is, I'm wearing a *kippah*, or head covering, but it's not required to wear a *kippah*. If you look at the class photos from Yeshiva University in the nineteen-forties, where students were graduating from the most prestigious and largest ordaining institution of Orthodox Rabbis, you see the men there weren't wearing *kippahs*. That was because at that particular time, many was felt it was not a good idea in America to show their Jewish distinctiveness by wearing a *kippah*. They might wear a fedora in the nineteen-forties or fifties but not a *kippah*, and there would be a lot of Jewish people who would go without any head covering at all.

Traditionally, to enter a synagogue you wear a *kippah* or a head covering of some sort as a sign of respect. It is sometimes possible to identify what subgroup of Jews you are looking at by the shape, the color, and styles of the *kippah* a person is wearing—people often choose their style of *kippah* based on how they identify with the community.

What about those men who wear the long coats and the big-brimmed hats. What's that all about? Well, that is a style that developed among the Polish nobility in the sixteenth or seventeenth century. Jews weren't allowed to wear those clothes at that particular time, but later one Jewish group took on that habit. It is only a custom among some Jewish communities within the general scope of Judaism. It is not only Hasidic Jews who dress like this, but also Jews who criticize Hasidic Jews; they also wear the same kind of coats. If you know the subtle details, you can tell one group from another by the cut, the style, the size of the brim of the hat, and how the hat is worn. You can tell which small community within that larger group, of what we would call today Haredi or ultra-Orthodox community, by the particular style of clothing.

Modesty is important in Jewish tradition—skin is not pretty, it's not supposed to be shown so you should cover your skin. This holds true for both men and women, but of course the issue of covering has come to be more of an oppressive function for women than for men. That has become a political issue. However, even in the Hebrew Bible there are a number of references to women who have their heads covered. Those references are used and understood in the Jewish tradition to refer to head coverings in general, and in some communities, Jewish women cover their hair after marriage but are not expected to do so before marriage.

The actual details of clothing distinction is largely self-imposed by Jewish communities, because there is very little organizational structure as a whole that could impose rules universally. The Jewish world functions as many semi-independent communities that have developed in different parts of the world and have been influenced by different cultures and different aesthetic styles. This sense of what "the Jews" do is something that is constantly being negotiated by various Jewish communities and individuals within those communities.

Amir Hussain, Loyola Marymount University

In terms of dress, the Qur'an speaks to men and women about dressing modestly and so if you're coming up with sacred norms for dress, or sacred dress, it's "dress modestly." The problem, of course, is the Qur'an never stipulates what that modest dress looks like. For that, you need to go to the *hadith* and the *Sunnah*, the sayings and traditions of the Prophet and you get different things there for men and for women. If you look at Islamic dress around the world, you need to remember that Islam is a world religion with over a billion people that stretches from the Balkans to the Bay of Bengal with different kinds of people, different temperatures, etc. But in general, that sense of dressing modestly for women typically means having your arms and legs covered to the wrists and to the ankles.

Modesty for men during prayer means having your shoulders covered and your legs covered up to the knees. So, a man can go to a mosque in a tee shirt and long shorts. However, you're not encouraged to do that—you're encouraged to wear a little more, but that's the bare minimum for what qualifies as "modesty" for a man. For a woman during prayer, it's typically the arms covered to the wrists, the legs covered to the ankles, and then the hair covering. For Muslim men you can pray with or without hair covering—it's more of a fashion aesthetic than a religious one. But for women, you are expected to cover your hair when you pray which, of course, then leads to the question: are you expected to cover your hair at all times? Some Muslim women cover their hair throughout the day, not just at times when they pray. There are also a variety of restrictions regarding which groups of people it is appropriate to have your hair uncovered around, but not everyone does that. There's a wide degree of interpretation on this issue of modesty and dress. There is also something similar in Islam to what Rabbi Firestone was saying about identifying the sort of community a person is a part of by their *kippah* and what Pim was saying about identifying different religious orders in the Catholic Church by their clothing. If you see someone wearing a particular kind of turban, you might be able to identify what Muslim community they are a part of.

Islam is more like Judaism when it comes to being an Imam. An Imam literally means one who stands in front and leads the prayer. A community will choose the best qualified person for that position, which may mean someone who has a very basic knowledge of the tradition but more than someone else in that congregation. Or it may mean choosing someone who has spent years at an institution of higher learning in the Islamic world. But there is no required dress for an Imam other than a sense of modest dress.

14

Constructive Tensions in Sacred Spaces and Sacred Clothing in Lived Religious Experience

An Interfaith Panel Discussion

MARGARET BARKER, E. WAYNE GADDIS,
EDINA LEKOVIC, PATRICK MASON, AND VARUN SONI

Sacred Space and Sacred Clothing in Lived Religion

Varun Soni, University of Southern California

In my role here at the University of Southern California (USC) as Dean of Religious Life, I oversee more than ninety different religious groups; that's more than any American university, more than fifty chaplains representing every faith tradition including a secular humanist chaplain for atheist and agnostic students. That's also more chaplains than any other secular American university and we do this work right here in the heart of Los Angeles, the most religiously diverse city in the history of the world.

My own background is that I'm a Hindu—the first Hindu in American history to hold a role like this and for the last nine years I've been the only non-Christian in the United States to do this work. So, the work that I do and I think the perspective that I bring really reflects a tremendous geo-religious diversity that we see on our campus and in our city.

On our campus we interpret secularism the way the United States interprets secularism, which means all religions are treated equally, where no one tradition is privileged over another. As Dean of Religious Life it is my responsibility to make sure that students from many different religious traditions have access to worship spaces on a campus that are meaningful for them so I work closely with our students to make sure that we have space on our campus. But we have spatial challenges; we're a campus of forty thousand on four square blocks, so space is a challenge. Some groups are bigger, some groups are smaller. Of course we have the stunning Caruso Catholic Center that was built over twelve years, a gorgeous sanctuary, but the Catholic community is our largest community on campus with over ten thousand Catholic students. Then we have, say a Baha'i student group, and they have ten or twelve students, so the way we think about sacred space for different groups varies based on what those groups look like, etc.

Right now, we have a few dedicated worship spaces on campus: we have a dedicated Hindu space, a dedicated Muslim space, a few dedicated Christian spaces, and a Jewish prayer space that many of our students use right across the street at Hebrew Union College. We have over seventy houses of worship within one square mile of our campus, so students often can walk to different houses of worship. We also have washing facilities on campus near our Muslim prayer space so those students can do *wudhu* before they pray. Of necessity, it's kind of a piece-meal approach to thinking about sacred space, where we often have to utilize different spaces for sacred spaces—multi-purpose spaces become worship spaces. One hour they could be used as a classroom, the next hour they could be used as a worship space. I think on a campus like ours we have to be very versatile and we have to make sure that students have access to meaningful space even if those spaces look different across the traditions.

In terms of sacred thread, we have students who identify often through garments or other articles of faith that are visible and that, I think, adds to the rich diversity in pluralism on our campus. But those threads aren't apolitical in this day and age. Many of our students display faith through articles of clothing—maybe they're Jewish students wearing a *yarmulke* or Muslim students wearing a *hijab* or Sikh students wearing a turban. Oftentimes those students can become targets of anti-semitism,

Islamaphobia, and anti-Sikh sentiment on campus. This is especially true for Muslim women who wear a *hijab* and Sikh men who wear turban in a post-9-11 era. I know many of our students have parents who, after a terrorist attack somewhere else around the world, will ask them to remove their article of faith out of concern for their safety. And our students who continue to represent themselves through their articles of faith I think display tremendous moral courage.

But once again, these items of sacred clothing aren't apolitical, even if a student is wearing an article of faith because of their religious tradition or obligation or identity—other people might see that in different ways and so what happens around the world happens on our campus. We have students representing over 120 different countries here, so we are always aware of what's happening around the world and how it will play out on our campus and oftentimes, I think our students use their article of faith for very positive purposes For example, we have Sikh students who have a "wear a turban day" and a lot of non-Sikhs will wear a turban for a day and then meet with Sikhs students to talk about what that was like. A lot of non-Muslim women at least once a semester will get together with Muslim women and wear a *hijab* for a day and then meet up and talk about what their experiences were like.

On a campus, every opportunity should be an educational one and oftentimes these conversations are very educational. But sometimes they're not—sometimes they bring attention to students that isn't always positive and so that's something that I'm aware of when I think about sacred threads on our campus.

One final point is that you know on our campus we reflect the national American trend, which is that 20 percent of Americans are not formally affiliated with a religion, almost 40 percent of millennials or our students are not formally affiliated with a religion and almost 70 percent of our students describe themselves as "more spiritual than religious." So I'm often thinking about what does a new sacred space look like for a community that's not formally affiliated with religion? How do we use meaningful stories about USC or the notion of a USC family as a sacred community to talk about values and ethics, to talk about service and empathy—all the things that our great faiths do, but to do it using the language of a secular research university.

I draw very heavily upon the discourse of an American civil religion when I think about what that looks like on our campus. For those of you unfamiliar with the idea of a civil religion, that's the idea that our

American political system in and of itself is a religion. When we go to vote, it's a sacred act. Our pilgrimages are to Washington DC or to Mt. Rushmore. So that's an idea of an America where the secular aspect that connects us with civil rituals becomes sacred and I think we can think about civil religion as it applies on our campus through the a USC "family."

Edina Lekovic, Muslim Public Affairs Council

My name is Edina Lekovic and I formally work with the Muslim Public Affairs Council. Informally I work with a host of American-Muslim, national, regional and local groups, both within the religious spaces in our communities and in the advocacy spaces within our communities. My family came from the former Yugoslavia and so my family's been Muslim for generations, but when people see my complexion or hear my voice, they can't quite compute that I'm Muslim. In terms of thinking about sacred clothing, the way that I wear my sacred clothing, I often get mistaken for being an Orthodox Jewish woman rather than a Muslim woman. The lines between identities here in Los Angeles are often blurred, and the assumptions that people make can set them back rather than forward in many spaces.

My family and I were cultural Muslims growing up and when I was in college is when I went on my spiritual journey. I went on my professional journey and my spiritual journey at the same time only to feel that once I started to wear a hijab that my choices became limited. Not because of who I was, but because of the symbolism of wearing your religion on your head, especially in a sphere like media, which I was studying.

Instead, my life took me in the direction of working in Muslim activism. The Muslim Public Affairs Council had worked to create a political and social voice, an inter-faith voice for American Muslims since 1988. The American Muslim community is about 3.5 million people strong, just one percent of the overall U.S. population. We skew the youngest among all faith groups. Forty percent of American Muslims are under the age of forty and we're also one of the fastest growing faiths within the country both through conversion and through birth rate; immigration or migration has less to do with it. And within the American Muslim community, the single largest group of American Muslims is African-American, which is another place for misconceptions to take place, followed by

South Asians, followed by Arabs, followed by people of other groups. In America, we have Muslims from all around the world.

My experience with Muslims here in Los Angeles has reflected the global experience of Muslims, but working in Muslim advocacy has given me the lens to be able to see Muslim communities around the country and to also be a bridge-builder. My work largely deals with community building, so I work with the Muslim Public Affairs Council; I also work with an Islamic Center called the Islamic Center of Southern California here in Los Angeles. It's one of over two thousand mosques across America.

The sacred spaces that exist in Muslim communities are very diverse. They are spaces that are not just for worship, but for communal gathering and for identity preservation (like many other sacred spaces), so they have many, many different functions. But at their core, they are places of meditation, of prayer, of self-renewal, and of self-reflection. In mosques, this spiritual process takes place in prayer, not in pews; it takes place on open carpet. But this sort of prayer can take place where people gather shoulder-to-shoulder or where they sit alone and contemplate in prayer. So, in some way all space is sacred for a Muslim. Any place in the world can serve as a mosque—a place of prayer—if it's simply clean, so that you can pray with purity and cleanliness. Traditional mosques are supposed to reflect this kind of space; they're supposed to be open, beautiful, awe-inspiring places that are filled with people who are connected to one another.

And yet mosques are also places of tension in America because of the political nature of what it means to be an American-Muslim today. So, while these spaces are supposed to be sacred, our conversations within mosques are often interrupted or infused by politics, by Islamophobia, by xenophobia, by fear. Just last week in the Islamic Center of Southern California, the mosque I'm connected with, there was a local man who was arrested for making repeated death threats against the staff there. The police served a search warrant on his home and found over a dozen different kinds of weapons with over 200 lbs. of ammunition, so this man was ready and able to make good on his threat.

Now, my community in the aftermath of that has to come back into a sacred space and to feel safe there. Such concerns about security are particularly acute in non-Judaeo-christian faiths and houses of worship create a particular kind of anxiety, and that's something that I see that has invaded many mosques, especially within the United States which is what

I'm most familiar with. This sense of anxiety that has come to be connected to your spiritual life, your sacred space, and your sacred clothing. It takes courage to be faithful to your values. It takes courage to wear your sacred cloth out in public. It takes courage to say that you're a Muslim and our sacred spaces are supposed to provide these kinds of sanctuaries and for many people they do, but in this day and age, we're seeing all kinds of attacks—arson attacks, vandalism, you name it—against mosques, let alone the kinds of deadly threats that I just described to you. There is a host of complex challenges that are out there regarding sacred space and sacred clothing.

On the other hand, American Muslims are heavily involved in inter-faith engagement. Probably one in three of American Muslims are affiliated with a mosque or go to a mosque on a regular basis, so we're right in line with other faiths in terms of more people being unaffiliated institutionally than being affiliated. But for those who do go to mosques regularly, 85 percent of them report being involved in inter-faith engagement, service engagement, and of considering themselves American, so there's a positive relationship in accepting yourself and feeling pride in who you are because of this sacred space of a mosque. But because mosques are giving people opportunities to connect with other houses of worship, Muslims are getting access to multiple sacred spaces and for me, that's part of where my faith has been elevated to new levels beyond my Muslim consciousness—in my exposure to other faiths and also other houses of worship; it has only elevated my own relationship to the divine.

The other thing I wanted to talk about is that there is perhaps no item of sacred clothing more politicized today than a *hijab*, a woman's head covering. The stereotypes are abundant and apparent; I won't repeat them, but the lived reality of American Muslim women is the opposite of those stereotypes. The fact is, American Muslim women are the second highest educated group of women in the United States. This is a conference about symbolism and the power of symbolism; the *hijab* supposed to be a symbol of modesty so that a woman can be considered for her mind, for her intellect, rather than for her body or her sexuality. It's a way of publicizing your intellect and privatizing your sexuality in its purest sense. This is the idea behind the sacred clothing; it's supposed to be a reminder. And for me the reason I decided to start wearing a hijab in college, and I wore it the more traditional way back then, was because I wanted to be identified as a Muslim. I wanted to wear my faith more openly. I knew that I could pass as somebody who wasn't Muslim. I didn't have to wear it on my sleeve but I opted in because I wanted to represent the kind of Muslim women that I knew existed all around me every day. So, in this way, my journey has been elevated by both sacred spaces and sacred clothing while it has also been extremely challenged by them.

Patrick Mason, Claremont Graduate University

I want to offer just a few reflections about sacred space and sacred clothing in the Mormon tradition, particularly the Church of Jesus Christ of Latter-day Saints. In addition to my work in Mormon Studies, I have done some work over the years in the field of religion, conflict and peacebuilding, so I'm particularly interested in the ways that sacred space and sacred clothing become sites of tension and conflict.

The Mormon experience with sacred space has been an interesting one. Mormonism was born in the United States in the early nineteenth century in upstate New York. Because of conflicts with their neighbors, the religion and the movement was forced to move from New York to Ohio to Missouri to Illinois and then to Utah; from there it has spread around the world. In each of those places there was a feeling among the Mormons that, this could be our place of worship, this could be a place where this new movement—this sense of new revelation from God—could take root.

But very early in the movement, Joseph Smith, the founding prophet of Mormonism, declared by revelation that a particular place in Missouri represented an especially sacred place that related to both the beginnings of the earth with the Garden of Eden and also with the end times when Jesus would come again to the earth. Typically, when we think of sacred spaces we often think of Jerusalem, Rome, Mecca, and Medina. But Joseph Smith by revelation said this place in Western Missouri, totally undeveloped, on the frontier, this is sacred space.

We have to remember that sacred spaces aren't always sacred. Somebody made them sacred. Something happened in that place. Either a sacred word was spoken or some kind of sacred act occurred—some kind of irruption of the divine into the terrestrial that made that place sacred and that created a community of faith. So then a community of believers sense that this place is holy. This is a place where heaven touched earth, and we can approach heaven by communing in this place.

However, there are real problems associated with any particular community saying, "this ground"—however demarcated—"is sacred and, in fact, it's our sacred space," meaning "it's not your sacred space." That becomes a real problem, especially when many Eastern, Native American, and other indigenous traditions have a sense that if you can't make it, you can't own it. Because land was not made by us, it's difficult for us to say we own it. But in the Euro-American legal tradition we could own private property. So we have these two competing traditions of our relationship to land, and so we see how this can become a problem with sacred space when we draw a line and say this space—this sacred space—is ours (not yours).

Going back to Mormonism in particular, Mormons were forced to leave Missouri and Illinois and then moved to Utah. However, Utah does not function as sacred space in quite the same way that Missouri does in the Mormon religious imagination. Utah is where the LDS Church headquarters was set up and still is today. It's home to the largest Latter-day Saint community, so there is a kind of sacredness there, partly by virtue of the concentration of the community, by the history that is there, by the sacred history of Mormon pioneers coming and settling into what they considered to be a wilderness. But we also need to keep in mind that in order for these Mormons to set up a new sacred community, they had to displace other people who were already there. Many of those native people had their own sacred places, and when Mormons came into their sacred space—what is now called Utah—and set up their community, they displaced others as well. So, we have to think about how the creation of one person's sacred space might impact the communities that preceded them. This becomes especially fraught when they are still neighbors.

For Mormons today the most sacred places are temples. They began building these in Ohio, tried to build one in Missouri, built one in Illinois, and then several in Utah, and now are building temples around the world. Unlike the regular buildings that Mormons worship in every Sunday, temples are reserved only for the faithful, for those who subscribe to core Mormon beliefs and live their lives in a certain way to meet standards for entry, what Mormons call "worthiness." These temples become places not only of reflection and of worship, but also where Mormons make sacred covenants or promises with God.

At the heart of Mormon theology, there is a sense that God and humans are ontologically more similar than different. Therefore, temples become the place where humans access divinity and learn the lessons that help them prepare for it. In this way, they become very powerful places for reflection and prayer. Within these sacred spaces, there is also a ritual aspect where Mormons enter into a kind of sacred and cosmic drama and recognize not only the dignity but the divinity of their lives. This sacred space provides a place where Mormons can transcend the mundaneness of everyday life and enter into a higher sense of reality, after which they can bring that sense of divinity back into their ordinary lives.

Mormons who have been initiated in the religion's temples come back having been clothed in sacred undergarments. Mormons do not wear sacred garments on the exterior, but most Mormons, including myself, wear sacred undergarments. These are sometimes derided and mocked like other forms of sacred clothing—people joke about "magic underwear." But for Mormons, the daily wearing of a sacred vestment clothes them with divinity. It gives them the sense that God has given us the gift of life and he calls us all to be priests and priestesses. This is one of the fundamental teachings of Mormon temples. There's a sort of democratization of sacred authority, wherein everybody can access the divine and operate in a divine fashion and with divine authority as priests and priestesses. They leave the temple having been clothed in these sacred garments or vestments which reminds them of their priest- or priestess-hood. And they take that into the world, into their daily lives, so that there remains an aura of the sacred in regards to all the things they do in their families, in their workplace, in their civic duties, and so forth. They do all of this as priests and priestesses who have been initiated in God's temples.

Pastor Wayne Gaddis, California Missionary Baptist State Convention

My name is Pastor Wayne Gaddis of the Greater True Light Missionary Baptist Church and President of the California Missionary Baptist State Convention here in the California area from San Diego to Sacramento. In the Baptist tradition, sacred space simply means a space or place that you have chosen where you can communicate with God. In being connected to God, we all need a sacred place for more reasons than one.

As a Baptist, I believe in Eph 4:5–6, which says that there is one Lord, one faith, one baptism and one God of all of us. God has given us each a choice to serve him or not serve him, whether you are a Christian or a non-Christian. Some call these sacred spaces temples, some call them mosques, some call them churches. Personally, I believe in the church. I believe in the church being the body of our Lord and Savior Jesus Christ. Yes, we all have our different beliefs, but in my religion, we believe that everybody ought to be respected for what they believe and who they believe in. We need to be able to look at our brothers and sisters and respect them for what they believe and who they are, and respect them for trying to make our world better. If we cannot, if we are going in our different sacred spaces and we're not seeking to make our community and our world better, I fear that we're all worshipping in vain.

In these different religious communities we all have our sacred space; and, in our individual sacred spaces, you'll be surprised as to what you can find there. Wherever it is—whether it be a mosque, a temple, a chapel, or a church, you will be surprised how peaceful it can be, how much love you can draw from your sacred space, and how much joy you can draw from your sacred space. Not only that, but in your sacred spaces you can find out that we all are God's children. We all are God's people and we are working for one common goal, and that is to strengthen our brothers and sisters.

We need to learn how to respect one another's beliefs, feelings; and most of all, how we worship and clothe ourselves. Now, Baptists don't have any particular clothing that we wear which we call sacred. We believe that everything that we do with a pure heart is sacred. However, we are learning how to respect those who wear their own sacred clothing.

Margaret Barker, Independent Scholar

I've been a Methodist preacher for over thirty years and I've also been tutor for trainee preachers in our area which is the area around the City of Derby in the middle of England. We go around to different churches every Sunday, so you get see many much-loved sacred places. Much of where I preach is former mining areas so the chapels are quite small. We have some new ones on the newer housing estates; they're modern and more spacious, but if you go to the older areas you find these little chapels, and the first thing that strikes you about them is that these are very special places. They've obviously been loved, and you go into these quite small chapels and they will have ordinary chairs and ordinary tables. There's a special table, a holy table at the front. There's also often a massive pulpit, because that's why we're there, and you will find around the room mementoes of families: "this vase was given in memory of so and so who served this church for seventy years," or whatever it was. You will also find a lot of needle work done by the women of the place—embroideries, some of them very old indeed.

Attached to a chapel invariably there will be a hall, which historically is called the school room because this was used for education purposes. It's usually used for a lot of other things as well—you have old people's luncheon clubs, you have play groups for children, you have centers where separated couples can meet and collect their children, etc. All these sort of things make life a little bit easier. So those are our sacred spaces; they're really homes to those communities and they're warm and they're welcoming.

Regarding sacred garments, preachers tend to wear something really to conform with the environment that we are going into, be it formal or otherwise. Now, we don't have any visible signs of what we are; there's no Methodist equivalent of the turban. Our visible sign, really, is a lifestyle rather than a particular sort of hat or something else. But that said, if you look at traditional Methodist hymns like those written by Charles Wesley, you will find they are full of what I call "temple theology." It's quite surprising. We don't dress our buildings up to look like temples, but we do actually shape our worship around that temple pattern.

One of the things that I have to do when I'm training Methodist preachers—the word we use is "enabling," you enable them to meet their call—is how you create the sense of a sacred situation simply by the words you use, your demeanor as you are leading public worship, the music you choose, the whole package. As Methodist preachers, we do have a number of very practical considerations, but part of the task of the preacher is to speak the words of the worship service and convey by how you act a sense that even in this little, tiny chapel (nothing very grand), this little building is actually a temple.

Tensions Created by Sacred Space and Sacred Clothing

Pastor Wayne Gaddis, California
Missionary Baptist State Convention

One of the biggest problems that I see as it relates to tension among people of different religious traditions is a lack of understanding and education about other religions, their sacred spaces, and their meanings of worship. I believe that one of the things we also have to look at is the passage in the Bible that says, "You reap what you sow" (Gal 6:7). Many people look at this scripture in a negative light, but you can also see it in a positive light as well. If you sow good things, you certainly are going to be looking to reap good things. If we actively try to understand another's religious forms, practices, clothing and places of worship, then it will be easier to appreciate them and the role of their faith in their lives.

Patrick Mason, Claremont Graduate University

In my mind the greatest danger to the sacred is when it becomes divorced from the ethical. The Christian author C. S. Lewis once wrote, "Next to the Blessed Sacrament itself, your neighbor is the holiest object presented to your senses." I understand the theology behind that for C. S. Lewis, based on his belief in the real presence of Jesus in the host. But from my own theological perspective as a Mormon, I would disagree with him somewhat. I would say that there is nothing that presents itself to you that is holier than your neighbor. Not the host, not a temple, not sacred clothing—there is literally nothing in this world that is holier than your neighbor. Now, this comes from the Mormon theological tradition that we are all children of God and therefore invested with true divinity, but it also comes from a deep commitment to human rights and human dignity which I think operates functionally as the closest thing we have to a kind of secular, civil religion, and as a moral code for a secular, pluralist world.

I think one of the greatest challenges of people who are religious—people who claim they are part of a religion—is when they divorce their religious lives from a sense of the ethical, of care and concern for the other, of care and concern for the earth, and of care and concern for the weak and the vulnerable. When we do that, then the sacred loses its power and then we have a problem with the next generation. So, I think the greatest challenge but also the greatest opportunity before us with the sacred today is to always imbue it with a powerful sense of the ethical.

Edina Lekovic, Muslim Public Affairs Council

When I think about tensions experienced by young American Muslims, there are plenty that have to do with their identity and the place that a mosque has in their life and whether or not it's relevant. I think that many of the reasons that it is difficult for young American Muslims to connect to mosque life has to do with the ability of mosque leadership to embrace or ignore tension within Islam. The challenge is how can we be civil and allow for the differences even inside of our faiths, rather than simply focusing on how we can get along with others. Sometimes we can make it a lot easier to get along with those of other faiths than with our own. This is something that I've seen over and over again at New Ground: A Muslim-Jewish Partnership for Change. During our exchanges people often have more tension with fellow Muslims and fellow Jews than with each other.

In regards to tensions that exist within mosques, the first is gender. Muslims in mosque life are coed except for during prayer. So, within prayer, men pray together and women pray together all at the same time but you stand gender segregated. All other time in mosque life is gender integrated, and that's by design. However, there are many mosques that have taken the practice of gender segregation that exists within prayer and have made it the standard within mosque life outside of prayer, and this creates tension. This also creates tension between culture and faith that exists in many different houses of worship and for young people especially. There aren't woman Imams in mainstream Muslim tradition, so while Muslim women often speak as educators in other spaces, they do not speak in the same way at mosques. If you take this dynamic and you universalize it within the mosque rather than particularize it for religious services and sermons, you create a culture that says that there is gender inequality rather than gender equity. This is an area in which young people are particularly sensitive today.

A second tension is sectarian differences between Sunni, Shia, Sufi, and Salafi. We have sect-different approaches to faith within our community and the minorities get persecuted. Shias make up ten to fifteen percent of Muslims worldwide, and they are persecuted in many places bad enough that they have fled a Muslim majority country for the persecution that they have received and many of those sub-communities under the Shia community have responded by turning inward, by creating the kind of protected sacred spaces that I believe that temples hold, where other Muslims can't come into those spaces because they are meant to be safe space for the persecuted minority within Islam.

Lastly, there is an intellectual tension. The Quran embraces the idea of critical thinking—we're supposed to think and rethink, yet the dominant narrative in Islamic interpretation is that the Quran is fixed rather than flexible. And that's not because the Quran describes itself that way, it's because that's what the recognized, respected majority of scholarship—mostly done by males—has produced over fifteen centuries. If you look at the Quran as being a message for all times and all places, then diversity is part of Islam and Islam is supposed to be practiced in a way that is relevant for each time and each place in which it is lived. These are some of the internal tensions that I think are hopefully creating progress because people are having to engage in the battle-place of ideas and I think that's what our young people are looking for—open dialogue, open debate around these issues rather than silence or resistance to addressing the tensions.

Varun Soni, University of Southern California

What's different about Hinduism as opposed to the other faiths represented here is that Hinduism is not an Abrahamic tradition. It's part of the so-called Dharma traditions that come out of South Asia, the four uniquely Indian religions: Hinduism, Buddhism, Sikhism, and Jainism. And just as Judaism, Christianity, and Islam share a common theological framework, so, too, do these traditions. One of the things that different about these traditions as opposed to the Abrahamic traditions is that our traditions don't believe in linear time; rather, we believe in cyclical time, so there's no beginning of time and there's no end of time. Time is in a cycle like the seasons; the universe contracts and expands over time. That's what our origin story is. And because of that, we also believe in reincarnation, that our soul is reincarnated over many lifetimes until it achieves liberation from the cycle of suffering—liberation from the cycle of rebirth. For Buddhists, that's called *nirvana*, for Hindus that's called *moksha*: once our soul, which is a reflection of God, achieves liberation, then our soul becomes one with God.

So, we believe that everyone has an individual soul, and that soul is a reflection of a larger soul, an over-soul, Godhead, cosmic consciousness, etc., and that the soul yearns to be with God and if we cultivate the right action, the right knowledge, the right devotion, the right contemplation in our life, then we can achieve liberation between lifetimes and become one with God. That's why if you go to a yoga class you might be greeted with a traditional Hindu greeting of "namaste." "Namaste" literally means "the divinity within me acknowledges and salutes the divinity within you." Just within a Hindu greeting you see a core theological concept, very different from the Western greeting of a handshake: I have no weapon, I will not kill you.

Because of that, temple life in Hinduism is oriented around something different. The goal of Hindu liberation is really to understand your own divinity, not that you are God but that you have God within you. That's why you see animals depicted as the divine in India. When people go to India and they come back they say, why do you worship the cow or the snake or the elephant? It's not that the cow is God or the elephant is God or the snake is God or the monkey is God; it is that there is God in the cow, in the snake, in the elephant, in the monkey. That's why many Hindus are vegetarian, because it's not just humans who have an inherently divine nature, it's all sentient beings that have an inherently divine nature.

The goal is to awaken the inner divinity within us, to understand our natures, which means the goal is more of a contemplative, inward process, as opposed to something that's externally facing. You must to look in to thought, not out. That's why Hindu practices and Buddhist practice is so focused on meditation, contemplation, prayer, etc., as an inward, introspective process.

When you go into a Hindu temple, the goal is really to awaken the divinity within you, the divine consciousness within you. According to Hindu traditions we have six sense doors—the five senses that we all know about: sight, taste, touch, smell, and hearing, and then the last one for Hindus is the mind. The mind itself is a sense-door to a type of consciousness. When you go into a Hindu temple, it's very different than other houses of worship because, like Hinduism itself, it's kind of a disorganized, chaotic scene. You have within the temple setting, within the worship setting, spiritual technologies that are aimed at activating the divine consciousness within you through your sense doors. So, there will be a bell-ringing, which opens up your sense of hearing. The incense is burning, which opens up your sense of smell. It's a spectacle of sight that opens up your eyes; you are looking at images of the divine. The *mantra* recitation, or the recitation of prayer, opens up your mind. The congregational nature of worship opens up the sense of touch. It's a full, sensory experience and overload by design.

If you've ever gone to a Hindu temple or gone to India, it's hard not to see the spectacle of devotion in Hindu religious life and it's there by design—to use what's outside of you to awaken what's inside of you. So I think that in our tradition, the connection between what's happening externally in temple life and what's happening internally in terms of your own consciousness is explicit. The external kinds of rituals of the world are meant to awaken the internal potentiality towards liberation that all of us possess.

In terms of the tension, I think what is also different from Hinduism as opposed to the other traditions up here is that we're not a trans-national religion. There are many Muslim majority countries; there are many Christian majority countries, and even now we're at a point where there are more Mormons outside the U.S. than inside the U.S., even though it's a uniquely American religion in many ways. Hinduism is very different. There are only two Hindu majority countries in the world: India and Nepal. Ninety-nine percent of Hindus live in India. So when we look at Hinduism in a diaspora context, we begin to see some of these tensions play out.

You can see how Hindus in America look to India as a sacred site. One example of this and the tensions it can create in the Hindu diaspora is the beautiful temple in Malibu; it's one of my favorite Hindu temples in the United States, took a long time to build. It's really interesting because it's modeled after Tirupatinath which is the holiest Hindu temple in India; it's the second biggest religious institution in the world after the Vatican. It's a huge temple complex. "Tirupati" means "the lord of seven hills." So, in Malibu, the Hindu community thirty years ago found a place that is surrounded by seven hills and they built a temple in this place because it looks like the topography of the main temple in India. They brought the artisans and the priests who were trained at the Tirupatinath temple to create the temple here in America, and the priests who run the worship ceremonies at Malibu were actually trained at the temple in India in Tirupati. In many ways, it's a recreation of an ancient and significant Hindu temple complex right here in the United States.

What's unique about it, though, and this illustrates some of the tensions within the diaspora community, is that in India you will find a temple to Vishnu or Shiva or the Goddess, and depending on who or how you worship, you will attend one of those temples. But in the diaspora, we have to cater to all Hindus and we don't have a critical mass to say, "I am a worshiper of Vishnu or Shiva or the Goddess." Instead, all we can say is, "I am a Hindu." And so, what you find at the Malibu temple is a Vishnu temple side-by-side with a Shiva temple. You would never see that in

India but you see that right here in Malibu because it's a way to engage all the Hindus in the community, not just those who specify with one tradition or another because we don't have a critical mass in the United States. We're even less than one percent of the U.S. population, about 2 million Hindus in the United States. So in some ways the Malibu temple is a recreation of an ancient complex; in other ways it's a reimagining of what temple worship looks like in a new context.

A second example of various tensions in the Hindu diaspora is a stunning new temple in Chino Hills, called the Baps Temple. When the Hindu community wanted to build it, they bought all this land, but there was tremendous opposition from Chino Hills as a city. Citizens were against it and the city council was against it. But the Hindu community was not deterred. They spent years building relationships with their neighbors and lobbying the city council. In some instances, they had to wait until certain city council members retired and were replaced by others who were more sympathetic to their cause. Finally, they received approval to build after five years of this intense public diplomacy.

The temple itself is spectacular. It took fifteen hundred artisans three years working full time to carve this temple out of marble and out of wood in India and then they brought it over here to America and they established it. Now this temple has become a center for Chino Hills, Hindu or not. When the Mayor brings in international guests, he brings them to the temple. When community members want to do events, they rent space from the temple. It has become a part of the fabric of the community itself. In many ways, I think the temple organizers were prescient in building those kinds of interfaith relationships, those civic relationships, and those political relationships so that when the temple was finally established, it would be established in a context and a diverse community that really cherished the temple; not just Hindus, but the non-Hindus as well. So I think these two examples, the Malibu Hindu Temple and the Baps Temple in Chino Hills, give us a sense of tension that happens in the diaspora concept, especially from a tradition like Hinduism that's not a trans-national tradition.

Margaret Barker, Independent Scholar

In my community, we have been a predominantly Methodist village for over two hundred years, so we don't actually experience these sorts of tensions which are the result of a society moving around and changing. Something else to consider is that our style of doing things isn't spectacular. Our idea of the sacred is something that is immediately obtainable to anybody who is familiar with the interior of a home, which is a very good thing because people do actually feel at home, having a cup of tea and the sort of things that remind them a little bit of their granny perhaps around the place. But when you get to working in difficult areas—I believe you call it "downtown"; we call them "city center churches"—where we're dealing with the homeless or the addicts, things are a bit different. We have a mantra which is: belong, believe, behave in that order. People come in to these city center churches because they know what it's like to be utterly alone and utterly desolate and on their own. But they can sleep in the church hall, they can have a wash, they can have a meal, and have people who talk to them. This is something that people really want: they want to talk to another human being.

When they come to these churches, they find themselves part of the Christian community and they start learning how to behave and get terribly cross with themselves when they start using bad language. One of our preachers was recently accompanying one of these new people to a court hearing. On the way, they were met by a drug pusher, and this new member of the church community said, "I don't need that stuff anymore—I've got Jesus now." This is lovely. No one ever said to him, "You've got to stop this and you've got to stop that." But he realized that his new family lived in a certain way, and there were certain things that his new friends really wouldn't want him to be doing. This happens time and time again.

So I think in my Methodist community we avoid a lot of the conflict and the tensions that exist elsewhere and in other religious traditions simply by being ordinary people and making people feel at home. Methodist ministers and preachers look like members of the human race, you know. We don't have things that set us apart except we are countercultural in many, many ways because we oppose a lot of things that we don't like happening in our society—domestic violence, for example. We were pioneers in taking a stand against that. So, I think it's our ordinariness that enables us to be sacred in a very secular world.

The "Sacred" and Questions of Meaning and Individual Purpose

Varun Soni, University of Southern California

In my work as Dean of Religious Life I see a unique aspect of the University. I see a lot of inspiring, powerful examples of service and empathy and religious reconciliation, but I also see the dark side. I see students in my office every week who are struggling with real trauma and much of the trauma I see emerges from existential angst that comes out of a struggle to answer the ultimate questions in their life: Who am I? What does my life mean? What is the nature of God? How do I translate my values into action? These are questions of meaning and purpose, of significance and authenticity.

What we've done here at the University of Southern California that makes us very different than other Offices of Religious Life or university Chaplains' Offices is that we've chosen not to orient our work explicitly around "God," but around these ultimate questions of meaning and purpose and significance and authenticity. I want to be a resource for everyone at the university, not just those who self-identify as religious. For those who do self-identify as religious we have as many chaplains and opportunities to participate in religious life of any university, but for those who don't, we still want them to think deeply about these big questions of meaning and purpose in their life because I see how disconnection from these big questions leads to particular angst and trauma that makes a university experience very difficult for our students. And when they graduate, they often don't know where they're standing.

Why are these questions of what is sacred important? I think they're really important for people who do not consider themselves religious and I challenge my non-religious students to identify what "religion" looks like for them. When people would mention that the "real" religion on campus is football, I thought it was a joke but it's not—you go to the USC Coliseum on pilgrimage, you have rituals, you have a mythology, you have a tradition, and you are part of a community. It is many of the things that our religious communities provide for us. So I want to challenge my students to think about what is sacred to them, even if it's so-called a secular song or game or tradition because if they can find what is sacred to them, even if they are not religious, even if they don't believe in God, I do believe that that then helps them orient their own lives around questions of meaning and purpose and significance and authenticity. I'll emphasize questions because I want my students to live those questions, not necessarily to find those answers. Now that's at odds with what's happening at the rest of the University. In every class they're looking for their answers, but I think in spiritual life the questions are often more important. The answers may change but the questions don't change. And if I can do anything, it's to challenge my students to think deeply about the big questions in their life, to cultivate a sense of the sacred as they define it in their lives, and to connect the dots between what they think personally and how they move professionally through the world.

Edina Lekovic, Muslim Public Affairs Council

I think that stories give us meaning. I've always believed in the power of stories to help connect us with people who we think that we have nothing in common with; that we ultimately can find a thread of something that connects us to another human being and that our sacred stories, no matter where they come from—whether they're Native American or Eastern or Western or Judeo-Christian or Dharmic traditions—they give us a well of stories to draw lessons from and to derive meaning from and to derive inspiration from. I think that in today's climate where things are moving faster than ever, and it's hard to feel like our feet are still attached to the earth, when our heads are in our phones and we're trying to deal with current events and we're trying to think about the future of our country and we're trying to get home on time—all at the same time—that the sacred is a place that can give us stillness and that can help us find a moment of quiet in that day to reconnect to ourselves and to reconnect to something larger than us. When we find such a place, then this sense of the sacred can come back into our daily lives.

One of my sacred memories growing up is coming home after school and finding my mom watching Oprah. In the later years of her program, Oprah would have this segment at the end of each show that was about discovering your spirit or finding your spirit; it had to do with this idea of tapping into your spirit. This gave my mother and me a daily practice of thinking about the sacred it because I would get home just in time for that segment, and it gave us something to talk about and a moment of quiet and stillness that was rooted in somebody else's story and helped us connect back to our own story and where we were trying to go.

It was that moment of remembrance. And so, for me, the sacred spaces, the sacred clothing, it's all minutia. Frankly, as a person who is trying to live my faith, these places and this clothing are not about people, and ultimately my belief in God is rooted in my belief in other people and in the values of courage, compassion, mercy, and justice that are all rooted in the relational.

Ultimately, I hope that the power of stories today can be more relevant than ever in providing something sacred and helping people to think about what is sacred in their own lives because, as I say in my own community all the time, it's great that we're building more and more mosques. It's great that there are over 2000 mosques in America, but if there's nobody to inherit those mosques, if there aren't any children running around in those mosques and aren't able to transfer leadership to the next generation, then we will only have real estate that we own that no one is going to inherit. And that will be the greatest tragedy of all because our sacred spaces, our sacred clothing, all of this is a means to an end; it's not an end in and of itself.

Patrick Mason, Claremont Graduate University

In my mind the greatest danger to the sacred is when it becomes divorced from the ethical. The Christian author C. S. Lewis once wrote, "Next to the Blessed Sacrament itself, your neighbor is the holiest object presented to your senses." I understand the theology behind that for C. S. Lewis as belief in divine presence and the real presence of Jesus in the host, but from my own theological perspective as a Mormon, I would disagree with him somewhat and I would say that there is nothing that presents itself to you that is holier than your neighbor. Not the host, not a temple, not sacred clothing—there is literally nothing in this world that is holier than your neighbor. Now, this comes from the Mormon theological tradition that we are all children of God and therefore invested with true divinity, but it also comes from a deep commitment to human rights and human dignity which I think operates functionally as the closest thing we have to a kind of secular, civil religion, and as a moral code for a secular, pluralist world.

I think one of the greatest challenges to people who are religious—people who claim they are part of a religion—is when they divorce their religious lives from a sense of the ethical, of care and concern for the other, of care and concern for the earth, and of care and concern for the weak and the vulnerable. When we do that, then the sacred loses its power and then we have a problem with the next generation. So, I think the greatest challenge but also the greatest opportunity before us with the sacred today is to always imbue it with a powerful sense of the ethical.

Pastor Wayne Gaddis, California Missionary Baptist State Convention

The question that I keep coming back to is: How can we grow in this? What are the next steps? What can we do in the future to bring understanding, love and appreciation for people of all faiths? I'm reminded of the prayer that Jesus prayed in John chapter 17, "Lord make us one—make them one, as we are one." And therefore, we need to create an understanding between people who find it difficult to understand each other. This is something that is imperative, especially in my own Baptist community, so that we can appreciate the importance of others' places of worship, their sacred place to them. If we do this, then we will also come to appreciate the commonalities of worship we all have, and the need to work together to protect all of our places of worship.

Our task is to bring people of all faiths together in a way where each of us treats their modes and places of worship as being of equal value to those who worship in them. I believe that none of our sacred places has any more authority, or any more power than any other, as long as we are all reaching out to the God that we believe in. I believe that there is a God, and not only is there is a God, but this God wants us to look at every human being with complete dignity and respect for whatever they are and whoever they are. And to those who are burning churches and mosques, I ask them to enter their sacred space, and ask forgiveness. If we are going to better our community both locally and globally, there must be an active end to violence, and a beginning of a dialogue where we can come together to understand one another; where we can be an answer to Jesus' prayer that we love one another, as he has loved us.

Margaret Barker, Independent Scholar

I believe that these existential questions can be boiled down to a question of "where to I belong?" Much of this existential anxiety today, certainly in

England, comes from the fact that we are a society adrift. We are just free from everything, free from any sense of direction and all sorts of things have gone wrong. Freedom has gone wild. I think that if we can live with familiar patterns, with established symbols and shared stories, instead of allowing our so-clever media to chip away at the very foundations of our society; if we can learn more about these sacred spaces and sacred clothing that have kept us together for such a long time, then I think a lot more people will be a lot happier.

In England, I blame our media for a lot of our societal problems. They have been too clever. They have been chopping away at the branch that supported them; they have been undermining the foundations of the world that they lived in and they thought it was clever. And now, of course, they've succeeded, and the branches are falling off the tree and the buildings are falling down. So I think we've got to recover, restate, and, if you like, reassert the sacred stories, shapes, and patterns in our societies and our different cultures side by side so that we actually know where we belong, and that we can't actually do exactly as we like all the time. We've got to think about other people; we need to respect boundaries and the sacred places and clothing of others. And there are a lot of challenges there.

www.ingramcontent.com/pod-product-compliance
Lightning Source LLC
Chambersburg PA
CBHW050440240426
43661CB00055B/2452